Good Toys, Bad Toys

Good Toys, Bad Toys

How Safety, Society, Politics and Fashion Have Reshaped Children's Playthings

ANDREW MCCLARY

McFarland & Company, Inc., Publishers
Jefferson, North Carolina, and London

LIBRARY OF CONGRESS CATALOGUING-IN-PUBLICATION DATA

McClary, Andrew, 1927–
    Good toys, bad toys : how safety, society, politics and fashion have reshaped children's playthings / Andrew McClary.
    p.   cm.
    Includes bibliographical references and index.

    ISBN 0-7864-1837-0 (softcover : 50# alkaline paper)

    1. Toys—Materials. [1. Toys—Design and construction.]
I. Title.
TS2301.T7M277   2004
688.7'2—dc22   2004006357

British Library cataloguing data are available

©2004 Andrew McClary. All rights reserved

No part of this book may be reproduced or transmitted in any form or by any means, electronic or mechanical, including photocopying or recording, or by any information storage and retrieval system, without permission in writing from the publisher.

Cover photograph: ©2004 Digital Vision

Manufactured in the United States of America

McFarland & Company, Inc., Publishers
   Box 611, Jefferson, North Carolina 28640
   www.mcfarlandpub.com

To all the parents who are worried
about their children's toys.

Acknowledgments

I would like to thank the following for their help in making this book possible: the librarians at Michigan State University, and at the East Lansing Library, who have been most helpful; Val Berryman, curator of history at Michigan State, who provided me with hard-to-get materials; and, above all, my wife, Jane. With her insights, editorial ability, and general support and patience, she is equally a creator of this book.

Contents

Acknowledgments vii
Preface 1

I. Troubled Toys
 1. The Changing World of Toys 5
 2. Toy Weapons 7
 3. Fashion Dolls and Action Figures 28
 4. Toys That Come Alive 43
 5. Toys That Teach 58
 6. Hazardous Toys 76
 7. Racist Toys 93
 8. Gender Toys 106

II. Toys Past, Present, and Future
 9. Toys of the World We Have Lost 127
 10. The Commercialization of Toys 148
 11. The John Burroughs Toy 166

III. Afterthoughts
 12. The Special Problem of Media Bias 173
 13. The Plight of the Parent 177

Chapter Notes 181
Selected Bibliography 193
Index 197

Preface

How does a retired professor of natural science end up writing about toys?

When I began college, a career in engineering was my goal. But a first course in that field told me that I wanted another career. What would it be? A trip to New York and a vocational advisor gave me my answer. His advice: "If you don't satisfy all those interests you have, you will spend the rest of your life going from one career to another. Be a city planner. It draws on many different interests." And so I majored in art and sociology and joined a big city planning commission. Fine people, fine mission, but, unfortunately, my interests led me off to a year or so as a shrimp fisherman in Florida. Then back to school: A master's in anthropology and a shift (that dreaded interest itch again) to zoology and a Ph.D.

Teaching zoology at a university in Wisconsin was fine: the students were great and I had tenure. But the same thing happened again: something was missing. A friend at Michigan State University saved me. "Come over here," he said. "You belong in a generalist program. University College at MSU is just right for you." And indeed it was. It had four departments: social science, humanities, American thought and language, and natural science. We often team-taught, crossing from one department to another. Unlike specialists, who limit themselves to one area of study, our interests ranged across many fields. The same was true for a book I wrote: *Biology and Society: The Evolution of Man and His Technology* (Macmillan, 1975).

But then came retirement. What might a generalist do to keep busy? The answer lay in an entirely unsuspected place: the world of toys.

Why toys? The store is right; toys are, indeed, "us." Just like humans, toys have moods, interests, eccentricities, and personalities. They are a mad hatter's world, full of fun, surprises and challenges—a world that is perfectly suited for the generalist to explore.

A brief look at some toy books and their variety will suggest this. Richard O'Brien's *The Story of American Toys* is a classic work, which traces the strange pathways our toys have taken through time. *I Had One of Those Toys*, by Robin Sommer, is a more personal approach. David Longest's *Character Toys as Collectibles* is aimed at a special interest group. *Toys As Culture*, by Brian Sutton-Smith, examines the many roles toy can play in our lives. Three of his chapters are "The Toy as Solitariness," "The Toy as Achievement," and "The Toy as Bond and Obligation." The *Whole Fun Catalog of 1929* is full of zany toys. And further back in history, one can find books such as the *Handy Books* by the Beards, which emphasize handmade toys. Finally, there are books on toy personalities. *Forever Barbie* and *The Story of G.I. Joe* are examples.

With all this variety, it was easy for me to become interested in the world of toys. I helped my grandchildren make some, did the same with other children at the Michigan State Museum, and began to give toy talks to audiences, from children to retirees.

I also wrote articles on toys and gave a paper at an invited presentation at Emory University. There, six participants discussed the possibility of a Smithsonian Institution–sponsored "Festival on the Mall," where children from around the world would make toys. Out of all this came a book titled *Toys with Nine Lives: A Social History of Toys* (Linnett, 1997). It has been recommended as a core book for young adults and was even translated into Japanese. Why? I am not sure!

As I delved more deeply into the toy literature, I learned something unexpected: Most of those who wrote about our toys saw them as full of fun and wonder. But not all. To some writers, our toys were altogether too dangerous. To others, they were racist or too mindless. And still others were afraid of toys that seemed to come alive: did they deprive children of their natural itch to imagine?

How valid are criticisms such as these? A look at history can give us a partial answer, for it helps us to ask this key question: Have our toys always come under criticism?

In the book's first section, "Troubled Toys," we will look at concerns about toys. In the next section, "Toys Past, Present, and Future," we put these concerns into historical perspective. How are these problems changing? Instead of losing ground, might today's toys be about to enter a time when they will be better than ever?

The third section, "Afterthoughts," has two chapters. The first, "The Special Problem of Media Bias," argues that many media toy watchers have been biased toward the negative, giving our toys more of a black eye than they deserve. The second chapter, "The Plight of the Parent," looks at the challenges that face today's parents as they try to choose the best toys for their children.

I. Troubled Toys

1

The Changing World of Toys

In early America, most children owned only a few toys. For example, Dorothy Howard, who lived a hundred years ago on the western frontier, had around a dozen toys in her "pretty box."[1]

Why did Dorothy own so few toys? There were several reasons for this. First, most children had to make their own toys, and this took time. Second, most early American families could not have afforded to buy many toys for their children, even if they had been available in stores. And finally, most children left their time of play at an early age to become working members of the household.

By the early 1900s, all this had begun to change, for the Industrial Revolution was creating a new world of toys. More and more toys were machine-made and store-bought. And the Industrial Revolution was giving more and more parents the wealth to buy these toys. Because of this, by the 1970s the average American suburban child owned more than ninety of these machine-made toys.[2]

Back in early America when toys were handmade, parents might get advice from family or friends about the best ways for their children to make and use a toy. But in the new world of machine-made, store-bought toys, the mass media became the primary advisor. By the early 1900s, more and more parents were reading articles in magazines and newspapers that told them about toys. Some of these articles sound almost modern. One talked of toys as teachers, and another described some popular toys. But other early toy articles sound out of date. For example, one writer of a hundred years ago lauded the German toy makers. It made sense back then, for many of our children had toys that had been made in the Tyrol region of Germany. However, German toys were to lose their favored place in our toy world. By 1918, one could find articles with titles such as "German Toys Not Wanted," for we were involved in World War I.

Most of these early toy articles had a positive tone. It was a time of great technological innovation. America was becoming industrialized and new inventions were appearing everywhere. Toys were a part of this new world and media writers talked about all the new and exciting toys that were appearing in stores. One writer described an interesting new toy musical instrument, the bugle. Another told readers about that marvelous new invention, the windup toy. In 1905, they were all the rage.

These new toys could help children in so many ways! There were toys to entertain children in their "leisure hour," toys that were "quaint and artistic," toys for Christmas, and educational toys, such as those that taught peace to children. And the bargains! Some of these toys could be bought for a penny.

These early articles tell us about the toys of their time. But they also can tell us something else. The *Reader's Guide to Periodicals* listed only twenty toy articles for the decade 1890–1899. But fifty years later, the number of toy articles had grown dramatically. Over the two-year span of 1953–1955, almost a hundred toy articles were listed.[3] In part, this reflected an overall growth of media articles. But it said something else: toys were becoming a much more important part of our lives.

In earlier times, media writers talked about how wonderful our toys were. But by the mid-1900s, the tone of their writing had changed. Now, many of them used the media to tell us about toy problems. In the next section of this book, we will be looking at some of these problems.

2

Toy Weapons

THE HANDMADE TOY WEAPONS OF EARLY AMERICA

When America was young, boys, and some girls, played with toy weapons that would make the hair of today's parents stand on end. Some such as snowballs, corn cobs, acorns, and stones, were ephemeral toys, weapons of the moment that were picked off the ground or gathered and hurled at the enemy (Fig. 2.1A and 2.1B). But others, such as pea shooters, spears, bows and arrows, and slingshots, took time and care to make. In earlier years, many of these toy weapons were fashioned from natural materials. For example, a bow might be made from a hickory stalk, which was springy, and an arrow might be made from false dogwood, which had straight branches. As pioneers became more settled and began to accumulate odds and ends around the house, toy weapons were made from these leftovers. Now, a bow might be made of an old umbrella rib, and an arrow would be tipped with a used nail.

There were many ways to use these "toys," and many reasons to use them. Sometimes, it was a matter of showing your manhood. Charles Eastman, a Sioux Indian who grew up in the mid-1800s, remembered mud and willow fights. Boys would place a large lump of clay on the end of a springy stick. Then they would form into "armies" of up to a hundred boys on a side. As Eastman said, the battle became warm, but that was for the better, for it tested a boy's mettle.[1]

Sometimes, it was a matter of defending yourself against strangers who were out to get you. In the late 1800s, Charley O'Kieffe, aged five, joined hundreds of others moving west to find a better life. The O'Kieffe party consisted of Charley, his widowed mother, two brothers, and a sister. Their wagon, filled with baggage and trailing the family cows, made an attractive target for those who were up to no good. The O'Kieffes did not know it, but in our early West, a favorite pastime of town boys was to make trouble for the pioneers who rolled through their towns.

I. Troubled Toys

Top: Fig. 2.1A. A snow fort. *Bottom:* Fig. 2.1B. A snowball gun. Sometimes battle became mechanized.

When the O'Kieffes reached Johnstown, Nebraska, a gang of town boys came running up to their wagon, and tried to stampede their cows. Charley remembered what happened next. Brother Ira dug out his slingshot, loaded it with an iron spike head, and shot at the gang, hitting one boy on the ear. "The sight of the blood spurting out cooled off the others, and we went on our way with no more trouble," said Charley.[2]

Once they had settled in the West, pioneer boys faced other enemies. Jesse Applegate, an Oregon pioneer of the 1840s, remembered what he called some "unpleasantness ... between us White boys and the Indian boys." One day, the boys were trading things back and forth. The settler boys got a sweet-tasting root from the Indian boys, who got nails and scraps of iron from the settler boys. There must have been tension, however, for a settler boy tripped an Indian, and — as Jesse wrote — "a race war now broke out instantly, and the battle became general."³ The settlers threw big pebbles and Irish potatoes at the Indians, who returned fire with pebbles and arrows. Before it got too dangerous, the fight was broken up by a Mr. McKinley, who was in charge of the local trading post.

The Wild West was not the only place of boyhood violence, for the same could be said of just about anywhere in early America. Jack Conroy was a miner's son who grew up at the end of the 1800s in Missouri. As Jack put it, the farmer boys "were our natural enemies."⁴ Jack and his friends would ambush the farmer boys, attacking them with spears made of the horseweed that grew along creek bottoms.

Maintaining turf was also an important matter for boys in America's towns and cities. William Dean Howells grew up in a small Ohio town in the mid-1800s. Howells and his friends did not get along with the German children who lived in town. "There was a family of German boys living across the street, that you could stone whenever they came out of their front gate," he said.⁵ Henry MacCracken, who grew up in New York and later became president of Vassar College, remembered using a dangerous weapon in turf battles. His gang fought "the great whip war" with the Irish kids, lashing away at their enemies with the long whips that were used to drive horses.⁶

Not all city battles were that rough. Sometimes, toys were used less to hurt than as a way of telling intruders to stay away. Jimmy Savo's weapon was an example. Jimmy grew up in New York City in the late 1800s. At Halloween time, he did what many other city kids would do. "We put flour in a long stocking, and when a kid from another block passed by, we would sock him. It left a white mark on his clothing."⁷

Toy weapons were used to show your bravery and to defend your turf against outsiders. But they could also be used to challenge the world of adults, to test the system. And school was a good place to do this. Edward Hale, who grew up in Boston during the 1830s, remembered how he was transferred to a new room in school. "We were pleased," said Hale, "because it was known that the new Master was very easy, and that the fellows did as they chose." Indeed they did. One boy went across the room to a pail. It held snow which provided drinking water for the class. "From this, he then made little snowballs with which to pelt the other boys, all without interruption from the Master."⁸

Many years later, Arthur Davis of Georgia remembered using peashooters in school (Fig. 2.2). Instead of peas, he and his friends would use newspaper wads as missiles. Our teacher would take every one away … we'd go home, make some more, take them back the next day.⁹ Sometimes, it seemed to be a no-win proposition for the teacher. Dorothy Smith

Fig. 2.2. Using a peashooter on the way home from school.

of Hanover, Indiana, recalled what her grandfather did when he was in school during the 1880s. All the boys carried rubber slingshots to class even though they were prohibited. Every week, the teacher would call each boy by name and ask if he'd brought a slingshot to school. Like George Washington, her grandfather couldn't tell a lie, so he'd confess that he had, and hand his over. But, said Dorothy, "Granddad got around the problem. He always brought two slings to school, a good one and a poor one he could turn in."[10]

Sometimes, toys became weapons simply by accident. Dan Beard, later to become a famous writer and naturalist as well as a co-founder of the Boy Scouts of America, tested his new slingshot by shooting at the door of the house across the street. Then the unexpected happened. "My missile fled straight to its mark but a man took that most inopportune instant to open his door, and the pebble hit him on the fleshy part of his nose." As he put it, Beard "made a center run for the opposite fence."[11]

Although it had diminished by then, play with dangerous weapons continued into the mid-1900s. For example, Michael Cox remembered playing out in the "field," a place of sinkholes, cattails, and mounds of earth. Cox and his friends "borrowed" their family's ashcan lids for shields. Then they pulled horseweed stalks from the ground to make javelins. Hurling these at each other, they played "Roman soldier." It could be dangerous. As Cox remembered, "Aldy nearly tore out my eye once, his spear embedding itself in my cheek." In a macabre finish to his story, Cox says, "All this was good training, for as they grew older, as the end of high school approached, these boys knew what lay ahead. Most would find themselves 12,000 miles across the earth, where they would be wending their way through the jungles and rice paddies of Viet Nam.[12]

How common was play such as this? One has to be careful, for autobiographical memory can be tricky. Many an "old-timer" probably exaggerated the daring and dangerous exploits of his childhood, for violence is always interesting to readers. Even if autobiographical bias does exist, it seems safe to say that the combat play of earlier America was more violent than it is today, for America was still a frontier society. Unlike today's suburban children, who are drafted into organized play at an early age, the country children of an earlier America were largely free to roam, to invent their own brands of play, which often involved violence. And our early cities were also frontier societies of a sort, teeming with immigrants of many nationalities. Children would roam the streets and could become just as violent as children in the country.

Interestingly, all frontier societies seem to spawn youthful violence. New Zealand of the 1800s was an example of this. As described in his classic book, *A History of Children's Play*, Brian Sutton-Smith has given us a picture of New Zealand children who were eerily like those of early America in their violent play.[13]

What did grown-ups, particularly parents, think about rough play of this sort? We have no statistics, but all evidence suggests that today's concern about toy weapons lay far in the future. After all, Pa had used these very same toys, and considered them simply a part of growing up. Sometimes, parents did use a quiet kind of discipline on children who became too careless with a toy weapon. James Hearst, who grew up in Iowa, remembered what happened when he accidentally shot one of the family pigs with his bow and arrow. "My father pulled out the arrow and gave it to me without a word, but I got the message," he said.[14]

Toy Weapons Become Machine-Made

This earlier world of war play, with its handmade toys, was to be swept away by the Industrial Revolution, for it created a new world of machine-made toys, including toy weapons. At first, only wealthy families could afford to buy these new toys, but by the late 1800s, almost every child had machine-made toys, including one or more of the new toy weapons.

These new toy weapons were completely different from the handmade toy weapons of earlier times. Even if you were a skilled whittler, it was very hard to make a realistic toy version of that most common weapon of all, the gun. But machines could do this easily, and toy guns largely replaced the older types of toy weapons. Toy companies worked hard to invent new kinds of toy guns. In the years between 1861 and 1865, seventeen toy patents were issued in America, and nearly half were for toy guns.[15]

Children loved these guns, but something was missing. Where were the missiles? After all, a good bit of the thrill and even the danger of earlier toy weapon play had come from real battles in which children had used spears, slingshots, or corn cobs.

One of the best answers to the real missile dilemma was invented by children. It was a hybrid — half handmade and half machine-made. To make a rubber band gun, you would whittle a crude pistol out of any handy piece of wood, then arm it with machine-made rubber-band missiles. Rubber-band guns provided hours of real, yet very safe battles. The toy companies then went to work, and came up with some ingenious missiles. One was the "Harmless Pistol," which shot a rod of wood tipped with a soft rubber suction cup. It was supposed to be fired at a cardboard target. But even if a boy used it in war play, it would be harmless (Fig. 2.3).

Toy companies also thought up a variety of squirt guns. One of the strangest is shown in Figure 2.4. It was less than three inches long, and would fit into a woman's purse. As its ad said, "Ladies sometimes fill it with scent, and derive much amusement spraying their friends."

Suction cups and squirt guns were two answers to the challenge of inventing toy weapons that shot real missiles. Another was the BB gun, for at least in the eyes of the toy companies, BBs could do no harm.

The first BB guns were wooden. In 1888, Clarence Hamilton, a young watch and clock repairman who worked for a Michigan company, thought that boys would like an all-metal BB gun, rather than a wooden one. He designed a metal one, and showed it to the board of directors. The general manager was so impressed that he cried, "Clarence, it's a daisy!" And in just a few years the Daisy BB gun was on every American boy's want list.

But was the BB gun just a toy? As a boy in Nebraska, Wright Morris remembered playing "Western front" during World War I. He was hit just below the eyeball by a BB that just stuck there. When it fell out, it left a big freckle. Were the BB gun makers responsible for accidents such as this? The BB gun companies thought not. To them, parents should train their

HARMLESS PISTOL.

Top: Fig. 2.3. A rubber suction cap at its end supposedly made this missile harmless. *Bottom:* Fig. 2.4. This little gun was just right for a lady's purse!

boys to use a BB gun safely. But how do you teach BB gun safety to a child? Writing in 1967, Joe Brown remembered what must have been one of the starkest examples of discipline ever recorded. Joe had just received a new BB gun. As he remembered it, "I admired Mr. Ellard, and I've never been quite certain why I shot him. Maybe it was because I was delirious with joy and pride and would have done anything to call attention to my brand-new nickel-plated rifle…." Anyway, when Joe came stalking up the alley and saw Mr. Ellard bending over burning some trash, Joe shot Mr. Ellard in his rotund rear. Mr. Ellard walked over, took Joe's rifle, stepped back, and shot Joe in his right leg. He handed Joe back his rifle, and said pleasantly, "O.K., buddy, now watch where you go pointing that thing." Gross perhaps, but it worked. "It was the only lesson on gun handling I ever had as a boy," said Joe, "and for a long time afterward I felt hot around the ears when I recalled that I needed it."[16]

At first, BB guns were tolerated, but just as had happened with other potentially dangerous toys, public opinion about who should be responsible began to change. Now, it was up to the toy company or the government to make sure that BB guns were safe. BB gun makers tried various strategies that were aimed at getting the public, and hopefully the government, off their collective backs. For example, the Daisy company tried to make its BB gun into a family toy (Fig. 2.5). But most public officials saw the gun in a different light. Several states banned them, and increasingly, courts have found BB gun companies responsible for injuries. Today, BB guns are no longer on the toy shelves of stores. Instead, they have been banished to the gun department.

Rubber-band guns, suction cup guns, and squirt guns all shot safe missiles. But unexpectedly, the most successful toy gun of all shot no missile. When you pulled a cap gun's trigger, the cap would explode with a satisfying bang and a smell of powder. Even if no missile were fired, it would be fun to use. Very quickly after their invention in the mid-1800s, cap guns became "all the rage."

Toy guns were fun, and became immensely popular. And so did a different kind of war toy which carried a tiny weapon. (Fig. 2.6) Toy soldiers were not new. In times past, they had been playthings for the rich and royal. But machines could make toy soldiers by the thousands, as well as all their paraphernalia, from horses to cannons, and so boys could afford toy soldiers. They were completely safe to play with, and you could dream up all sorts of bloody battles. These little toys became just as popular as the cap gun. Eleanor Abbot, who grew up in Cambridge, Massachusetts, during the 1870s, remembered going to play soldiers with Arthur, a friend of hers who had just received toy soldiers and a fort as a birthday gift. "The fort itself proved everything that we had dreamed … leaden soldiers of every warring nation of the World seemed represented. For fully a hour of peace and innocence we sat cross-legged … waging such wars as we could improvise."[17] Out in Oklahoma, Robert Rutland also had toy soldiers. "My favorite pastime was playing war games with lead soldiers. Most

Chapter 2—Toy Weapons

Fig. 2.5. A BB gun ad of the 1930s. It says, "Once in every two or three years, along comes one Christmas gift that's just the thing for everyone on your list."

of the soldiers were infantrymen who withstood a barrage of small pebbles until all the arms and legs were broken off. I knew just enough history to have a favorite, a mounted 'General Pershing'…. I sent him out into deadly battle until finally the general's head was knocked off in mortal combat. I buried him in the backyard with full honors."[18]

The new machine-made war toys seemed better in every way than the older handmade ones. But their realism could make them dangerous in a

Fig. 2.6. Mom and Sister watch while he blows the soldiers away with his cannon. It shoots rubber bullets.

way that had been impossible with the earlier toys. Police, particularly those patrolling inner city neighborhoods, just might think that a child with a toy gun was carrying the real thing (Fig. 2.7). Mercifully, it did not happen very often, but in a few instances this led to a fatal shooting. Even one mistake was too many, and in 1988, Congress passed a bill that made toy guns have an orange plug on their barrels so that they could not be mistaken for the real thing.[19]

This made toy guns less realistic. In addition, another development made them even more fanciful. Movies and television have increasingly led children into fantasy worlds. The heroes of *Star Wars*, and fantasy figures such as the Teenage Mutant Ninja Turtles carry otherworldly weapons, and their popularity has led toy makers to make more and more otherworldly toy weapons. The Super Soaker is one example.

A New Kind of Play

The Industrial Revolution changed the appearance of toy weapons, and it also changed the way in which these toys were used. The older war play, which had used real missiles, began to fade away. In earlier times, Jack

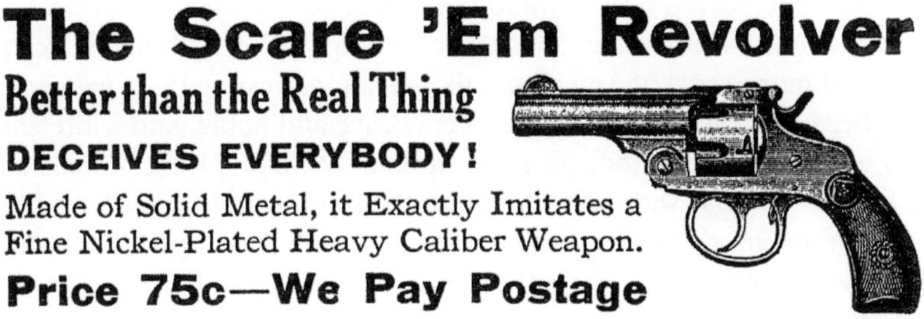

The Scare 'Em Revolver
Better than the Real Thing
DECEIVES EVERYBODY!
Made of Solid Metal, it Exactly Imitates a Fine Nickel-Plated Heavy Caliber Weapon.
Price 75c—We Pay Postage

Fig. 2.7. The "Scare 'Em" Revolver. Its ad says, "It's just the thing to scare a burglar." But might it deceive a policeman?

Conroy of Missouri had hurled spears at enemy children, and Henry MacCracken of New York City had battled Irish children with horsewhips. But in the increasingly gentrified America, which was growing out of the Industrial Revolution, play of this sort became less and less tolerated. Instead, play in which the enemy was purely imaginary became more and more common. William Dean Howells, who was mentioned earlier, would stone the German children who lived in his town. But he also played pretend games of war. When he was a boy, the veterans of our 1812 war with the British would proudly march through town, and there were even a few Revolutionary War veterans still around. Howells and his friends wished that there would be another war with England, and so, they would make weapons of wood and march about, fighting imaginary "bridish," as he called them. The bridish always lost, said Howells. [20] As a young boy during the Civil War, Dan Beard played army games to celebrate its glory. He made a Fort Sumter of mud and wooden blocks, put clothespin soldiers in the fort, and fired at it with pebbles. [21] For Hamlin Garland, who was born during that war, it had "a mingled air of romance and sorrow, history and song." He and his sister Harriett carried wooden sabres and hammered on dishpans, imitating the young drummers of that war. [22] But by Bruce Catton's time in the early 1900s, the Civil War was a fast-fading memory, although he and his friends still recalled it in their play. "We got along without officers, because nobody was ever willing to take orders, and the enemy of course was always imaginary. We were inevitably the Union Army, and we never lost."[23]

In the late 1800s, children replayed the Indian Wars. Anne Sneller, who grew up in New York state at the turn of the century, did not really believe Indians were coming her way, but it helped to imagine it was so. She and her friends would climb to the roof of the corn crib. Then, said Anne, "We drew our bows, and aimed our arrows at the first brave who showed his feathered head around the corner of the barn. "There! There he is!' we cried to each other. Shoot! Shoot!"(Fig. 2.8).[24] As Indians became more and more a part of American folklore, an interesting thing happened. They became larger than life. They were brave and noble, and white children wished that they, too, could be Indians. William Dean Howells and his friends felt that way. "If they could, the boys would rather have been Indians than anything else, but, as there was really no hope of this whatever, they were willing to be settlers and fight the Indians." [25]

World War I had its share of pretend war play. World War II also had its followers. As Barbara Holland remembered, "We were good, Nazis were bad, Hitler was crazy."[26] She and her friends lay in the grass watching for German bombers, and dug trenches to trap invading Germans. The boys practiced hand-to-hand combat; while the girls made booby traps of clothesline and coat hangers, which occasionally netted the mailman. During the Korean War, Ed Stivender and his friends used toy machine guns to fight the enemy. They also played Strategic Air Command by running across lawns until they got to a hill, where they launched themselves into space.[27]

In earlier times, children had learned to play war games from family and friends, or by listening to soldiers who came back home as heroes. But by the late 1800s, a new teacher had begun to appear — the media. At first, this media consisted of magazines and the cheap "pulps," which featured hair-raising stories of the sort that children loved. By the early 1900s, a more powerful media teacher had appeared. The early movies, "nickelodeons," they were called, gave children lots of ideas about how to play. The Westerns, with their gamblers, half-breeds, marauding Indians, heroic cowboys, chases, and battles were popular. John O'Dell, who has written a classic book about play in America's Depression years, remembered how children of the time were influenced by cowboy heroes. In books, comics and films, the bigger the hero, the fancier his rubber-band gun. Therefore, all kids worked at packing a gun that was neater than anyone else's.[28]

The Gangster films featuring John Dillinger, Pretty Boy Floyd, or Machine Gun Kelly, as villains, and "G-Men" as heroes, were also popular models for war play. In later years, war movies with their heroes and fantasy films featuring heroes such as Superman were also popular and gave kids countless ideas about combat play.

These movies, and later the radio and then TV, told kids just what to say and how to act when playing. You said things like "cheese it, the cops," or "hold 'em up," when you played cops and robbers. And you knew just how to fall when you were hit. Michael Kernan remembered the rules: "When you were shot and finished with your operatic death scene (complete with a 'Gaaaaah!' and a bravura collapse), you were honor-bound

Fig. 2.8. Anne Sneller on a corn crib roof with her bow and arrow. The enemy is imaginary. From *A Vanished World*, by Anne Gertrude Sneller, Syracuse University Press, 1974. By permission of the publisher. Illustration by Nancy B. Perkins.

not to jump up and be someone else."[29] Ed Stivender remembered World War II play; how you would cry, "I'm shot, men, carry on without me," and how to walk with a wounded leg.[30] Sometimes, children went about as far as they could go in their wish to be like the heroes and villains they saw in the media. They would bring their cap guns to the movies, and shoot at the villains who appeared on the screen. [31]

Is War Play Moral?

Free of danger, and full of innocent symbolism, it would seem that today's toy weapons should live in a golden age. But this has not happened, for they have faced a paradox: as war play became safer and more imaginative, it came under increasing criticism. This criticism began after the First World War. The Spanish-American War which preceded it may have been, to use Teddy Roosevelt's words, a "splendid little war." But that was not so for the "Great War" of 1914–18. Now, war was total. Everyone, even those who did not want to be involved, were in it. And new technologies, particularly the machine gun, made war a slaughterhouse. Verdun has become a symbol for this, a place where over a million French and German soldiers died, fighting over a ring of forts that had been pounded into rubble.

If war was a mindless horror, was it fitting, even moral, for children to play "war"? This question arose in unexpected places. The lyrics of the song shown in Figure 2.9 went this way:

> Dear little boy, with your soldiers of play
> How you shout as you give your commands
> "Forward!" and "Charge!" in your brave boyish way.
> Soldier boy, wait for the changing years,
> For the crash and the roll of the drums,
> As the trial of the battle comes. Will the
> Smoke and the flame still be just a game?
>
> Can you feel the ache of the hearts you break;
> My big little soldier boy?

Maudlin perhaps, but the worry would not go away. Once a concern such as this arises, it is sure to be featured in the media, for violence, especially when children are involved, is sure to attract reader attention. Accordingly, concerns about the morality of war play began to appear in popular magazines, and continued into the 1940s. For example, a 1940 article in *The Rotarian* featured several views about the subject. Josephine Powell of California said, "I feel that … constant association with playthings of a martial nature would make war seem reasonable," and Mary Phillips of New York agreed. She said, "Martial toys are uncivilized, and give importance to the savage, brutal side of a child." But others felt differently. "I think the danger from military toys is greatly exaggerated," said a clergyman from New Hampshire. And an Arizona superintendent of schools said, "After watching children for many years, I believe this is all much ado about nothing."[32] However, World War II brought a new round of concern. Writing in 1944, Arthur Rautman, a psychologist, warned parents against encouraging war play. He said that when a child is playing soldier, it indicates an unhealthy state of mind and considerable worry on the part of the child because of the war.[33] Did worry about toy weapons affect their sales? Apparently not. During World War I, the sale of war toys actually increased, presumably in response to war fever. Although toy weapons did not do so well during World War II, this did not seem to result from any publicity against war play. Instead, it was a

Fig. 2.8. A 1915 song.

reflection of the poor quality of the toys produced during the war. The shortage of metal forced toymakers to use wood and cardboard as substitute materials, and war toys did not look very real. [34]

Vietnam was different. In the early 1960s, when the war was beginning, war fever, coupled with television's emphasis on the war, led to a boom in toy weapons. Some of this boom may have also resulted from a kind of military action, for War Department officials went to toy fairs and helped to promote toy weapons. But in the last years of the Vietnam War, sales collapsed. In part, this was due to a rising disillusionment about the war. But something else was involved. During the Vietnam War, very visible, sometimes even violent, peace advocates became a powerful political force. Their anti-war demonstrations in cities and on college campuses are well-known, but fewer people realize that peace activists also attacked war toys. The Women's Strike for Peace, the Women's International League for Peace and Freedom, the California Toy Company, the War Resisters League and others distributed anti-war materials and organized protests against toy weapons at toy makers' conventions. And protests against these toys continued long after the Vietnam War ended. [35]

Do Play Guns Turn Children Into Killers?

In the late 1990s, a rash of killing plagued America's high schools. Students, often thought of as "nerds" who did not belong, would pull a weapon and gun down some of their fellow students. What had driven these students, often "outsiders," to become killers?

There are many answers. Here were some: America had long been a gun culture. Could it be that more and more of America's young people were joining this culture and were carrying guns, which they sometimes used? There was some evidence for this notion. While juvenile crime has decreased, the number of juveniles who use guns has actually increased.[36]

Family breakdown was also suggested as a cause for these killings, as more of today's teens grow up in unstable family environments. [37]

Could the media, especially television, create a "mean world syndrome" which might make children more violent? A recent study does seem to support this view, for it has found that children who watch a lot of television do seem to commit more aggressive acts.

The study followed the behavior of 707 children from very early childhood until they became teenagers. There was a significant association between the time they spent watching television, and violence in later years. The study was designed to eliminate childhood neglect, family income, neighborhood violence, parental education, and mental instability as possible causes for this violence. [38]

Gun-carrying adolescents, family breakdown, and media violence have all been suggested as causes for these school killings. But there was another seemingly unlikely possibility: could playing "Bang, bang, you're dead" with toy guns train children to be killers? At first, this seemed absurd, but the idea that toy guns could be the culprit gained rapid media attention, and soon, everyone was talking about this possibility.

Some people thought the whole issue of teen violence was overdone. One teen put it this way: "I am angry with the media for devoting too much time and coverage to (the school shootings). The media do not truthfully portray teens and teen issues. The truth is that my friends and I are more worried about getting into a decent college and finding an after-school job to pay for the prom than getting revenge (on) a classmate who teased us." [39]

But the woman at Turtle Park thought otherwise. She was walking along Turtle Park in northwest Washington, D.C. Suddenly, there they were: Three boys around five years old, playing "Bang, bang, you're dead" with their plastic guns, and their mothers just sat there, doing nothing. When she got home, the woman called Bob Levy of the *Washington Post*. Should she start a petition to ban toy weapons at Turtle Park? Or might she call the police? Levy was dubious. "Cops don't sit in judgment of parents," he said. But perhaps the woman's concern was justified. After all, it was the very day that the teens who died in the Columbine shooting were being buried. [40]

Many of us would sympathize with the woman. Lisa Suhay, who lives in Medford, New Jersey, put it this way: "There is no way that you can convince me that little boys cannot be steered past gun play, and further, that gun play did not beget the string of shooting sprees our country is experiencing."[41] Do professionals who deal with children agree with Suhay? Some do. For example, Ron Slaby, a Harvard psychologist, says that play with toy weapons is a "rehearsal for real-life violence."[42]

But many people disagree. "Toy guns are a small issue," says Kathleen Heide, a criminologist at the University of South Florida. "The real concern should be helping kids deal with negative feelings and resolving conflicts." And parents see toy guns as an inevitable part of childhood. "Our children have water guns and cowboy guns," said one mother. "If you don't give them guns, they build them"(Fig. 2.10). When one father banned toy guns, his four-year-old ate his peanut-butter sandwich into the shape of a gun and began to shoot it. [43]

Diane Levin, co-author of the *War Play Dilemma*, sees toy guns in yet a different way: "If it's a gun one day, and a telescope the next, and if they were fighting aliens in the morning and wild animals in the afternoon, you know there's creativity at work ... that's healthy."[44]

Although there is no definitive proof that play with toy guns will turn children into future killers, most Americans are fed up with violence, and so, anything, even something as seemingly innocent as a toy gun, has become suspect. Activist groups such as the Lion and Lamb Project circulate lists of violent toys to avoid at Christmas. Daphne White, its founder, conducts workshops telling parents about the dangers of toy weapons. Sometimes, she notes, parents say that gunfighting, like that between cowboys and Indians, has always been a part of Americana. White's response: "This is a different time with much more violence in all parts of the culture. The merchandising of violence did not exist then the way it does now."[45]

Toy gun turn-ins have appeared across the country. For example, in Marquette, Michigan, The Salvation Army traded leftover Christmas gifts for toy guns. "We feel strongly that this ... might get toys to kids which aren't associated with death and destruction," said one Army official. And children swap toy guns for T-shirts at anti-violence days in Los Angeles and other cities.[46]

Children have even helped to run turn-ins. Cody Hill, age 16, is the founder of Guns Aren't Fun, a toy exchange program in Portland, Oregon. Children under twelve turn in toy guns for sports equipment, books, art supplies and other non-violent playthings. Children who turn in more than one gun can enter a ra°e for a chance to win a bicycle or CD player. But some children do have mixed feelings about these turn-ins. At a Washington, D.C., event, Sam Ziman, age six, dropped his plastic ray gun into the bin, saying proudly, "That was my last one." But then, he looked about conspiratorially and added in a whisper, "I'm keeping all my swords, though."[47]

Schools have become leaders in the battle to reduce play with toy guns. By 1998, 94 percent of all American schools had rules banning all firearms, whether real or toy, from school premises. Children who bring toy guns to school can be suspended. Some schools have extended their control over toy guns beyond the school. In a Massachusetts case, two twelve-year-old boys were suspended for after-hours play with war toys in the woods adjacent to their school. Sometimes, there are no weapons involved. Kindergarten boys in New Jersey were suspended for playing cops and robbers at recess. Their guns consisted of fingers pointed at each other.[48]

But it just may be that some schools have overreached themselves in taking action against toy guns. In May 2000, a Washington judge ruled that school officials violated a nine-year-old's constitutional rights when they suspended him for bringing a small toy gun to school.[49]

In the spring of 2001, Jeremy Hix became a test case for the weapons issue. Hix, a sixteen-year-old student at Holt High School in Michigan, had become interested in Scottish bagpipes. He was taking bagpipe lessons, and had acquired the traditional regalia worn by a bagpipe player.

Chapter 2 — Toy Weapons

Fig. 2.10. Five boys at play in the early 1930s. Why do two of them have swords?

Hix decided to go to the school's spring prom dressed in his regalia as a bagpiper. As part of the dress, he wore a sgian dubh, a three-and-a-half-inch knife, which was tucked into one of his socks. When they saw the knife handle sticking out of his sock, Holt school officials suspended Hix from school. In their view, he had violated Michigan's zero tolerance policy for weapons.

Was the sgian dubh a weapon, or was it merely a ceremonial object, long a part of the bagpiper's costume? Jeremy's plight attracted national attention, and may well become a test case for the zero tolerance policy against any kind of weapon that so many schools and states have now adopted. [50]

A New-Age Toy Weapon?

Children still play "Bang, bang, you're dead" outdoors. But play of this kind may soon be history. By Christmas 2001, toy weapons were almost absent from toy stores. In part, this was a result of our national campaign against these "toys."

But another reason is that children are spending more and more time indoors. What are they doing there? Today, the average American child lives in an electronic household, surrounded by three TVs, two VCRs, three radios, two tape players, two CD players, a computer and a video game player. And a recent study has found that the video game industry has won thirty percent of the American toy and game market. [51]

What are computer and video games like? Many are superb, with stimulating story lines and sophisticated graphics. Myst and Riven are examples. But others, like Doom and Quake, are very different, for they are full of gore and violence, games in which the player tries to maim or kill an opponent.

How important are these violent games in a teen's life? About half of all teens in a CNN poll said yes, they have played violent games. How often do they play? About ten percent play violent games regularly. Sometimes, it's hard to quit video play. Over two-thirds of the teens polled played video games one to four times a week, and a third of the boys polled felt as if they were addicted.

What do teens think about violent video games? "You don't think about it as as killing a person," says one. And another says, "I never met a male teenager who didn't like violent games … I'd wonder about one if I did." Finally, what do parents have to say about video games? Over one-half of the teens polled said their parents had no rules about their children's video play. [52]

Eric Harris, one of the Columbine killers, was addicted to violent video games. Was this just a coincidence? David Grossman thinks not.

A retired army officer and professor at West Point, Grossman spent years teaching infantry recruits to kill. "Believe me," he says, "it does not come naturally. You have to be taught to kill."[53] How does the army do this?

By a process of conditioning, says Grossman. How is an infantry recruit's normal aversion to shooting or bayoneting an enemy overcome? Among other ways, says Grossman, the army uses videos that are eerily like those played by so many of today's teens.

3

Fashion Dolls and Action Figures

Fashion Dolls

Ruth Handler, who was on vacation in Europe, first saw Lilli in Switzerland. As she remembered it, they were walking down the street in Lucerne, and there was a doll — an adult doll with a woman's body — sitting on a rope swing. Lilli was a mildly pornographic doll, the kind of thing that men might buy as a gag gift. But Handler saw something else in Lilli. She would create an adult doll like Lilli, but she would be for little girls, not men. And so, Barbie was born.

When people talk about her, they like to say "Barbie Doll," but to Handler and her co-workers at the Mattel Toy Company, she was not to be a doll at all, at least not the traditional kind. Instead, she was to be a new kind of doll — a fashionable image of what young girls would like to be when they grew up.

Early Paper Dolls

But Barbie was not the first fashion doll. Even in country America, girls had fashion dolls. Housebound on a cold winter day, Dorothy Howard, of Sabine Bottom, Texas, would turn to the family Sears catalog. She would search its pages until she found pictures of elegant ladies in the very latest of fashions. She would cut them out, brace them with some cardboard, and dream of a world that she would never know.

The well-known Carl P. Stirn Company of New York City offered a box of French paper dolls. They came in six kinds. "The dresses are perfectly beautiful," said the Stirn catalog.[1] In many boxed sets, the doll itself would be in underclothes, so that you could outfit her with a dress you could dream about. One set came with the elegant gowns that had been worn by president's wives at inauguration time. No matter how glamorous, paper dolls never seemed quite as much fun as their more expensive sisters, for they were harder to play with. The old song *She's Only a Paper Doll* said it all.

When did the first "real" fashion dolls appear? As early as the fifteenth century, the French were using elaborately outfitted dolls to advertise the latest in French clothing. These dolls were shipped abroad to the royal courts of Europe so that the ladies of these courts could see, envy, and then buy the latest French fashions, for the French court at Versailles was universally acknowledged to be the world center for fashion. These dolls, some of which were life-size, were equipped with every article of clothing, right on down to their underwear.

Fig. 3.1. An early American fashion doll.

Long after these dolls had gone, the term "French fashion doll" remained. But now, it meant no more than a rich child's doll (Fig. 3.1). By the 1880s, these dolls were favorites among the well-to-do children of England and America. These dolls were not dolls at all, but little adults. In England, Queen Victoria herself was turned into a little fashion doll. Sometimes, media figures of the time became models for these dolls. Among others, there was a Jenny Lind doll, who looked just like the famous singer. Regardless of whom the doll represented, she was sure to be fashionable. Her porcelain head would be delicately painted, with real hair that was elaborately coiffed, and these dolls came with all sorts of possessions—combs, sewing kits, miniature sheet music, books, and playing cards.

These early fashion dolls were much more than just dolls. As Kristina Haugland of the Philadelphia Museum of Art has put it, "They were meant to shape the expectations of the little girls who owned them and teach them all the things they'd need to know to succeed in the most ostentatious era ever."[2] Just as did all elegant ladies of the time, fashion dolls wore corsets to keep their figures in shape (Fig. 3.2). These dolls were similar to Barbie in many ways. But they differed in one very important respect. Unlike the Barbies of today, they were meant for rich and royal children, and were far too costly for everyday families to buy.

In later years, fashion dolls began to change. For one thing, fewer and fewer dignitaries such as Queen Victoria were represented. Instead, media celebs such as Shirley Temple became the norm. Just as does Barbie, these later fashion dolls kept up with all of the latest fads. Upscale doll Amaryllis Blanchard was a cloth doll who was dressed like a "flapper" of the 1920s. She had twelve suit coat and dress ensembles, several evening gowns, a velvet cape, sweaters, gloves, thirty-two pairs of shoes, twenty-eight hats, jewelry and purses. Besides her personal outfit, she had accessories such as a steamer trunk, a photo album, skis, a bathing suit, and a pet dog.

The Triumph of Barbie

Fashion dolls such as Amaryillis had been around for years. But none of these dolls ever swept across America as Barbie did. What was the secret of Barbie's triumph? First of all, it was her affordability. By the mid-1900s, the promise of the Industrial Revolution was finally becoming a reality for most Americans. Until then, the Industrial Revolution had still not reached all American families. Girls who lived in poorer families might dream of having a fashion doll, but their fate would be to have a doll of rags, and perhaps a paper doll or two. And some of these girls might have no dolls at all, for work on the

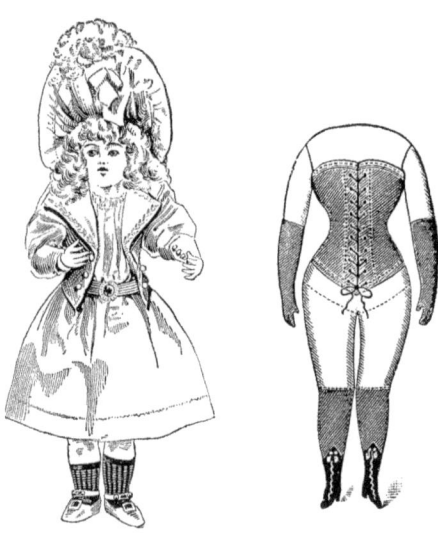

Fig. 3. 2. This doll of the 1890s wore a corset.

fields or in the mills would take their childhood away from them at an early age. But in the years following World War II, life finally became a time of hope for poorer Americans. Just as did those who were better off, they could hope for a home in the suburbs, and a car, or even two, in every garage. Now, there were many gadgets, from power mowers to washing machines to buy. For girls, there were affordable fashion dolls. In earlier times, fashion dolls such as Amaryllis were made by highly skilled craftsmen and were too expensive for most girls to have. But now, machines could make these dolls by the thousands, and a girl who belonged to a family of modest means could afford to have a Barbie.

Although affordability was one reason why Barbie became a success, there was another reason that was even more important. By the early 1960s, every little girl across America was talking about Barbie, for she was the image of what little girls wanted to be when they were older. With a curvaceous body, a glamorous if indefinite face, a huge closet of clothes and other accessories, and a handsome boyfriend named Ken, she was every girl's dream doll.

Liz Berg remembered how it was when she was a girl. "I *loved* that doll! ... I had it on the best authority from my friend Vicky, a doll connoisseur, that the Barbie doll was *it*." And so, Liz robbed her cigar-box bank and headed off to the toy store with Vicky. "There she is," Vicky said respectfully. "That one." I stared at Barbie wide-eyed, dry-throated, and probably faint with desire. Barbie had everything—a long silk ponytail, a fetching black and white swimsuit, tiny pearl earrings, painted nails. And all those accessories: blue underwear, a girdle, a slinky black evening gown, a pink chiffon scarf. "Let me tell you, I got a good cheap thrill putting *that* thing on Barbie," remembered Berg (Fig. 3.3).[3]

Why was Barbie was so attractive to young girls like Berg? By midcentury, when Berg was young, American girls were becoming increasingly obsessed with their appearance. As Joan Brumberg notes, the "girls of today make the body into an all-consuming project in ways young women of the past did not," which was something of a social revolution. In earlier times, says Brumberg, "many parents tried to limit their daughter's interests in superficial things, such as hairdos, dresses, or the size of their waists, because character was considered more important than beauty by both parents and community." All that changed, and as Wendy Jones notes, Barbie became immensely desirable to young girls because "her main job is to work on her own body."[4]

Barbie offered young girls much more than just the allure of looking cool. Lisa Zeiger remembers her as "the slate on which we etched our future womanhood." To Zeiger, she was "the first grown-up confidant for girls accustomed to tending charges like Raggedy Ann." Barbie was also the first emancipated doll. Zeiger remembered the toy called Barbie's Dream House as a shrine to independence. It was her second skin, said Zeiger, where she lived *alone*.[5]

And it was the media that told girls about Barbie and bound them in their desire for the doll. By the 1960s, the media had created a mass culture among the young, banding them in their lifestyles and wants. A young girl who was growing up on the frontier of early America might have a few girl friends, but she would be largely unaware of what other girls across the country were playing with. But by the 1960s, all girls saw the same cool images on TV, and wanted the products it advertised. And those who didn't see these messages were "uncool," out of it. Today's definition of a lonely child is the little boy or girl who does not have a television to watch, and does not know what everyone else is talking about.

Her affordability, coupled with the voices of thousands of girls, all clamoring for a Barbie, made it hard for mothers to say no when their daughters asked for the doll. But something else made it even harder. In earlier times, parents decided what was good for a child, and that was that, even if a child was unhappy about their decisions. But by the 1960s, the older, more Puritan way of decision had been replaced by the "fun morality," described in the chapter Commercialization of Toys. Now, if your child was happy, all was well. If not, you must be doing something wrong. Thus, it became very hard for many mothers to refuse a daughter who pouted because she could not have a Barbie. And if a mother did say no, a child could find ways to have one anyway. Judy Attfield, who is a Barbie expert, remembered what happened. As she said, friends of hers who were refused Barbies

Fig. 3.3. An early Barbie. She is coming home from the beach.

"resorted to playing with them clandestinely,"[6] smuggling borrowed dolls into their house, or going over to play with a friend's or collecting them later in life.

Her affordability, the mass culture of childhood, and the rise of fun morality all helped to make Barbie a smashing success. Something else helped. This was the sophisticated marketing strategy that Mattel developed to sell her. There were several parts to this strategy. First, Barbie was to be a walking clothes hanger, a young lady who had all of those goodies young girls might dream of having. In short, she was to be the ultimate girl consumer. Amaryllis and other early fashion dolls may have flaunted their rich assortment of clothes, but Barbie has owned so many costumes and accessories that she makes Amaryllis look like a pauper. Over the years, Barbie has gone through literally thousands of outfits, and in doing so, she has made Mattel the fourth biggest user of garment cloth in the United States.[7] In addition to her outfits, Barbie has owned a vast array of accessories, far more than Amaryllis ever dreamed of owning. They have included dream houses, cars, yachts, swimming pools, health clubs, airplanes, ice cream shops, town houses, a ski chalet, and animals such as lion cubs, pandas, chimps, and parrots.

Besides creating a huge range of accessories, Mattel has used two other marketing strategies. The first is called segmentation. Instead of one Barbie, Mattel has created many different Barbies, each with her own personality, wardrobe, and accessories. In effect, segmentation asks children to buy more than one Barbie. Mattel's second marketing strategy is licensing, which is mentioned in the chapter The Commercialization of Toys. In this marketing strategy, Mattel sold Barbie's image (for a fee), to makers of backpacks, sweaters, socks, hats, sleeping bags, watches, cosmetics, bicycles, and foods. This increased sales of the licensed product and at the same time kept Barbie's image before the public eye. Finally, in a reverse sort of licensing, Mattel struck a deal with nineteen colleges. Barbie dolls wore the colors of these colleges. Then the college and Mattel shared the profits from sales of these collegiate Barbies.[8]

Just how successful has Barbie been? When Barbie first appeared, there were two hundred toy companies in America that sold dolls. Ten years later, only sixty remained, for the others could not survive Barbie's increasing domination of the doll market. In 1990, Barbie had become a $700 million business, and in 1993, Barbie sales hit the $1 billion mark. By 1996, Jill Barad, who was Mattel's president, could say that ninety-nine percent of all American girls between the ages of three and ten owned a Barbie, and the average girl owned eight of them. If they were lined up head to toe, all the Barbies ever sold would circle the earth more than eleven times.[9]

Bad Barbies?

Any person who is somehow different is sure to face social challenges. And the same will be true for a new kind of doll like Barbie. When she first appeared, some girls thought Barbie was too worldly. One girl said, "I would like her if there was a little less eye makeup ... if she was a little less glamorous. But how else could she attract boy dolls?"[10] But most girls had no reservations about Barbie. To them, she was a fairy princess, a doll to dream with.

But many grownups were dubious about Barbie. A writer in *Nation* magazine put it this way: "Big sister is watching your little daughters. She is Barbie, the 'teen-age fashion doll' [who is] rearranging the souls of girls between the ages of 6 and 15."[11] Many adults were concerned about Barbie's figure. Her dimensions, 5½ inches, 3 inches and 4¾ inches, translated into a full-size Barbie with a 39-inch bosom, a waist of 21 inches and hips of 33 inches. When Barbie first appeared, her somewhat voluptuous figure bothered many people. M.L. Lord, who wrote *Forever Barbie*, includes an interview with a mother of an eight-year-old. When shown Barbie, she seemed embarrassed and actually blushed. "One thing ... my daughter would be fascinated. She loves dolls with figures. I don't think I would buy this for that reason. It has too much of a figure.... (She stared at the doll for a long time) ... I'm sure she would like to have one, but I wouldn't buy it. All these kids talk about is how the teachers jiggle. I think that would be all that she would observe...."[12]

Interestingly, some men were particularly worried about Barbie's figure. In the 1960s, most toy buyers for retail stores were men. Because Barbie had breasts, they assumed that she would be a market failure, because most mothers would refuse to buy Barbie. But that's not what happened. The buyers had forgotten to ask young girls what they thought of Barbie, and in spite of their reservations, Barbie became an instant hit with pre-teen girls, and the buyers were caught short-handed. It took three years before stores could catch up with the demand for Barbie.[13]

Barbie was responsible for many a mother's upset, and she may have been responsible for something much more serious. Many American girls are dissatisfied with their figures. For example, a University of Arizona study found that nine out of ten express dissatisfaction with their bodies.[14] Given this and similar findings, is it possible that Barbie's unreal figure is, in part at least, responsible for the epidemic of anorexia that has swept across American girlhood in the last thirty years? Do girls say, "I want to be as skinny as Barbie," and so, enter into eating habits that get them in trouble?

The rag dolls of early America were very simple in form, and could represent just about anyone. But Barbie is different. Her clothes and accessories tell little girls exactly who she is. Does this deprive a girl of the chance to use her own imagination? Edward Nelson, president of Vogue Dolls, thought so. He said, "A simple doll gives the child a greater opportunity to express her own personality." Nelson thought that much of the problem stemmed from TV: "Youngsters are brought up watching TV almost from birth ... they learn to be passive and let someone else do things for them, so it's not surprising they respond to this type of doll."[15] But others have felt that children may see Barbie's very complexity as providing all sorts of cues for imaginative play. Child psychologist Brian Sutton-Smith has warned that we must be careful not to project our own anxieties upon children, who can see the world in a very different way.[16] It may be that the realism of Barbie does not restrict a child's imagination. Instead, this realism may provide all sorts of cues for imaginative play that are not present in a simple baby doll.

If you are a world celebrity, it's inevitable that you will be watched all the time by media gossips who will report all the weird things that you have done. And this has happened to Barbie. In the late 1980s, Carine Guillot, a nurse from Tinton Falls, New Jersey, bought a Ken doll, and discovered something unexpected: Ken had Barbie's clothes on. Her reaction was, "Oh my God! Now we have a cross-dressed Ken!" Guillot and her daughter collect Barbies and Kens, and are sure this Ken will become very valuable.[17]

Another embarrassing thing happened with Mattel's "Teen Talk" Barbie. Mattel had created 270 phrases for Teen Talk Barbie, and four of these would go into each doll. Unfortunately, one of these phrases was "Math class is tough." Harmless enough, except that the talking Kens did not say this. The American Association of University Women, the National Council of Teachers of Mathematics, and other similar groups complained, and Barbie, the dumb blonde, became a national joke.[18]

And then there were the swappers. Imagine you had bought a Teen Talk Barbie for your young daughter, who then comes running into your room in tears. She pushes the talk button, and Barbie roars "Attack!" "Vengeance is mine!" and "Eat lead, Cobra!" It turned out that a group of performance artists living in Manhattan's East Village had purchased G.I. Joe and Barbie dolls, and swapped their voice boxes. The mutant Barbies were then put back on store shelves. "It's a cheap shot, and it's unfair to the kids," said Joanne Oppenheim of the Oppenheim Toy Portfolio, but the media thought it was great.[19]

Good Barbies

From the very day she appeared, Barbie came under criticism. She was a hedonist, a seeker of earthly pleasures, and a sensualist who was interested only in her body. Because of this, Barbie might give young girls bad values. But might she also be a good role model for young girls? In one study, researchers found that this was so. They watched girls at play with dolls, and recorded negative behaviors such as hitting, kicking, pushing, grabbing, and teasing. Girls who played with ordinary dolls showed much more negative behavior than those who were playing with Barbie.[20]

Barbie could be more than just a hedonistic airhead. She could teach girls to get along with each other. What else might Barbie teach? In earlier times many dolls had helped train girls to be mothers. But these were new times in which more and more girls were thinking about entering a career beyond that of being a mother. Thus, Barbie began to turn into a career girl. By the mid-1980s, Mattel had created "Day to Night" Barbie. She came with a fashionable skirt which she could wear when she went out at night. But she also had a business suit to wear when at the office during the day.[21]

Fig. 3.4. Thirty years later, Barbie has grown up and become an airline pilot.

But Day to Night Barbie was just the beginning. Under the tutelage of Jill Barad, who was President of Mattel, Barbie became a ballerina, airline pilot, chef, veterinarian, doctor, and even an astronaut (Fig. 3.4). Many of these new Barbies came equipped with videos that gave girls a chance to explore the career that each Barbie represented. For example, Fashion Designer Barbie had a video that let girls create 15,000 different outfits, which Barbie could then wear.[22]

Barbie's change from airhead to career girl reflected the increasing interest that most of today's girls have in entering a career of some kind. But Mattel's new Barbies were more than just a response to the desires of today's girls. Mattel was being challenged by other companies that had also begun to make career dolls. If unchallenged, these other companies were certain to capture more and more of the doll market. As Mattel fought back by creating career Barbies, the company had an inspiration: why not create a Barbie that was at the very top of the career pyramid? And so, a Barbie for President doll was born. Barbie for President was well received by feminists. For example, Andree Brooks, founder of the Women's Campaign School at Yale University said "there is reason for rejoicing to learn that Mattel is coming out with a Barbie for President.... It is difficult enough to persuade good women to look upon elective office as a worthwhile option.... Perhaps Barbie can now overcome that reluctance by making it a trendy career choice."[23]

BARBIE AND HER FRIENDS: CHANGING TO MEET CHANGE

In the 1950s, it was fashionable for women to be broad-shouldered, narrow-hipped, and to have a high bosom. And that's how Barbie was built. Ten years later, the "Natural Look" was in, and so Mattel gave Barbie a softer, more natural body.

What else has Mattel done? What about introducing some Barbie friends who break away from the Barbie stereotype? In 1997, Mattel did just that, and introduced Wheelchair Becky, a doll with a disability. Later, she became Becky, the Paralympic Champion, which made her even more a part of our mainstream (Fig. 3.5).

What about creating other friends who break the Barbie stereotype? As Kathleen Lawrence of State University College at Cortland, New York, said, "I'd rather give Barbie some friends who are really different ... maybe one who's sensitive and one who's very good at school, and one who's very funny, so who cares how she looks."[24]

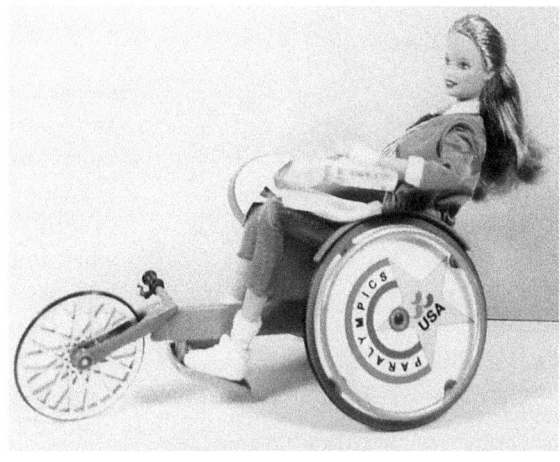

3.5. Paralympic Champion Becky

Mattel has listened to comments such as these, and has worked hard at diversifying Barbie. One example was the "Rock Diva Jam n' Glam Barbie," aimed at older girls. Another Barbie helped Hispanic girls celebrate the teen rite of passage called Quinceanera. And there was even a Barbie who starred in a full-length video of *The Nutcracker*.[25]

In spite of these innovations, Barbie's sales have fallen off. Why is this? In large part it is the result of two changes that are beyond Mattel's control. Years ago, girls as old as twelve would play with Barbie and her friends. Today, young girls have become much more sophisticated. Now, Barbie's primary user is between five and seven years old. And even seven-year-olds often think of Barbie as babyish, for many of them would rather watch MTV than play with dolls.

A second change has been of equal importance. When she first appeared in the 1960s, Barbie stood alone as a new kind of fashion doll. Now, there are dozens of competitors. The Bratz are one example. In 2001 and 2002, they outsold Barbie in the fashion doll category (Fig. 3.6).[26]

Finally, some Americans think that we are overly concerned with looks, sex, and material goods. Suppose these concerns became strong enough to reshape our cultural values. What kind of doll would replace Barbie and her competitors such as the Bratz? Could Laila give us a hint? Laila is very different from Barbie and the Bratz. Her body is that of a ten-year-old. And unlike Barbie and the Bratz with their designer clothes, Laila wears a simple short-sleeved blouse and skirt. Laila is made in Cairo, Egypt, and is designed with Arab sensitivities in mind. "There is a cultural gap when an Arab girl plays with a doll like Barbie," says Abla Ibrahim, who is director of the Arab League's department of childhood. "The average Arab girl's reality is different from Barbie's, with her swimming pool, Cadillac, blond hair, and boyfriend

Fig. 3.6. With their "in your face" look and dozens of fashion accessories, the Bratz dolls seem more hedonistic than Barbie has ever been. But they have not been attacked as happened to Barbie. In fact, in 2001 and 2002, they outsold her.

Ken," he says. If America ever became as culturally conservative as are the Arab nations, would Barbie and the Bratz then become Lailas?[27]

ACTION FIGURES

Girls have their Barbies and Bratz dolls. Boys also have their dolls, but they would never use that word. Instead, their dolls are "action figures."

Who invented action figures? Could toy soldiers have slowly evolved into little action men? There is no evidence for this, although it does seem significant that as action figures became more popular, toy soldiers declined.

In all likelihood, the ancestors of the action figures were born in the media. What kind of media? The first may have been books. In 1887, Palmer Cox published a fantasy book called *The Brownies*.[28] The Brownies were strange but likable little people, who emerged every evening from their forest haunts to play games and get into all kinds of trouble. At first, the Brownies existed only in their book, but soon, they became a simple cardboard standup toy (Fig 3.7).

The Brownies were followed by a host of other stand-up figures which had also begun their lives in the media. Many, like Andy Gump, Maggie and Jiggs, and Barney Google came out of comic strips or books. Some of these characters, such as Popeye, are still to be found in toy stores. Full of fun and folly, these comic stand-up toys were used by both girls and boys.

But that began to change. After all, as the old rhyme has put it, girls are made of sugar and spice, but little boys are made of frogs, snails and puppy dog tails. And so, cartoon characters began to specialize. Some, the kinder and gentler action figures like Little Orphan Annie, were aimed at girls, But other action figures, the rough and ready ones, were for boys. Heroes of the Wild West were just right for boys. And so, Matt Dillon, Roy Rogers, and other legendary cowboys were turned into small gun-toting action figures that little boys could admire.

At first, action figures aimed at boys came out of comic strips or comic books. But soon, that began to change, for more and more of these rugged action figures were beginning their lives in the movies or on television.

By the 1960s, most boys were familiar with the antics of these action figures, for almost all boys were going to the movies and watching television. Because of this, when toy versions of these rugged heroes entered stores as action figures, they were already celebrities. And so, they were snapped up by boys who wanted to play with "real life" versions of their media heroes. By the 1970s, an endless variety of these action figures were filling the shelves of toy stores.

How to play with these toys? That was easily answered, for each came with a story line that had been developed in the movies or on television. The Power Rangers action figure which flooded the toy stores during the Christmas season of 1994, had this story line: Rita Repulsa, a horned witch who lived on the moon, had sent her evil aliens to conquer the earth. A small group of clean-cut American teenagers vowed to fight the aliens. As they did that, the teens morphed into kick-boxing super heroes, the Power Rangers, who whacked the evil invaders into oblivion.[29]

The Incredible Hulk (Fig. 3.8), who is another popular action figure, had a very different origin. The Hulk began as a normal human named Bruce Banner, who found that he could turn into a hulking green monster and use his incredible strength to lash out at a variety of evildoers.[30]

As we saw a bit earlier, Barbie has had her ups and downs. Barbie's early success stemmed from the fact that she was unique. And her current problems are largely due to competition from an increasing number of fashion dolls that resemble her.

The action figures have a very different problem to contend with: if we think aggression in toys is acceptable, the action figures will thrive. But if we think aggressive toys give children bad habits, the sales of action figures will go down.

Ever since they first appeared, toy watchers have worried about aggressive toys such as the action figures. Nancy Carlsson Paige and Diane Levin, who are professors of education, have been particularly outspoken. In their 1987 book, *The War Play Dilemma*, they argued that these television action figures create an entirely new kind of war play. In their words, "The

Fig. 3.7. You name the trouble, the Brownies could get into it! Inset shows one of the very first action figures: Brownie of the 1890s.

Fig. 3.8. The Incredible Hulk

nature of the war toys themselves has been changing more dramatically in recent years than in any time since the invention of the 'cap gun.'... Whereas, with the basic cap or water gun, children in the past were required to create their own play around the 'shooting' theme, children can now buy a whole range of war-related toys that are based on the violent television shows they are watching. Thus, for most children's programs, a line of toys that includes the main characters, scenery, and weapons is marketed, with elaborate packaging describing the attributes of each toy. These 'program-based' toys allow and even encourage children to reproduce in play the scripts they have seen on the programs, rather than to invent their own play content."[31] To Carlsson Paige and Levin, this content is no longer one of heroic battles and good guys versus bad ones. Instead, the message these television action figures have for children is that mindless violence is acceptable, even good. The schoolchildren that the authors watched did seem to be mindless in their play, and in interviews, teachers said that they had seen the same sort of thing in their own students.

But others feel that children do not mindlessly mimic violence when they play with their action figures. Child psychologist Brian Sutton-Smith had students survey nine preschools, watching the war play of children. Each student kept a record of what he or she had seen. Television seemed to play only a minor role in directing their play. When they did engage in war play, these children made up their own scenarios, and did not mimic television. If they became violent, it was over the use of some toy, and not the result of anything on a television program.[32].

Sometimes, criticism of action figures has been very focused. For example, some toy watchers have argued that G.I. Joe (Fig. 3.9) has no business being a high-tech world policeman, especially when some of his victims look like Arabs.[33]

But most opposition to the warlike habits of action figures is more generalized. G.I. Joe is a fine example of this. When he first came out in 1969, the Vietnam War was getting underway, and Joe thrived. But by 1968, our hostility to what many saw as a failed war hurt Joe's sales badly. By the 1970s, and the appearance of the Flower Generation, Joe's looks had changed completely. Now he wore a peace medal, had a bushy beard, and longish fuzzy hair.

With the advent of the first Persian Gulf War and its widespread public support, Joe's persona changed once more, and he became a military figure. Today, following 9-11 and the second Gulf War, Joe is doing very well.[34]

When she first hit the stores, Barbie's somewhat voluptuous body created a storm of protest. What about the action figures? Some of them, such as the Hulk, are impossibly muscular. Even those who are closer to real males in their body build still have physiques that most of us males would envy. Might this pose a problem for young boys? Dr. Harrison Pope of Harvard University's McClean Hospital notes that action figures might induce young boys to take dangerous drugs such as anabolic steroids.[35]

Fig. 3.9. Over the years, G.I. Joe has been a military policeman, action marine, action sailor, astronaut, land adventurer, and infantryman.

4
Toys That Come Alive

"Alive" is one of those words that is easy to say, but hard to define. Just what does it mean to be alive? A thesaurus suggests these as meanings: vital, lively, active, animated, and aware. How might a toy be given these characteristics? One way is through television.

THE LIVING TV TOY

The earliest regular television broadcasts began in the 1930s. At first, television sets were expensive, and programming was limited. For the next ten years, television grew very slowly. By 1940, there were still only four thousand television sets in America. But after World War II, television began to grow, and by the 1980s, almost 99 percent of America's households had television.[1]

In its early days, television was seen as part of the family circle. It could promote family togetherness. Advertisements and magazine articles often showed the family clustered about the television set, which was in the living room or the family room. Television, said many experts, would bring the family closer together, for family members could join in watching its rich variety of programs. One 1949 study found that television viewers had "an awareness of enhanced family solidarity." Parents hoped it might be a way of teaching children values such as honesty, respect and hard work. Television programs such as *The Waltons* or *Little House on the Prairie* were examples of how television could do this. Furthermore, television might help fight juvenile delinquency, for it kept children off the streets.

But as television matured, this image of togetherness faded away, for each member of the family sought his or her particular kind of TV show. For example, young children were increasingly drawn to cartoons and to the action shows mentioned in the last chapter. As television became increasingly important to children, business people began to ask themselves how they could best use television to advertise their wares to young people. Before they could answer this, they had to learn more about the viewing habits of children. When in the day did they watch television, and how much time did they spend in front of the tube? Here is a summary of what researchers have found: Children watch a great deal of television. Some say it's as much as four hours a day.[2] Saturday morning is a favorite viewing time. So is after school, when they are likely to grab a snack and begin watching television. Researchers have learned about the times when children watch television, but they have also learned something else, which is even more important: most of a child's viewing is done when parents are absent. In more and more homes, parents are away at work or, if at home, are busy about the house. Consequently, television has become a baby sitter. But it is more than just a baby sitter. With parents absent, toy makers saw how television could talk freely with children.

Could toys be sold on television? Would children actually go out and buy the toys they saw on television? As they sought answers to this question, researchers discovered that a new world of toy buying had developed in America. In earlier times, parents would choose and buy toys for their children. But by the mid-1900s, the notion of "fun morality," which was cited in the last chapter, was telling parents that they must do things to keep their children happy. In the past, parents would choose those toys they thought would be "educational" for their children. But fun morality told parents that children should decide what toys they wanted.

Even if a parent did not want to buy the toy a child wanted, the child often went ahead and bought the toy him or herself. Children could do this, for more and more of them were getting handsome allowances. By the mid-1990s, five-year-olds in comfortable families were receiving $1 or $2 a week, and would receive $5 by age twelve. In earlier times, an allowance was seen as a nest egg for the future. However, many baby boomer parents saw allowances as money to be spent as a reward for a child's good behavior, or as a way to keep children happy. And so, children became powerful players in the world of toy buying. One recent report estimates that today's children either buy or influence the buying of $220 billion of goods every year, and a significant portion of those goods are toys.[3]

Very early on, toy makers saw how television might become a toy salesman of unprecedented power. Millions of children were addicted to television. Why not get them to ask for toys that they had seen on television? Or better yet, get them to spend their allowances on a television-touted toy?

What would a TV toy salesman be like? Children had always loved comic characters such as Mickey Mouse. If Mickey was on television, could he sell toys to children? In 1955, Elliot and Ruth Handler, the owners of the Mattel Toy Company, decided to find out. They invested $500,000 in a new television show, *The Mickey Mouse Club*. Their investment would give the Handlers the right to decide on the advertising that went with the show. It really was a risk for the Handlers, for Mattel was still a small company and $500,000 represented its total value. Could Mickey really sell Mattel toys? To see what would happen, the Handlers had Mickey sponsor a few of their toys, including one called the Burp Gun.

At first, the Handlers were disappointed at the lack of results, for the sales of the Burp Gun did not go up. But the Handlers had not allowed for the inevitable time lag that almost always occurs between a new advertisement and the sales it might create. Six weeks after their Burp Gun advertisement had first appeared, Mattel staff people went to work one morning, and found that they could not get into the front door of their building, because it was piled high with envelopes. When they finally did enter, phones were ringing off the hook. The letters and phone calls were coming from people who were asking Mattel for Burp Guns. Mattel's advertisement on *The Mickey Mouse Club* television show was a fantastic success.[4]

A show could act as a salesperson on TV, telling children about some new toy they might like. But it could do more than this. What if the toy sold itself? In the 1980s, Mattel built a show that did just this. It created one of the very first of the action figure shows that were described in the last chapter. The show was called *He-Man and the Masters of the Universe*. In it, all sorts of toys came alive, doing dangerous and heroic things. Children loved their adventures. But children could do more than just watch these toys in action, for the show told them that He-Man toys were available in stores. Soon, Mattel's show was on 120 television stations across America, and He-Man toy sales were booming.[5] Today, TV advertising of this kind dominates the marketing strategy of Mattel and other large toy companies.[6] One result, as we saw in the chapter on toy weapons, is that action figures have become a major part of a young boy's life.

Are TV Toys Deceptive?

These advertisements were very different than the advertisements that had earlier appeared in newspapers or magazines, for those had simply pictured a toy. But with television, a toymaker could show his toy in action, and make it do all sorts of things that would entice the watching child to go out and buy the toy. Do these advertisements tend to be deceptive? Do they show a toy doing things that could never take place in real life? Sometimes, this has happened. For example, one television show featured Hasbro's G.I. Joe Battle Copter. On television, the helicopter flew and hovered just as real ones do. What the viewer did not know was that Hasbro's television helicopter was rigged, for it was suspended by invisible wires. The Consumer Union filed a complaint with the Federal Trade Commission, which forced Hasbro to change its helicopter's behavior and pay a $175,000 civil penalty.[7]

Children are supposed to be more innocent than are adults. Are they more likely to be deceived by rigged television toys than an adult? In the early 1990s, there was a television special which asked whether television toys really did fool children. It was called *Buy Me That Too! A Kid's Survival Guide to T.V. Advertising.* The journal *Advertising Age* asked a panel for its opinion about the special. Two of the panelists were children. One was Alison Dowdle, aged eight. When the journal asked her if she liked the show, Alison said, "It was OK. Now, I know not to ask Mom for things on television." She also talked about a program which showed a doll that made pictures on the ceiling and had a magical sound: "I don't really believe it makes that sound, and it probably costs a lot." Before they watched the special, both Alison and her brother, Brian, aged 10, said that they believed most shows were honest. What did they think about them after they saw the special? Alison: "It's not nice to do to kids." Brian: "I think they shouldn't advertise on television."

Many of the adult viewers who had watched the special worked in areas related to marketing. Bob Garfield, editor at large of *Advertising Age*, said this of the special: "No harm done if kids harbor a healthy skepticism about the motives and ethics of American marketers. The problem is, however, that kids are apt to leave this show with an *unhealthy* suspicion about the business world." And John OToole, president of the American Association of Advertising Agencies said "Where are the parents who are saying 'No, we're not going to give you the money to buy that. You don't need that?'"[8]

The general public seems to be ambivalent about television shows that are directed toward children, for the findings are contradictory. A 1994 poll found that eight of ten adults agreed that business marketing exploits children. But a still later poll, taken in 1997, found that over eighty percent of adults felt these toy advertisements were acceptable at any time on television.[9]

As for children, some earlier work seemed to show that they were often deceived by television shows. But more recent work suggests that by the time they are five, many, perhaps most, children understand that advertising can be deceptive. For example, Maire Davis, who did research on children's understanding of television, found that 92 percent of her subjects knew that the Superman and Batman shown in television shows could not really fly, and 78 percent agreed that television shows make toys look better than they really are.[10]

Do TV Toys Brainwash Children?

Because children sit and watch a television toy doing something, does this mean that they will buy the toy and mechanically re-enact its television adventures, rather than thinking up new things for the toy to do? As Diane Levin, a professor at Boston's Wheelock College, said, television toys "promote play that is imitative rather than creative," that children "mimic the dialogue they have heard and re-enact scenes instead of creating their own."[11] In his research, Stephen Kline, who wrote *Out of the Garden: Toys, TV, and Children's Culture in the Age of Marketing*, found that his young subjects even used television dialogue in their play. As he says, these toys and their fantasy play "are not designed to enhance children's creativity." Instead, they merely encourage children to imitate what they see on television.[12]

Is this concern a valid one? Do TV toys really condition children to carry out copycat behavior, blindly imitating what they have seen on the tube? Tom Engelhardt, who has written in the area of popular culture, including toys, thinks it's a mistaken concern. He says the idea that the TV toy is some kind of all-powerful monster that forces children to follow its dictates is simply wrong. Speaking of children's play, Engelhardt says this: "Just a look at the weird things they do with the melange of toys on their floors can remind a parent that the toy company's selling-story may not be the only fantasy on a child's mind."[13]

There is evidence in support of Englehardt's view. Ironically, some of it comes right out of Kline's book. Here is what Kline says about television as a conditioner of children: "Although critics have launched many assaults, researchers have been unable to demonstrate clear and consistent behavioral effects of television."[14] And this, with respect to the idea that children replay what they see a TV toy do: "We interviewed, observed, and studied over 200 children between the ages of six and eight in order to assess whether television helps to tip the balance between discovery and mimicry in children's play." His findings: Only fifteen percent of the children said that they structured their play to be just like that on television. All the rest either incorporated a few elements from the television show into their play, or ignored its message. And these children were very much aware that the television shows were fantasy, and nothing more. If asked "Do Inhumanoids exist," or "Could you go and see Barbie at a rock concert?" the children thought the researchers were being stupid and laughed at them.[15]

And Wayne Charness, a spokesperson for Hasbro said, "Anyone who thinks children only mimic what they see on television … hasn't watched how kids play."[16]

DO TV TOYS INSTILL BAD VALUES IN CHILDREN?

Besides depriving children of a chance to imagine, numerous critics feel that these programs give children bad values; that their toys are all too often in bad taste. Sometimes, rather gross toys do appear on television. Back in the 1980s, the hulking monster Great Garloo showed up on television, where he went about wrecking trains and causing other damage. Mercifully, TV monsters such as Garloo were short lived. And in their brief existence, a few might even have helped, rather than harmed children. Speaking of another TV monster, Aurora's Frankenstein, one mother did think he helped her young son. "He was always imagining monsters were close at hand," she said. "Now, he realizes his fears were silly."[17]

Some critics feel television toy shows pay too little attention to religious values. In his book, *Turmoil in the Toybox*, Phil Phillips said, "Television generally does not give much credence to Christian beliefs or concepts. As you know, television gives credence to the occult and psychic power by presenting it and not trying to disprove it. Many shows, especially cartoons, are 'saturated' with the occult."[18]

Operating at a more secular level, some critics think children's television promotes a desire for instant gratification, and makes children too status conscious. As Russel Laczniak, a professor of Marketing at Iowa State University says, all too often, kids want a television toy not because of the fun they will have, but because others have the toy, and they want to be part of the "in crowd." Anna Simulinas, a New York mother of two, says "My girls see a toy they recognize from television … and right away, they're asking for it."[19]

Have the producers of children's network television made much of an attempt to improve children's television? Many people think not, and this failing has prodded the federal government into action. It has mandated that each television station must demonstrate to the Federal Communications Commission that it has served the "educational and informational needs" of children. Stations can either do this through three hours per week of educational shows or by some other method that is acceptable to the FCC. This rule was implemented in the fall of 1997. Assuming that it will remain in force, it will be interesting to see how much television will change under this rule.

What about parents? After all, they represent the "front line" in deciding what children should watch. Parents do complain about the quality of children's television, but that does not mean that they are willing to do much about it. When CBS canceled *Captain Kangaroo*, which everyone considered a fine, educational program, there was a public outcry — this fine children's show should not be allowed to die! Yet its ratings told another story, for they had been low for years.

THE ROBOTIC TOY

For thousands of years, children had to make do with toys that were powerless. A child might use his own power to make a toy work, as was so for a jumping jack. But the minute he or she stopped, so did the toy. Sometimes, nature would help out. A strong wind could fly a kite, a river send a toy boat on its way. But nature is fickle, and when the wind or water stopped, so did the toy.

Very early on, inventors began to design toys which contained built in sources of power. An inventive genius must have looked at the water wheels which helped to irrigate fields and asked himself: If the wheel were very small and powered by sand, could it be used to power a toy? And indeed it could. Figure 4.1A and 4.1B shows how sand can make a wheel turn. As the sand falls through the wheel, it makes a small figure on the front of the box seem to be alive, for he turns, just as does a real acrobat.

By the early 1800s, these little acrobat toys had become a popular American toy. They were called Leotards, after a real Leotard, who was a famous French acrobat. The Leotard toy would be placed on the parlor table, where everyone in the family could marvel at his ability to turn circles in unpredictable ways. Kenneth Grahame, the English author of *Wind in the Willows*, remembered his Leotard: "He was an acrobat, this Leotard, who lived in a glass fronted box. His loose-jointed limbs were cardboard, his slender trunk and his hands eternally grasped the bar of a trapeze. You turned the box around five or six times; the wonderful unsolved machinery worked and Leotard swung and leapt backwards and forwards, now

Top left: Fig. 4.1A. When the box is turned in a circle and then placed on a table, the Leotard figure turns somersaults. ***Top right:*** Fig. 4.1B. How the toy works: A sand wheel is hidden inside the box. When the box is turned, the sand goes above the wheel, and flows down onto it, so that the wheel turns back and forth, which turns the toy.

astride the bar, now flying free; iron jointed, supple sinewed, unceasingly novel in his invention of new unguessable attitudes...."[20]

But sand toys stopped moving as soon as their sand gave out. And toy sailboats did the same in a calm. Could there be a toy that carried internal power, which allowed it to walk, talk, and do all the other things living things do? In an earlier America, this idea would have belonged to science fiction. But today, toys of this sort have become a reality. What can these "robotic" toys do? Furby, one of the best-known of these new toys, danced when it heard music, and used infared technology to chat with other Furbies (Fig. 4.2).[21] The B.I.O. Bugs made by Hasbro were another example. Giant robot insects for use on the floor, the B.I.O.s learned to avoid obstacles such as a wall or chair. And they fought each other. A dog called i-Cybie was even more sophisticated. It could learn to do tricks, and had moods just as humans do. When it was dark and wintery, i-Cybie's tail went down, and its mouth closed. And yet another dog, Poo-Chi, also came alive. It could sit, stand, dance and bark.

And the dolls! More and more of them are chattering away. Even supposedly dumb Barbie has come alive, for she can dance to music. And the Amazing Dolls can remember dates, tell stories, and play games. Children love these toys, and so do those who make and sell them. "The whole concept of a machine being alive is enthralling," says robot inventor Harry Thorne.[22]

Predictions are always risky. But it seems likely that electronic toys such as the B.I.O. Bugs and i-Cybie will soon dominate the playroom. As one toy watcher says, "The robotic category is going to be very crowded." [23] And this electronic ability will take many forms. By the year 2000 about half of all American toys were voice activated.[24]

When did all of this start? About two hundred years ago, toys started to come alive. As one might expect, dolls

Fig. 4.2. Furby

were the first to do this. To come alive, dolls need to walk about. But it proved difficult to make this happen. After all, it's about year before a baby can walk, and a baby is much more sophisticated than a doll. Walking dolls did appear in the early 1800s, but most of them cheated. For example, the Waterbury Clock Company invented a walking doll, but it had oversize feet that were set on rollers. You wound its clockwork motor up, and the doll glided across the floor. Another doll of the 1800s had movable legs, but you had to grab its arm and help it along. The "Autoperipatetikos" was another early attempt at creating a walking doll. Its unlikely name is Greek for "self-walking." Its heavy bottom, which was full of machinery, helped to give it stability, and the doll did waddle along, although the instructions warned that its feet could become entangled (Fig. 4.3).[25]

These were nineteenth-century dolls, but there have been more recent attempts to create a walking doll. Pauline and Dick Madigan, who are doll watchers and collectors, found a rare French walking doll that was made in the 1920s. Making it walk was an exercise in frustration. If the floor was too slippery, or if the doll's motor was out of adjustment, or if its clothes were out of balance, "the darn thing wouldn't work."[26]

While some inventors worked to make dolls walk, others tried their hands at making them talk. The most famous of these was Thomas Edison, the inventor of the phonograph. To make his doll talk, you wound up a small phonograph in the doll's body, and it would say rhymes such as "Mary had a little lamb." Edison may not have been the first to use a phonograph in a doll, and he was not the last to do so. A later version outdid Edison's doll, for it had a seventy-five word vocabulary and spoke in three languages. The trouble with all these dolls was that they were not particularly cuddly. For example, Edison's doll weighed four pounds and was twenty-two inches tall. And it had a metal key sticking out of its back (Fig. 4.4).

In addition to a phonograph, there were other ways to make a doll talk. In some, bellows and reeds were used. But really successful talking dolls were not to come until the 1950s. By then, small batteries and computer chips had become available. Doll makers were quick to take advantage of this new technology. Noma was an example. Using the new technology, she could say, "My name is Noma, and my mommy taught me a rhyme,"[27] and another 1950s doll would clap her hands when hugged.[28]

In the 1960s, Cheerful Tearful smiled when her arms were held up, and cried when they were held down. By the 1970s, Peggy Pen Pal could write along with her owner. Baby Walk N' Play bounced a yo-yo, and Baby Luv 'N Care complained of acid digestion until you put a hot water bottle on her tummy.[29] But this was only the beginning. In the 1990s, dolls could poop, burp, cry tears, get a cold (her cheeks got red), blush, sneeze, and eat cereal.[30]

Barney, the big purple dinosaur, came out in 1998, but he remains in toy stores, and is a good example of how powerful these new dolls have become. He's big, about sixteen inches from head to toe. That gives him enough room for the six "AA" batteries he carries in his seat. Animation technology in

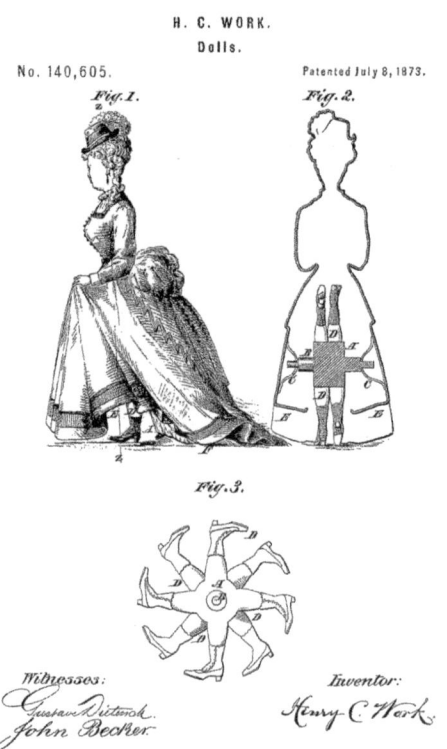

Fig. 4.3. An 1873 patent for a walking doll. Do you think it would work?

Chapter 4—Toys That Come Alive 53

Barney's hands, feet and eyes lets him do things in response to a child's commands. And finally, a voice synthesizer lets him sing and talk. A built-in transmitter lets Barney interact with PC and VCR programs. Thus, Barney is both a technological system, and a doll that is very close to coming alive. Press his hand, and he will say "Let's play!" Put him in the dark, and Barney says "Are you still there? It sure is dark." Then he says, "Let's play something different. Please let me see you." By squeezing Barney in different ways, you can get him to play twelve different games with you. And he will suggest the games: "I know a great imagination game. Think of something that flies in the sky." Barney can also sing seventeen songs. And he's no dummy, for he knows two thousand words, more than some of his owners do.[31]

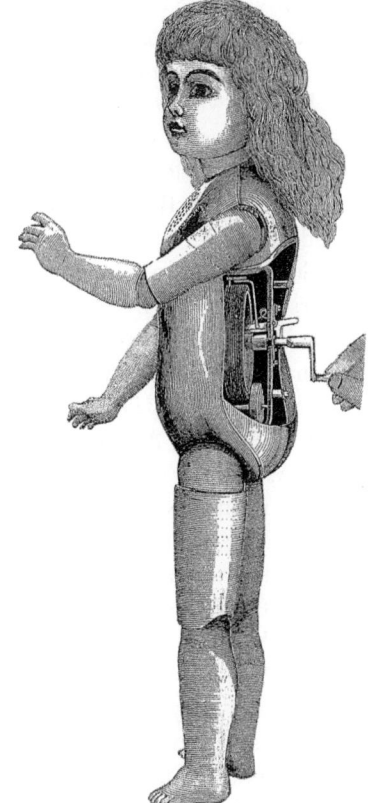

PROBLEMS WITH ROBOTIC TOYS

Fig. 4.4. Edison's talking doll. A crank winds the small phonograph inside the doll. It just did not sem to be very cuddly.

These robotic toys are fun, but they can also be very irritating. Barney is an example. If you lift him by a paw, he starts talking. Squeezing a foot and hand will shut him up, but if you don't know that, you are in trouble. In the old days, when your daughter went out, she dumped her doll on her bed, and that was that. But today, mom has to be a baby sitter. The virtual pets of a few years ago were an example. Even though they were tiny, and not very doll-like, the virtual pets were hard to baby-sit. To keep them alive, you had to clean them up, feed them, even put them to bed. If you did not do these things, the pet would die, and mom would be on one of her guilt trips when daughter came home.

And it's not just mom, for robotic toys can irritate teachers. The virtual pets were so small that children could easily bring them to class. "Kids were going to the bathroom to feed their pets," said one principal. And if confiscated by the teacher, they could go off in her desk.[32]

Robotic toys might irritate school teachers, but they can also irritate the children who own them. Amy Duncan, aged eight, loved her robotic doll who was also called Amy. But little Amy could get under her skin. "When she asks for something, you have to give it to her right then and there ... I think they should change her name to Annoying Amy. That would fit her better."[33]

Sometimes, robotic toys almost act as if they are superior to their owners. When you first turned a Furby on, it did not even bother to talk to you in English. Instead, it spoke in Furbish. But after a few days, it condescended to come down to your level and speak English.

In early 1999, Furby's language oddities got it into trouble. The National Security Agency and the Norfolk Naval Shipyard issued Furby alerts. As the Navy said, "If you see one ... you are to take proper action ... seize it and its owner ... this is a security violation." What was the problem? Apparently, it was a fear that Furby might pick up classified information and take it to some foreign country. But Roger Shipman, president of Tiger Electronics which makes Furby, was perplexed. As he said, "Although Furby is a clever toy, it does not record or mimic voices." And one child who was writing in a school newspaper asked this question: "How does Furby get into the NSA in the first place? Do they just break out Furbys at National Security meetings? Do we really want someone who does something like that protecting our country?"[34]

Beyond their ability to irritate and the silliness of Furbys, do robotic toys pose more serious problems for their owners? Some toy watchers think so. Earlier in this chapter, we heard from people who thought TV toys could stifle a child's imagination. What about a doll that can talk with you, telling you how to play, and what to do next? Would it be even more of a threat to a child's ability to imagine scenarios for the doll? Educators and others have been worrying about this for years. Dr. Benjamin Spock, the legendary children's doctor, said "Children usually love simple toys best and play with them longest. This isn't because children are simple. It's because they have so much imagination."[35] Dorothy and Jerome Singer, who are two of the leading child psychologists of our time, noted that robotic toys which come alive "often end up at the bottom of the toy chest, their batteries dead."[36] And a psychiatrist at the famed Menninger Foundation in Topeka, Kansas, said, "Young children have galloping imaginations. They can give a doll whatever kind of life they choose. It isn't desirable to have the doll supply the action." More recently, another toy watcher wrote, "Modern toys don't leave much to the imagination. Computer chips do the thinking." And psychologist David Walsh, founder and president of The National Institute on Media and the Family, adds his views: "The question is, do we want the toys to be clever, or our kids?" [37]

Could robotic dolls that interact with television pick up bad behavior and transmit it to a child? Some people think this is already happening. A recent toy, which was a replica of a World Wrestling Federation wrestler called "Stone Cold" Steve Austin, could pick up dialog from the Internet. It could also bark out taunts heard the night before on television. Should the trash-talk of wrestling be in a toy that might be used by a three-year-old? "I wouldn't buy them," said one mother. And another added, "I think it's a poor role model for children." But others thought this kind of worry was uncalled for. Kathryn Maciel, vice president of Toy Biz, which made Tuff Talking Wrestlers, said, "If kids are watching the shows, they're seeing far more."[38]

For many toy watchers, the wrestler toys have done something that's more serious than talking trash. Al Snow was a real wrestler, who entered the wrestling arena with a women's head skewered on a stick. "Help me" was written on its forehead. Swinging it around, he yelled, "What do you want?" at the audience. "Head!" they yelled back.

When a replica of Al and his head entered toy stores, an outcry resulted. Could this toy lead kids toward a later habit of spouse abuse? Under pressure, the World Wrestling Federation removed Al and his head from toy stores. However, they did so with some reluctance, because merchandise, including toys, accounts for about a third of the WWF's income. But other dubious wrestling toys remained. For example, the Bashing Brawler invited kids to smash a head and make it scream. Did these toys condition kids to be violent? No, said Maureen Kassell, a spokeswoman for the WWF. She argued that kids know the difference between reality and faked mayhem. Furthermore, toys like these are for older children. But Daphne White, founding director of the Lion and Lamb Project, an advocacy group that is concerned about violent children's entertainment, disagreed. What are parents supposed to do, asked White. Are they supposed to lock a child in a closet until his eighteenth birthday?[39]

Could robotic dolls that come alive be insulting to children? One toy watcher thought so. She was looking at the Rosie O'Donnell show on television. It was airing a segment about a doll called Baby Go Boom. As the woman said, "Rosie's intended promotion of this doll turned into a horrific display of degradation and unsympathetic bad taste." What had happened? Baby Go Boom was shown giggling, falling down, wiggling and shaking, all while on her back. Rosie's band leader laughed at the doll's antics, and said, "She has a seizure!" But the woman saw nothing funny about the doll's behavior. As she put it, "We were astonished at Ms O'Donnell's lack of sensitivity to her television audience." After all, she said, "Some children who were watching might suffer from epilepsy, and this would hurt their feelings." Was the woman overreacting?[40]

Bonding is a part of being human. We bond with each other in many ways. Belonging to clubs and societies is one example. Many of us bond with our pets. We give them names, brag about their intelligence, and cry when they die.

What about robotic toys? Why would anyone want to bond with them? The very idea seems silly, yet it is beginning to happen. Linda Spice has cerebral palsy. Even the simplest movement is hurtful. And so, she is largely housebound. But her two robotic pets, Faith and Hope, are a constant source of inspiration.[41]

Aibo was a robotic dog that became a favorite of technology lovers. Clubs sprang up across the country, where members could swap stories about their Aibos. Robbie Ann Kohn, who was in the Boston club, said this of his Aibos: "Intellectually, I know they're not alive … and yet, I feel for them. I feel guilty and sad if I neglect them. I get a charge out of asking 'do you love me?'" [42]

As do most robotic toys, Aibo contained a library of behaviors, and so, constant use of an Aibo could make it change its personality. As Gary Wilkes, a Los Angeles Aibo owner put it, "Maybe I'm fooling myself, but if you put all the Aibos in a room together, I can usually tell which is mine." And so, owners get together to compare notes and as Kohn said, they can see whether they are parenting correctly.[43]

All these Aibo owners were adults. Presumably, they were able to take the "aliveness" of an Aibo in their stride. Even though they might have had emotional feelings about their toys, these adults understood that their toys are not really alive.

But what about children? In the near future, children may spend much of their time playing with toys such as Aibo and Furby. What might these toys do to a child's concept of "aliveness"? Will they understand that a robotic toy is not really alive?

Research has shown that young children are not fooled by such things as garage doors that open by themselves or dishwashers that suddenly start washing. Children know that these machines are not alive. But what of toys that act as though they are real people? There is some evidence that children may see robotic toys in a very different way than do adults. For example, Dean Creehan, aged forty-four, takes Da Vinci and his other dogs to elementary schools, where children can play with them. Once, a child broke one of Da Vinci's legs. The children felt terrible about it. They asked, "Does it hurt?" and "Will he be OK?" All Creehan's dogs are robots.[44]

Psychologist Sherry Turkle and her associate, Jennifer Audley, have used Furbys to explore the ways in which children view this robotic doll. One of their questions has been: "Is it alive?" Children often said, "It's not alive in a human sort of way, but in a Furby sort of way." To Turkle, the response "sort of alive" broke new ground, for it suggested that children who played with robotic dolls have trouble understanding "life" and "death," at least as most of us would understand these concepts.

What happened when their Furby "died"? Some children panicked, refusing to believe that Furby had really gone. Others would refuse to accept a new Furby, for they were unwilling to again go through the anguish that the "death" of their Furby had caused them.

What about immortality? One child said that a different toy, her robotic dog, was better than a real dog, because it would never die and plunge her into grief.

As Turkle said, "The possibilities of engaging emotionally with creatures that will not die, whose loss we will never need to face, presents potentially dramatic changes in our psychology."[45]

Robotic toys will surely continue as a mainstream plaything for children. But it may be that these new toys will become less faddish and more responsible than are the robotic toys of today. In the American International Toy Fair of 2002, there were signs that this was already happening. There were not as many robotic toys as in earlier years, but they were better toys. "People have to realize that technology is only useful if it's used to enhance a good toy," said Chris Byrne, toy consultant. "Kids are technology agnostic. They live in a world where microwaves talk to them. Technology has to add magical interaction to a toy in order for it to appeal to them," he said.[46] But what is "magical?" More and more interaction, and more sophistication seem likely bets. But something else is happening: As we shall see in the next chapter, these toys are becoming educators.

5

Toys That Teach

The "Educational" Toy

Toys can do many good things. Some feel that a toy adds to the individual dignity of a child. And others think that toys teach love. Finally there are many that say a good toy should be educational. But what is a toy that teaches dignity or love like? And what about an "educational toy"? Karen Hewitt and Louise Roomet had a problem with this last question when they set out to define an "educational" toy. They were developing an exhibit to be accompanied by a book titled *Educational Toys in America: 1800 to the Present*. Their first task was to decide what an educational toy was. But they never did find an acceptable definition. As Hewitt and Roomet put it, "We learned that the term meant different things at different periods."[1]

If they thought about it that way at all, earlier Americans would probably have seen toys as doing two things. First of all, toys were simply fun for children to make and use. And secondly, they helped train children toward their future duties as providers. When they sewed dolls, girls gained a skill which would be valuable in later life when they made clothes for their family. Using plants as playthings would help them when they maintained the family vegetable garden. Boys played with a bow and arrow or slingshot, and this gave them the skills needed when they hunted game for the family larder. Whittling toys taught them how to use a knife, a skill which would be valuable when they made household implements for their families.

But there were always some people, usually philosophers or educators, who saw other uses for toys. In 1693, the great English philosopher John Locke said he knew of a friend who had taken ordinary building blocks and placed a letter on each of their sides. The friend then had his children throw the blocks into a line on the floor, trying to make them spell out a word. Speaking of his oldest son, Locke's friend said the child "played himself into spelling, with great eagerness, and ... without having been forced into doing it."[2] So Locke's blocks may have been the first educational toy as we understand the term today. A hundred years later, the educator Maria Edgeworth saw toys as having a very different educational value. To her it was the act of making them that was important, for it challenged a child to be creative. This was not a particularly meaningful argument for country people. After all, their children had no choice but to make their toys. But Maria Edgeworth was of the upper middle class, where toy buying was already becoming common. And so, she was directing her comments toward families who were buying toys for their children.[3]

By the mid-1800s, toys had come to have still another educational value. Friederich Froebel, a German philosopher of education and something of a mystic, had developed a concept of toy value that was very different from those of Locke and Edgeworth. To Froebel, play was a spiritual activity. If done properly, Froebel thought that play could lead children toward a divine unity with God. Children could achieve this unity, said Froebel, if they played with a variety of geometric toys he called "gifts." These were to be presented to children in an evolving sequence. The first gift, a simple ball, symbolized the idea of a divine, all-inclusive unity. The second, a cylinder, cube, and sphere, helped a child to understand the unity of all objects. Froebel's system progressed through a series of twenty gifts. These were made of sticks, modeling clay, folded paper, and building blocks that resembled the TinkerToys, which were to come much later. Each set of gifts was designed to illustrate a single concept, such as beauty or growth (Fig. 5.1).

Froebel's gifts were to be used in what he called children's gardens, which later came to be known as "kindergartens." Froebel never came to America, but his ideas did. German intellectuals who had come here in the mid-1800s brought them, and they were received with excitement by American educators. In part, this was because many were Transcendentalists who believed, as did Froebel, that children had a "divine spark" that needed nurturing. A child's garden, where little children could learn, also seemed a good idea. Consequently, Froebelian kindergartens were started in America, and by the late 1800s, there were hundreds of them.

How effective was Froebel's system of education? Did his gifts really teach children about beauty, a oneness with nature, and ultimately with God? We can't be sure, but there is good evidence that his gifts did teach some children, and in a way that had never been intended. Milton Bradley, a maker of toys, arranged to sell Froebel's gifts to the public, and Anna Wright of Boston was one of those who bought a set. Her young son, Frank

Top: Fig. 5.1. Children used Froebel's "Gifts" to study concepts such as unity in nature. *Bottom:* In their work, children built objects such as these.

Lloyd Wright, loved them, and after he became America's most famous architect he recalled that Froebel's gifts had started him on the road to developing his particular style of architecture. And Wright may not have been alone. Norman Brosterman, who has spent years in a study of Froebel's work, argues that Froebel's gifts may have influenced the course of art history, for when they were young children, world-famous artists and architects such as Georges Braque, Piet Mondrian, Paul Klee, and Le Corbusier had all used Froebel's gifts, and all became leaders in developing what most of us think of as "Modern Art."[4]

But Froebel's gifts, with their moral message, were not to last. By the early 1900s, a new educational philosophy took root in America. Influenced by the developing sciences of sociology and psychology, educators such as

Fig. 5.2. In the 1930s, schoolchildren developed social awareness by using blocks. He's not just piling them. Instead, he is building a skyscraper.

John Dewey felt that a successful educational system and its toys would teach children to be socially aware, and would develop their ability to become productive members of society. To help do this, the gifts of Froebel were replaced with large building block construction toys. These could be used in the classroom to help children understand how the things about us look. (Fig. 5.2)

Today's experts have a variety of ideas about educational toys. Jane Gibson, professor of educational and developmental psychology, says to look for a toy that captures a child's attention and stimulates his curiosity. Seek out toys that show a child what he is capable of doing, says Joy Puckett Cain, parenting editor of *Essence* magazine. Toys that encourage make-believe are creative, says Aricha Slade, an associate professor of clinical psychology, for they encourage cognitive skills. A good toy challenges a child to do, think, or feel, says Diana Huss Green, editor of *Parent's Choice*.[5]

After they have read endless articles advising them to buy educational toys, today's parents hurry to the toy store to buy one. But what does an educational toy *look* like? Because "educational" is such an ambiguous word, some companies have exploited it as a way to induce the public to buy their toys. In doing this, they often make outlandish claims, says Robert Quiltech. He found that ads for the Mattel-A-Time Clock claimed that "it responds to your child's desire to learn to tell time — all by itself." As Quilitech said, "Despite breathless ads that claim 'educational' toys will make Junior's I.Q. soar, no one has yet proved that these playthings have the slightest effect on brainpower."[6]

THE CREATIVE TOY

In recent years, "creativity" has become a favored word when toy makers and educators talk about the qualities a good toy should possess. In one survey, parents placed creative right up with educational as one of the two qualities a good toy should have.[7] Why creativity? One reason is that we worship creativity. Whether in the form of a new use for computers, the ability to start a company and make it grow, or the knack of designing a garden that is different from all others, creativity in all its forms is today a prime American value.

But just what is it that makes a toy creative? How does a toy go about imparting its creativeness to a child? These are, to say the very least, challenging questions. To begin, the word itself has many different meanings. Some of its synonyms are invent, originate, develop, fashion, design, cause, establish, organize, and appoint. And when writers advise parents to buy their children creative toys, they add still further meanings. In the toy advice literature, one finds that a creative toy encourages imagination, improvisation, problem solving, fantasy, and pretending. How then, can a parent go about identifying toys which have these magic qualities? After all, creativity does not show up on a toy as some kind of color or bump.

The question, "Is this toy creative?" may be less important than most of us think. As child psychologist Brian Sutton-Smith has suggested, it is a mistake to think of toys as instructors who can teach a child to be creative. Instead, a child's toy may actually be less of a teacher than a passive plaything. One child can take a given toy and play very creatively with it, while another plays with the same toy in ways that are not creative at all. Creativity does not reside in toys, but in children. If this is so, many parents may be doing the wrong thing when they ask, "Will this toy help my child to be creative?" Instead, they should ask themselves, "Does our home environment encourage our child to be creative, regardless of the toys he plays with?" Some parents also seem to think that they should look beyond toys to find creativity. Said Susan Tempelman, mother of Ryan, 5; Joshua, 3; and Nathan, 11 weeks, "They didn't play a lot with toys. They did a lot of dress-up kinds of things, a lot of imaginative kind of play. I encouraged that by giving them things that they wanted to use — boxes and sheets."[8]

The Physical Fitness Toy

Most people don't think of them that way, but toys can be very useful in teaching physical fitness. The hoop is one such toy. It is nothing more than a circle of plastic or wood until you try to make it work. Then it becomes a very challenging physical fitness toy. People have devised many, many things to do with hoops, all of which draw upon physical skills. It's a very old toy. For exercise, Roman men would run down roads, rolling their hoops and leaping through them as they went along. And they may well have been watched by others who were critical of their style. As one writer of the time put it, "A man who does not understand games and is unskilled with ball or hoop keeps quiet, for fear that the crowds of spectators standing round will burst out laughing."[9]

Two thousand years later, American girls practiced a gentler, more ladylike hoop exercise called Graces. As shown in Figure 5.3, each player held two sticks that were crossed, rather like open scissors. Pulling them

Fig. 5.3. The Graces

apart sent the small hoop, which was often banded with a ribbon, flying across to the other player, who tried to catch and return it. Imported from France, Graces supposedly developed a graceful posture in young ladies.

Could hoops do more than give girls graceful posture? During the 1800s, Dio Lewis, a physical education instructor, was an outspoken believer in the importance of physical education for women. As he said, "The graduate of a young lady's seminary should be as much improved in body as in mind by student life.... Girls who leave school pale, thin, and bent, no matter what their knowledge of mathematics, languages, or music, have been outrageously humbugged."[10] Lewis' ideas changed girls' lives forever, for they were then given all sorts of physical workouts at school. In one of these Lewis used full-sized hoops in a strange exercise called "Hoop Drill," which really looks odd to us today. (Fig. 5.4)

When boys used hoops in class, they were expected to do something "manly" with them. In the early 1900s, one gym teacher had the boys in his classes learn to dive through hoops, ducking their head as they went through, and ending the exercise by rolling on a mat. Asked to put on a show for parents, the teacher, Ernest Balch, decided to modify his hoop drill to make it more exciting. His new drill, which he called the "Fiery Hoop of Death," needed special hoops. "Take a hoop and wind it with narrow strips of cloth or cotton," he said. Next, he soaked the cloth in alcohol. Then the show

Fig. 5.4. Hoop drill, as shown in W.P. Brown, *The Teaching of Elementary School Gymnastics, 1909.*

began. "The class lined up, the hoop was lighted, the efficient stage manager turned off the lights, and only the burning hoop lit the hall. Down charged the class, dived through it, rolled up to their feet, and ran back to the steps. After all were back in line, instantly the lights came on, and you should have heard the applause."[11]

By the 1920s, the traditional hoop was beginning to disappear. As cars increased in number, and open space decreased, it was harder to find places where they could be used. But in the late 1950s, the hoop returned with a vengeance. Two toymakers, who owned the Wham-o Toy Company, invented a new version of the old rolling hoop. Their innovation, the Hula Hoop, became an instant hit. As everyone knows, Hulas are spun around one's waist. It's good exercise, and takes quite a bit of skill to do properly. In earlier years, physical education instructors never had their students hula. Why not? No one really knows, but the late Elvis Presley may give us a hint. Not everyone was happy about Hulas. To some people, twisting one's hips made a child look just like Elvis. It was too sexy, and would not do. It just may be that in the more puritanical times of our past, gyrating one's hips with a hoop would have been more than unseemly, it would have been seen as downright evil.

How could this new-age hoop, the Hula, be used in schools? Teachers began to explore its possibilities, and one result was to use the Hula with physically challenged children. One teacher used them by having her charges practice basic movements, such as jumping in and out of the hoop, crawling through it, or rolling it back and forth. After mastering these drills, her children were challenged with more difficult exercises such as neck or waist spins.[12]

Other instructors have used Hula Hoops in swimming pools, and as targets to dive through. They have even been used outdoors as physical fitness toys. And soon after their introduction, Hulas became a fad in China, where people of all ages used them to keep fit and trim.[13]

The Physics Toy

Toys can be used as teaching aids in physics. They work well, because toys are familiar to children, who then feel comfortable with trying to decide what it is that makes the toy work. The tumbling man of Figure 5.5 was a popular physics toy of the nineteenth century. Figure 5.6 is also a gravity toy. Unless you know that lead exerts a heavy pull due to gravity, their balancing seems hard to explain.[14]

While the laws of physics do not change, they do operate differently in different environments. For instance, the pull of gravity is much weaker on the moon than on Earth. Until recently, physics teachers have not worried much about this because we were not able to escape our earthly environment. But astronauts have done so, and when in space, they have demonstrated how toys such as yo-yos will act very differently in a "weightless" environment. Carolyn Summers used this to design a class project in which her physics students would first set up experiments with toys, and then ask themselves how their results would have differed had they been in space.[15]

Physics is a difficult subject to teach. Patricia Janes, a science editor, has suggested that teachers have children bring to class wind-up toys that travel along a floor. The teacher then uses tape to make a six-foot track on the classroom floor, and has children measure how far their toy will travel in a minute. That distance becomes "A" for each child. Now, the children can do that wonder of science: Use a formula

Top: Fig. 5.5. If placed on an incline, the little man somersaults downhill. Why does this happen? There is a heavy weight (a blob of mercury) which rolls from one end of the toy to the other, pulling the man head over heels. *Bottom:* Fig. 5.6. Another gravity toy. The lead ball places the center of gravity under the boy and so both players stay where they are.

to predict something! How far will their toy travel in ten minutes? "A" times 10 gives them the answer.[16]

With older students, toys can be used to introduce more sophisticated concepts. Figure 5.7 shows a toy called the flipperdinger. The player blows through the pipe, and tries to lift the styrofoam ball up until it hooks onto the overhead hoop. But if the hoop is raised, no amount of blowing will do the trick, for the ball keeps falling off to one side. Bernoulli's Principle explains this failure. It states that the pressure of a column of fast moving air is lower than the pressure of the air that surrounds it. At the higher levels shown in Figure 5.7, the column gives out, and the ball falls away.

Toy makers have invented a variety of interesting toys that can be used in school physics classes. One company, Creative Playthings, developed a clear, tough plastic bag which can be filled with water to make an instant magnifying glass. And it also designed sets of transparent plexiglass paddles of different colors. These can be put together to show what happens when primary colors are mixed.[17] Fascinations, a Seattle company, developed a toy it called the Astro Blaster. The Blaster consists of a series of balls that are strung together on a rod. The lower balls are larger than the upper ones. When the Blaster is dropped, the balls shoot up. The smallest ball at the top will go much higher than the largest at the bottom. This is supposed to demonstrate the principle of momentum, but it also illustrates a problem faced by anyone who tries to teach physics. It's fun to play with the Astro Blaster, but how many students really learn the principle of momentum, which it is supposed to illustrate? Perhaps it's not fair to criticize the Astro Blaster, because it's really our problem, not the Astro Blaster's. As one science instructor wrote, "Many teachers approach science with trepidation ... some remember having had personal difficulties with the subject when they were students. Others are awed by the mystique that surrounds scientific thought. Still others view science as one area of curriculum that is simply beyond the comprehension of normal persons."[18]

Many of us would agree with this. We have been told by endless experts that young Americans have a mind block about science which is much greater than that of children in other countries. There, children are typically far ahead of ours in their understanding of the subject. Young children love toys, and unlike science, toys seem friendly to them. Could toys help to solve young America's problem with science? The balancing men cited earlier and the toy cars that Margaret Derr uses seem to work well in helping very young children understand the principles of physics. Perhaps a crash program at the kindergarten level, using "friendly science

The Wellness Toy

It started at Massachusetts General Hospital in the early 1980s. Gail Zayka's three-year-old boy Teddy had undergone surgery. His hospital roommate was also undergoing surgery, and needed a catheter. Having someone insert a tube into your body can be scary for a little boy. It might be painful, and what if the catheter never came out? Zayka, who had often made dolls and stuffed animals for her own children, decided to help out. She designed a doll that could show children what happened when they were catheterized. Before she was finished, Zayka had made dolls that also showed children what would happen in other medical procedures. When she showed her dolls to a doctor, he ran up and down the hospital halls saying, "Look what this lady has made!" Zaadi dolls, as Zayka called them, have been used in hospitals across the country. Even though they are cloth, the doll's organs are lifelike. In one doll, the heart is red, the lungs spongy and pink. And a kidney is removable, so that a new one can be transplanted. One arm is breakable, and fashioned so that it can be put in traction. The doll's face came in two styles. One was sleepy, to show children they will be asleep during an operation. The other face was sad, to tell children that its all right to feel bad when they are ill. The dolls are also designed to show side effects that can result from an operation. Sometimes, their hair is removable to show the effects of chemotherapy. Other companies

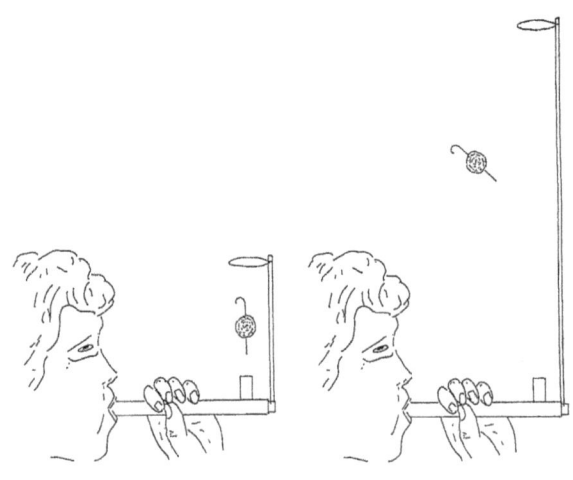

Fig. 5.7. The flipperdinger. Blowing through the tube forces the styrofoam ball into the air toward the hoop. The ball rides within a column of thin air. If the hoop is raised, as at the right, the column fades out, and the ball falls off to one side.

have entered the hospital doll business. Legacy offered a doll with a "bleeding knee," a joint that simulated the kind of hemorrhage that can occur in children with hemophilia.[19]

Dolls can also teach a child about dentistry. One imaginative Texas dentist took advantage of the Cabbage Patch fad of the late 1980s. His daughter, Jennifer, seemed to be afraid to have Dad fit her with braces. He noticed that Jennifer was inseparable from her Cabbage Patch doll. She would eat and even sleep with it. And that gave him an idea. As he said, "I heard Jennifer telling her doll how important it was to brush her teeth ... so I figured, why not." Both Jennifer and her doll got braces at the same time, and this changed his practice. "Pretty soon," he said, "the phone started ringing.. people would approach me asking for appointments for their kid's dolls." The dolls got a metal brace that was kept in place with Super Glue, and everyone, presumably including the doll, was happy.[20]

More recently, dentists have begun to use toys in a very different way. Ten years ago, the American Dental Association was suggesting that children should wait until they were at least three years old before seeing a dentist. However, the ADA and the American Academy of Pediatric Dentistry now recommend that children see a dentist by their first birthday. But this can be hard on little children. Parents such as Francine Swire well remember the image of a dentist she had as a little girl: "I have a picture in my mind of a green room, this horrible chair and a man in a white coat looming over me with pointy things," says Swire. She still feels that way about dentists, but not Jeremy, her child, who rushes in the door of his dentist's office. Toys are the secret behind Jeremy's attitude toward his dentist, for the office is full of them. More and more pediatric dentists have toys in their offices, and some even join in with their patients. "We'll play with a toy first," says pediatric dentist Dr. Lynn Halick. "We'll chat together. I try to have things on a personal level. It makes a pleasurable experience." It just may be that all of those dentist jokes will be a thing of the past.[21]

The Education for All Handicapped Children Act, which was passed in the 1970s, meant that more and more handicapped children were to enter newly mainstreamed classrooms. Often, young children are uncomfortable around other children who are different. To help them become more understanding, a doll called New Friends has helped teach children without handicaps what it is like to live with a disability. These dolls were first designed for use in North Carolina, but have been adopted by Head Start, day care and kindergarten programs throughout America. Some of the dolls have disabilities such as a broken leg. Others have a support device such as the helmet used by children with cerebral palsy. These dolls are used in many ways. Sometimes, they can help a teacher who wants to "introduce" a disabled child to a class before the disabled child even enters the classroom. The doll can be taken home by class members, so they can talk about it with their parents or caregivers.[22]

New Friends dolls pioneered the field, but others have followed. A small Colorado company called Hal's Pals has also made them. Like New Friends dolls, the Hal's Pals doll can be used in a classroom. But they have also been "personalized" to fit the needs of a particular handicapped child, who will then own the doll. For example, eight-year-old Aurelia, who was born with spina bifida and is paralyzed from the waist down, must wear braces. Her doll used look-alike "designer" braces of blue and silver. Aurelia thought Hal's Pals dolls were neat. "Because they're kind of like me," said Aurelia.[23]

In the last few years, major toy companies have entered this market, and are producing dolls with physical disabilities. One example of this was Mattel's Wheelchair Becky, which was mentioned in the Fashion Dolls and Action Figures chapter. What did children, and adults for that matter, think about Becky? Soon after she was introduced, Becky became a hot item, and was sold out in two weeks. By the late 1990s, Mattel had sold over 100,000 of these dolls.[24] Another example of a handicap doll is the Cabbage Patch Playtime Friend (Fig. 5.8)

The American Academy of Pediatrics estimates that there are at least six million children in America with some form of disability. These range from learning disorders to severe physical handicaps.[25] Thus, there is a market for handicap toys that may be worth as much as $3 billion a year to the toy makers who work in this area. Everyone agrees that making more of these toys is an important thing to do, but there is some disagreement over what they should be like. Should they be special toys for children who are handicapped, or is it best for them to be modifications of toys that already exist, such as Mattel's Becky? Perhaps the best answer is both. But there is evidence, at least with some handicapped children, that it is best to give them toys that are as close as possible in design to the toys used by children without handicaps. As Toy Manufacturers of America's David Miller says, there is "a burning desire on the part of (their) parents to do everything they can to mainstream the child."[26]

Everyone agrees that dolls with handicaps are fine. They show life as it really is, for many children do have physical problems that make them different from others. It seems only right to show people in all their forms, but can this be carried too far? Back in 1992, Danish toy makers began exporting Mommy-To-Be dolls to America. For those who are not familiar with her, Mommy-To-Be had a protruding abdomen that lifted off to reveal a baby boy or girl. When the baby was removed, Mommy's abdomen popped back into place—no stretch marks! Some thought Mommy-To-Be was a fine doll. Alexander Sanger, president of Planned Parenthood of New York City, said Mommy gave parents "an opportunity to discuss reproduction with their children." But others were not so happy about Mommy, because they thought she might send the wrong message to young girls. As Barbara Otto, a program director at the National Association of Working Women put it, "Are we trying to create another generation of breeders?"[27]

THE SOCIAL TOY

Educators have always said that toys can help children "socialize," but they have had different ideas about how toys can do this. Sixty years ago, Adeline Hill, author of *Learning Levels in the Nursery School*, simply said "toys should be shared." Twenty years later, a first grade teacher agreed, but added a bit more: if the toy was really good at socializing children, it would not only teach children to share, but would also ensure that children had fun in the process. But by 1965, things had become more complex. Toys, said the American Toy Institute, should not only teach children to socialize effectively with their peers, but should teach them to be sensitive to, and tolerant of those who live in other cultures. Irene Clepper, who wrote *Growing Up with Toys*, agreed with all of this, but she sounded a warning note: watch out for jargon. As she put it, experts tend to speak of "developing interpersonal relationships." Don't be frightened by this jargon, she said, it just means "getting along with other people."[28]

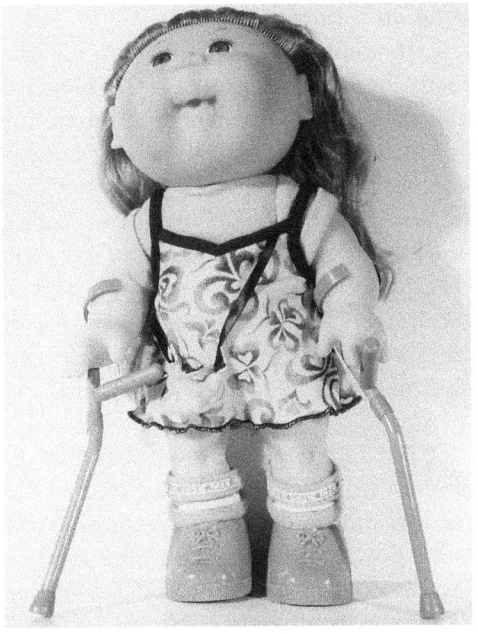

Fig. 5.8. The Cabbage Patch Playtime Friend. Its box says, "We like school, sports, drawing, reading—all sorts of things, just like you."

Toys can play a part in acquainting American children with the ways of children who live in other cultures. Africa is an example. Until recently, much of Africa was still a Third World area, lacking many of the machine-made products of the Industrial Revolution which are so familiar to us, and many African children still had to make their own toys. But somewhat paradoxically, they did this by making use of scrap materials thrown away by the industrialized world. Here in America, a school program for gifted students took advantage of these unique toys to teach American students about the children of Africa. Several of these African toys were shown to the American students. Then, the students discussed the ethical dimensions of these toys. Was it somehow immoral that African children had to use our waste to make toys? Next, the American children were challenged to try to make similar toys. This turned out to be quite a learning experience. "I think African children are smart," and "It's hard to build the toys that African kids do," were typical comments.[29]

Another teacher had her children collect toys from other cultures. A few of these were purchased, but most were on loan from friends or organizations such as UNICEF. In discovering how these toys resembled and differed from their own, her students had a way of visualizing differences between cultures.[30]

In addition to teaching children about other cultures, toys can tell them about an earlier America. There are many books and articles available which show teachers or children how to make early American toys. For instance, children can make a buzzer button, a toy of early America, and use it to learn forgotten things about early American life. In Revolutionary War times, the button was made of flattened musket bullets. Soldiers would make these toys for their own children, for many soldiers had their families with them in camp. In later years, when America's northern forests were being denuded to provide lumber for houses and other structures, the buzzer button took on a new life. Now, it was called a buzz saw, and mimicked the large circular saws that were cutting our forests (Fig. 5.9).[31]

But sometimes we have abandoned toys that help to teach children about history. Writing in the *New York Times*, Tom Englehardt bemoaned the loss of toys that once taught boys about American history. When he was a boy in the 1950s, says Englehardt, he spent hours reliving the battles between cowboys and Indians who once fought on our frontiers. But adult sensitivity about ethnicity has banned toys such as these. Instead of the grand old warriors, says Englehardt, boys now must play with fantasy figures that are disconnected from history.[32]

Chapter 5—Toys That Teach

ROBOTIC TOYS AS EDUCATORS

Children love robotic toys because they are so much fun to play with. But could they become more than just a plaything? For example, could they teach? Peggy Hernandez and her daughter, Sierra, 6, were having dinner one night when Sierra's robotic doll Amy piped up to say she needed a fresh diaper. Sierra's response was: "This baby's got to learn. I'm eating my dinner." It was hysterical, said Hernandez. "I told her, you either take care of her or pay a baby sitter." Another five-year-old put her Amy in "time-out" for being too bossy, and still another said "It's hard being a mommy," after just a few days of taking care of her Amy.[33]

But not all education need be that stressful. A toy called Little Leap can teach songs to its young owners, and helps them learn to read. Some of these robotic toys are even multilingual. For example, Niya is an African-American doll that speaks in three languages. "It's a fantastic learning instrument," says Diane Paige, who bought a Niya. "She speaks in different languages, which makes it educational. It's a doll way ahead of its time." GeoSafari is yet another educational robotic. It's a small world globe that asks children over 7,500 questions about countries, rivers and mountains.[34] Kasey the Kinderbot, which is a Fisher-Price toy, will help preschoolers learn more than forty skills, including numbers, shapes, and even the "Hokey Pokey."[35] And the Counting Pal can teach very young children both colors and numbers (Fig. 5.10).

Julian Maddox, age six, has cerebral palsy. He often visits Mount Washington Pediatric Hospital

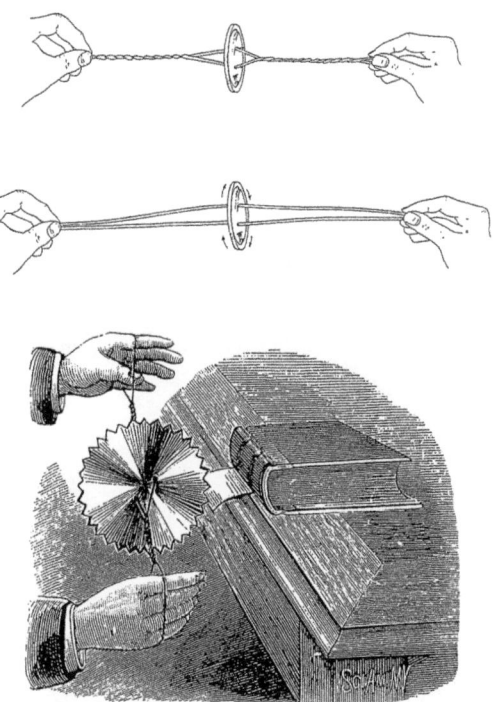

Top: Fig. 5.9. Working a buzzer toy. Pulling and relaxing the string makes the buzzer spin. *Bottom:* A buzzer toy of the 1800s. It was built like the saws used in lumber camps.

in Maryland for treatment. But today is very different, for Julian is going to work with Jester Bot, who is a Muppet-like stuffed toy.

Julian puts on a multi-colored hat which is equipped with an electronic device that can send signals which Jester Bot can pick up. Julian nods his head forward, then pushes it back, and Jester Bot copies everything Julian does. But this is only a beginning, for Jester Bot, the brainchild of Corinna Lathan, is only in his infancy. "Every day the technology is improving. We're constantly improving on it," Lathan says. What lies ahead? Jester Bots of the future will guide handicapped children through games like Simon Says. And surely, Jester Bots will someday be working with handicapped children in ways we have yet to imagine.[36]

In her fine book *When Toys Come Alive*, Lois Kuznets looked at a wide variety of literary toys. Pooh and his friends, who live in the classic Pooh books, were examples.[37] She found the toys of fiction to be just like humans. That is, some of them were noble, others selfish or even mean. In effect, they were us, with all our virtues and faults. If robotic toys were to have similar virtues and faults, might they help children understand human nature, and so become more tolerant of their peers?

THE CHILDREN'S TOY

American parents are besieged with advice, and a large part of this advice tells them about toys. Educators, teachers, talk show people, all these adults tell other adults about the pitfalls of bad toys and the merits of good ones. But what about children? Do they have any say in all of this? Should a child worry about whether he or she is learning to be creative when playing with a toy? As we have seen, most toy advisors do have such

Fig. 5.10. Pulling its string makes the Counting Pal come alive. When a child pushes one of its shoes, the Pal sings a song that tells the child what number and color that shoe is.

an agenda. Toys should *do* something for children; educate them or train them to be creative.

But what about fun? Here's the response of one advisor: "That is a limited, unsophisticated, and antiquated way (of thinking) ... toys provide valuable experiences other than amusement."[38] True, but Eda Leshan, who wrote in the 1960s, had a different idea about what toys should do. She began her argument with a view of the adults who were her contemporaries. "All too often," she said, "we adults work so hard at our 'recreation' and 'fun,' that we really don't enjoy them at all ... we've forgotten how to play." How do we recapture the secret of play? asked Leshan. Her conclusion: "After years of studying and observing young children—children at play—I'm convinced that they have the answers," she said. What is their secret? A child, said Leshan, "doesn't ask whether what he's doing is worthwhile. He plays for the sake of play, play as an end in itself."[39]

6

Hazardous Toys

If there is one issue about toys that has concerned people more than any other, it is the issue of toy safety. Why do some toys, which appear harmless, end up hurting children? Are today's toys safer than those of the past, or are they more dangerous? Can we learn to anticipate toy hazards? Who should be responsible for toy safety: the government, the toy maker or the parent? This chapter begins with a look at the child-made toys of country America to see how hazardous they were, for this can provide some perspective as we examine the toy hazards of today.

THE HAZARDS OF CHILD-MADE TOYS

There are no statistics that tell us how often the children of country America were hurt by their toys. But we can get some insight into the toy hazards of our country past by asking if the toys of that time had any characteristics that could have led to significant health risks.

Two such characteristics seem especially significant. One was that country children made their own toys. Dorothy Howard, who grew up in Sabine Bottom, Texas, at the turn of the twentieth century, remembered what happened when she was five years old. Dorothy did not want to wait for help in making her rag doll and went ahead alone, sewing on the family treadle machine. Unfortunately, she ran the needle through her finger, but soon recovered as only a five-year-old can.[1] Surely, Dorothy was not alone, for many other girls must also have come to grief as they, too, learned how to sew by making dolls.

What about boys? They would not be caught dead sewing, but they did use a jackknife. That was something else, for the jackknife was a status symbol for every boy in country America. Boys would save their pennies to buy one, whether from the general store in the nearby town, or from the Sears catalog. In 1908, the catalog had a full page which advertised jack- and penknives. The jackknife was useful for carving on school desks, and for whittling out all sorts of toys such as willow whistles or slingshots. We have no statistics, but many a boy must have cut himself when learning how to use his jackknife. Children can still hurt themselves when they make toys from model kits, or cut out the paper dolls from a booklet, but surely, self-inflicted injuries that came from toy making must have been far more common in our country past.

In addition to making their own toys, the children of country America faced a second potential hazard which is largely gone today. They spent most of their time outdoors, which exposed them to a range of hazards rarely encountered by the housebound children of today. When playing, they could fall under the wheels of wagons, be kicked by horses, or be burned by bonfires. As they played in the fields with their toys, burrs could cut their skin, and bees could sting. And danger lurked in unexpected places. Bessie Wilson, who grew up on the Kansas frontier, remembered crawling out onto the housetop to place her mud pies on a board which covered a hole in the roof. "On reaching the board, I sat down and turned it over. There coiled around the hole was a very large rattlesnake. It raised its head about five or six inches and began lolling its long red tongue at me. I was too young to be frightened, but called 'Oh Mamma! come see the snake.'" Mamma snatched Bessie away and killed the snake with a garden hoe.[2]

Out on the western prairie, Charles Jackson and his buddies made a dugout in an old buffalo wallow, and spent hours playing there. But they were almost trampled by a stampede of cattle. "Duck yore head, stampede o' steers is goin' right over the whole shebang," yelled Charles.[3]

Jesse Applegate, who grew up on the Western frontier, remembered how he and his friends once used an ox stomach as a kind of medicine ball. One boy backed off, lowered his head, and rammed it into the ox stomach. But, said Jesse, "he did not bound back. We gathered around to see what the matter was, and discovered that Andy had thrust his head into the stomach, which had closed so tightly around his neck that he could not withdraw his head. We took hold of his legs, and pulled him out, but the joke was on Andy...."[4]

The outdoors could be dangerous, and so could its toys. The jackknife was an example. It was used as a tool to make toys, but it was also used as a toy. Mumbly-peg was a jackknife game played by every boy. There were many variations of this game. All of them involved contests in which a group of boys would race each other, trying to be the first to complete a series of knife throws. This must have led to many an accident. For example, one throw involved tossing your knife over the shoulder so that it would land with its point driven into the ground. Mercifully, this really accident-prone game has gone away (Fig. 6.1).

The pyrotechnic toys of an earlier America must have caused many an injury. Pyrotechnic toys came in many forms. Out in Oregon, Jesse Applegate's brother, Elisha, who was good with machinery, cast a ten-inch lead cannon. It fired a long bullet, specially molded by Elisha. Jesse and Elisha kept increasing the cannon's powder charge to see what would happen. As Jesse said, "It was not safe to be near the cannon when it was undergoing a test of its strength." So they hid around the corner of the house, in case the cannon blew up. Once, just as they fired the cannon, an Indian came strolling up a path, and had just enough time to dodge as the bullet whizzed by him.[5]

Children loved to play with things that exploded. Dan Beard, who grew up in the mid-1800s, had a cousin who took gunpowder, mashed it into a fine dust with his mother's rolling pin, wrapped it in paper, added a fuse, and used it as a crude firecracker. It worked, but "started off spitting fire and chasing everybody."[6] And out in the mining camps of the old West, men would amuse themselves by blowing anvils into the air. Soon, children were doing the same thing. Where did children get the gunpowder for these pyrotechnics? Sometimes, they stole it from a cowboy's six-shooter (Fig. 6.2).

Children were endlessly ingenious about pyrotechnics. Writing about his boyhood in the mid-1850s, William Dean Howells remembered this: "Maybe the boys today do not throw fire-balls, or know about them. They were made of cotton rags wound tight and sewed, and then soaked in turpentine. When a ball was lighted a boy caught it quickly up, and threw it, and it made

Fig. 6.1. Playing mumbly-peg. Players compete with each other, trying to flip a knife over their head, so that it will stick into the ground.

Fig. 6.2. Fourth of July fun. Blowing an anvil into the air.

a splendid streaming blaze through the air, and a thrilling whir as it flew. A boy had to be very nimble not to get burned, and a great many boys dropped the ball for every boy that threw it."[7] Sixty years after Howell's time, when Halley's Comet was supposed to pass close to Earth, children reinvented the fireball. They wrapped cloth around rocks, added a tail, soaked their "comets" in kerosene, and threw them into the air, yelling Halley's Comet has come.

Other hazards were toy weapons. They were everywhere, but we have dealt with them in an earlier chapter.

When they played indoors, early American children could also invent hazardous toys. Edward Hale, a rather wealthy boy who grew up in Boston in the early 1800s, recalled burning his eyebrows off when he and his friends were igniting gunpowder in the Hale attic.[8] Although he does not say so in his book, Dan Beard probably invented the rather hazardous indoor toy shown in Figure 6.3.

A New Age of Danger

The machine-made toys that came out of the Industrial Revolution carried hidden hazards of a kind that were rare in the simple toys of homemade days. A homemade rag doll would not poison its user. But some of the new machine-made dolls were covered with poisonous paint. Small parts, such as a doll's eyes, could come off and choke a child. Toy steam engines, which became very popular in the late 1800s, had a safety valve, but it could malfunction, causing the steam engine to explode when it was run. And many of the new metal toys had sharp parts, which could cut a child if the toy was broken.

The goals of toy companies could also increase the potential for accidents. Toy companies had to compete with each other, and one way to do this was to save money by using cheap and potentially dangerous materials. For example, some companies made dolls and other toys of celluloid, which was an inexpensive material to use. Unfortunately, celluloid is highly flammable, and can easily burst into flames, burning a careless child.

But other toy companies worked at making their toys safer, for safety in toys was a good selling point. In the 1800s, toy balloons were filled with hydrogen and sold on the streets. The danger of explosion was real enough to cause a toy inventor to substitute helium, and these new and safer balloons were a big success at New York's Central Park.[9]

Toy companies try to make their toys safe, for it's good business to do so. But toy makers must serve two masters: the children who use their toys and the people who invest in them, hoping for a profit. Should the government be an active monitor of toy safety?

THE GOVERNMENT AS WATCHDOG

Today, we expect the government to monitor toy manufacturers and make sure that the toys they sell are safe for our children. But this is a relatively recent idea. For many years, it was assumed that parents should be responsible — that it was their duty, not the government's, to

Fig. 6.3. A hazardous house toy of the 1880s. When gas lighting came into houses, children could place a rubber tube over a gas jet and let the gas fill a soap bubble, which floated around the house.

ensure that toys were used safely. As late as 1945, magazines such as the *Ladies' Home Journal* told parents that they should be the ones who were responsible for protecting their children from unsafe toys. In that year, a *Journal* article had this to say: "Each Christmas, hundreds of children are killed or injured because of toys unwisely selected, or because grownups did not bother to teach their proper use."[10]

Parental watchfulness was one way to keep toys safe. But there was another approach. Perhaps toy safety was more than a parental responsibility. Perhaps it should be up to the government to ensure that all toys were safe. It could watch over toy companies and punish them if they produced unsafe toys. Consumerism, the idea that government should intervene to protect the public from inferior or unsafe products, began in the early 1900s, but it did not reach the toy world until mid-century. By the 1940s, state governments were beginning to enact laws banning hazardous toys. Some of these laws were rather naive. A 1948 law introduced in the New York State Senate banned the sale of any toy composed wholly or in part of inflammable material. This really upset toy makers. H.D. Clark, secretary of their trade organization, The Toy Manufacturers of America, said that he was astonished that the Senate had not consulted with toy makers before introducing the bill. Plastics might be dangerous, but wood and cloth toys will also burn, at least when they are tossed into a fire. Did the legislators intend to ban all but metal toys?[11]

As legislators became more sophisticated in crafting toy laws, they tended to become more focused, aiming their legislation at specific toys. For example, a New York law outlawed the sale of hollow-barreled toy guns that might be converted into dangerous weapons.[12]

Some of the toys that came under state fire were really gross. In 1965, the Connecticut State Department of Consumer Protection confiscated imported toy ducks that were suspected of carrying salmonella. The toys were made of real baby ducks that had been eviscerated and then stuffed.[13]

The states were not alone in controlling hazardous toys. By midcentury, the federal government had begun to do the same thing. The Federal Hazardous Substances Labeling Act, passed in 1960, allowed the Food and Drug Administration to act against household items that contained certain dangerous chemicals. And "household items" included toys. For example, in 1963, the FDA banned Flubber, a plastic toy, because it caused a mild skin rash.[14]

The year 1966 saw a watershed event for consumerism. In that year, President Johnson spoke to Congress, requesting it to enact a wide range of consumer safeguards. Beginning his speech with "The consumer's interest is the American interest," the president went on to call for legislation that would create government agencies to watch over everything from package labels, to drugs, to toys. "Children must be our first concern," said the president. "They are our hope and our future."[15]

Johnson urged legislation banning toys which contained hazardous substances, and by 1969, his wishes regarding toy safety had become law. In that year, President Nixon signed the Child Protection and Safety Act, which empowered the federal government to ban potentially dangerous toys. The act was not specific about what a dangerous toy might be, but those who had written the law had in mind as likely prospects toys such as electric ovens, rockets, dart guns, and toys with sharp or small parts.

The toy industry did not object to the proposal, but it did oppose one suggestion made by the Commission on Product Safety, which had been created by Congress to fine-tune the new legislation. The commission urged the government to test all new toys before they went to market, a venture that just might turn out to be very, very costly. Thus, the idea was not adopted.[16]

By the late 1960s, it seemed that the new laws were going to make dangerous toys a forgotten issue. Even before Johnson's speech, a 1965 article in *Good Housekeeping Magazine* could say, "At one time, toy safety was a serious problem. However, as a result of efforts by safety authorities and manufacturers groups, the great majority of toys today are safe when used properly." And a 1967 article in *Today's Health* noted that "toys represent only a relatively minor cause of home injuries."[17] But within a few years, Edward Swartz would change all of this.

The Activists Attack

The twentieth century has been a time of consumer activists. But there was no charismatic activist who championed the attack on hazardous toys until the time of Edward Swartz. A personal injury lawyer, Swartz first became aware of what he called "the death trap lurking in the toy box" when clients came to him seeking compensation for injuries their children had received from toys. Swartz and his wife looked at the toys of their own children. What they found led Swartz to further explore the toy world, and he became a toy safety expert who wrote two books, *Toys That Don't Care* and *Toys That Kill*.[18]

Swartz used dramatic statements in his attack on hazardous toys. There is a "death trap lurking in the toy box," said Swartz, for "stores and homes are filled with toys that can cause maiming, blindness, asphyxiation, burns and even death."[19]

Swartz' advice to parents has been equally dramatic. He was concerned about the durability of toys and so, "When you're shopping for toys, ask to open them up and stomp on them if you have to," he said. "If the store won't let you, then don't buy it."[20]

Swartz' hard-hitting style, coupled with his two books, made him something of a media celebrity. He had guest appearances on over twenty TV shows, including *60 Minutes*. Newspapers and magazines loved him. The whole issue of toy hazards became hot copy. In the 120 years preceding Swartz, the *New York Times* had contained only around twenty-five articles on toy hazards. But in 1971, when his first book came out, the *Times* gave him front-page coverage, and in the four years following, there were over fifty articles on toy hazards in the newspaper. The same sort of thing happened in magazines. In the years prior to Swartz, they gave only scant attention to toy hazards, but in the five years following his books, over forty-five such articles are listed in the *Reader's Guide to Periodical Literature*.

Prodded by Swartz, by the media and ultimately by public opinion, the federal government acted to further tighten controls over toys. In 1972, the Consumer Product Safety Commission was created. It could impose mandatory safety standards for toys, and could even recall faulty ones. In the late 1990s, the CPSC found faulty electrical systems in the Fisher-Price Power Wheel toy, and issued a recall of the toy which cost the company over $30 million.[21]

Sometimes, activists take their complaints to court. One way to do this is to sue a toy company. Swartz himself has been a leader in the field of product liability, and has made toy lawsuits a specialty. There is no doubt that lawsuits have put pressure on toy manufacturers, and have helped to reduce the number of potentially dangerous toys. But lawsuits have their limits. They benefit the litigant and the lawyers who are involved, but they are very costly for the toy manufacturers, and that can mean an increase in toy costs for the public.

Swartz was only one of many toy activists. Special interest groups also give toy company officials gray hairs, because their accusations are eagerly sought after and publicized by the media. The PVC controversy is an example. In 1997, Greenpeace, which is known for its concerns about the environment, announced that polyvinyl chloride, the plastic used in many toys, contained poisons that could endanger children. But the Consumer Product Safety Commission tested a small group of toys and found them to have either no dangerous chemicals or amounts that were too small to be harmful. Yet the PVC threat was simply too newsworthy to ignore, and it created a bandwagon of concern. Gina Solomon, who is with another activist group, the Natural Resources Defense Council, said, "why take the risk?" And Philip Clapp, president of the National Environmental Trust, said, "We learned about this potential almost two years ago. It's unacceptable that millions of Americans are out there buying toys for their children while the government is silent." Besides environmental groups, other consumer and even religious groups joined in the attack on PVC. And so, toy companies began to withdraw vinyl toys from stores. Pressured by all this negative publicity, the CPSC went to work, and did extensive testing. Its findings: it might be prudent to keep an eye on rattles and teething toys, which spend so much time in a child's mouth. But for all the other vinyl toys, the CPSC had this to say: The amount of problem chemicals that a child might ingest "does not even come close to a harmful level."

But few people outside the toy and chemical industries seem to read CPSC reports, because media giants such as ABC television and the *New York Times* continued to warn the public about vinyl toys. Encouraged by all this publicity, activist groups have widened their attack on toys to other vinyl products such as those used in medicine.[22]

THE TOY MAKERS RESPOND

Prodded by the government, by the activists, and ultimately by public opinion, toy companies have worked to make their toys as safe as possible. One way to do this is to keep safety in mind when designing toys. The toy called Boomerang Links was an example of how companies do this, for the Discovery Toy Company had to solve several safety problems. Boomerang Links were C-shaped, and made all kinds of colorful chains. But they must not break into small pieces that a child could swallow, and they had to snap together easily so as to avoid hurting small fingers. The toy designers found a special plastic that met these requirements. It was four times more expensive than the plastic used for most toys. The designers chose the special plastic. As Larry DeSequirant, director of quality assurance said, "There are certain buying and selection decisions that go beyond dollars and cents."[23]

When they choose a material that is be used in a new toy, toy designers must ask themselves what problems will arise if the toy is misused. No matter how carefully they are watched, toddlers will swallow things like small plastic toys. But plastic does not show up on x-rays, making the location of a swallowed plastic toy almost impossible to find. In 1979, the Mattel Toy Company found a way to mix barium sulphate with plastic, which would make its plastic toys visible to x-rays. Mattel gave the formula to a hundred other toy companies. As one executive said, "It is not competitive information."[24]

Sometimes well-meant design improvements can lead to unexpected problems. The antibacterial agent Microban was first introduced in 1988. It can be tightly bonded to plastics or fibers, and won't rub or wash off. Hospitals have used it in equipment such as bedding. In April 1997, the Playskool company added Microban to several toddler toys, such as Roll 'n Rattle Ball and Busy Band Walker. "There is a tremendous consumer awareness about germs and bacteria," said a Playskool official.[25] Adding Microban was a good decision for Playskool, for it would help both Playskool's image and its sales. But the government saw things differently. Because Microban had not been approved for toys, it fined Playskool $120,000 and ordered it to retract claims that its Microban toys protected children from germs. Was the government right in acting with caution, or was it unnecessarily strict?

Sometimes new toy designs are controversial, because the toy company, the government, and toy activists all have different ideas about what the toy will do to children. In 1997, the Nestle Chocolate company decided to put Disney toys inside a new chocolate candy it was developing. As Nestle saw it, the new candy would be a sure winner, for it was a treat within a treat. Nestle thought it had made sure that the toy would not pose a health threat. It would be too big to choke on, and would be made of a plastic that could not chip teeth. The new toy met Consumer Product Safety Commission standards. But the toy worried another government agency, the Food and Drug Administration. "We'd be very concerned about the safety aspects of this kind of toy," said an official of that agency. And some state officials were even more concerned. "This illegal product literally sugarcoats potential death and injury," said Connecticut Attorney General Richard Blumenthal.

And what if Nestle's idea started a trend? A competing company in Europe had sold two million chocolate-covered toys of its own design, and it was almost surely going to catch on here. Would other companies be as careful as Nestle? Finally, consumer advocate groups were unhappy. "Do kids need yet another incentive to eat candy?" asked a member of the Center for Science in the Public Interest.[26]

Laboratory testing is one strategy companies use to avoid safety problems. Another is to watch children at play with their toys, hoping that this will uncover hidden problems. Toy companies work hard at doing this, but it is never a foolproof process, as Mattel found in 1996. Mattel had created a new version of its popular Cabbage Patch doll. It was the "Snacktime Kid," which could eat plastic foods with its motorized mouth. Would children poke their fingers into the doll's mouth? They did so in Mattel's play lab, where children tried new toys. No problem, the doll's mouth was soft, and large enough so that fingers could not get stuck. As children were sure to give the Snacktime Kid real food, Mattel engineers designed the mouth to tolerate mushy food. What about a stop button, in case something happened? Too involved, said the engineers, and anyway, the doll's internal drive, which operated the mouth, would slip at the touch of a finger. As Jim Walter, Mattel's vice president for corporate product integrity, said, "There were no indications of any problem."

No one foresaw the possibility that the Snacktime Kid might snack on a child's hair. But to Mattel's dismay, it happened just often enough (several dozen complaints among half a million owners), to create a media frenzy that forced Mattel to announce a voluntary recall. Most parents did not return the doll, because their children wanted to keep it, and ironically, all the media hype made the Snacktime Kid something of a collector's item.[27]

Watching children with their toys is helpful, but as the Snacktime Kid showed, it is never foolproof. Why is this? One reason is that children use their toys in many different ways, doing things that they will not do when they are being watched. Here is an example. As we saw earlier, a number of tests have shown that when they play with a vinyl toy, children do not absorb enough vinyl to do them any harm. The CPSC does admit that a child who mouths his or her vinyl toy for an hour or more might be in trouble, but argues that this is not likely to happen. Not so, says Rick Hind of Greenpeace. A Disney movie is seventy-five minutes long, and thousands of little children may be watching with a vinyl toy in their mouth. Does this really happen? No one seems to really know.[28]

The limits of field testing and the variable playing habits of children can frustrate toy makers who are trying to anticipate toy hazards. But something else makes it even harder for them to uncover toy hazards.

Country America was a traditional world. Beliefs and ways of doing things remained much as they had been for generations. Some traditional toys, such as spears, could be dangerous, but their potential to do harm was well understood, for these toys had long been a part of children's play.

The new world created by the Industrial Revolution is different, for it is one of continuing change. Every year, new toys enter the market, and are eagerly sought after by children. But these new toys can bring new and often unanticipated dangers. Scooters have been an example of this. A popular toy of years past, scooters had almost vanished until they were reborn as a fad in the late 1900s. By the end of the year 2000, the toy industry had sold millions of scooters, but problems were showing up. "People don't think about the fact that these scooters can be as dangerous as bikes and skateboards," said Dr. Jill Posner, who practices emergency medicine in Philadelphia. By August 2000, the Consumer Product Safety Commission had received reports of over nine thousand scooter injuries. Some of these scooter accidents were the result of faulty design. For example, the handles of Kent and Kash scooters could give way. And so, these two scooter models were recalled by the CPSC.

But most scooter injuries result from careless use of the new toy. A helmet, wrist guards and knee and elbow pads would greatly reduce scooter injuries, but it may be hard to get children to wear this kind of protective gear.[29]

Today, thousands of new toys are invented every year. When this happens, the toy inventor faces a sea of unknown hazards. Pogo sticks that fly are an example. In August 2001, Razor USA introduced "Airgo," an air-powered pogo stick that could lift its owner up into the air. How safe is Airgo? No one really knows, for no testing seems to have been done.

What does the CPSC have to say about this new toy? Although the commission does try to identify dangerous toys before they hit the stores, its power to regulate begins only when a toy reaches the market. "If (the company claims) that you can jump ten or twenty feet with their sticks, this certainly seems like something we'd like to know about," says Mark Ross of the CPSC.[30]

The new world created by the Industrial Revolution is one of continuously changing toys. And it's also a world of changing beliefs about them. The toy called Rowan was a recent example. A noble knight, he was modeled after an action figure in TV's *Mystery Knights* show. Rowan was a toy that came in a McDonald's Happy Meal box. Was Rowan a hazard? Just a few years ago, when toy watchers looked at children who were playing with this toy, they found nothing to worry about. He had a little wheel that a child could work with his thumb so as to produce sparks. No one worried about the sparks; they were harmless. They did make Rowan look like a cigarette lighter, but that did not bother watchers, for smoking was considered to be a harmless habit. But once our views about smoking changed, so did our views of Rowan, and complaints about this "harmless" toy began to hit the media. Might he turn young children into smokers?[31]

Toy companies work hard at uncovering hidden toy dangers. And when they are found, most are quick to issue warnings or even recall orders. After all, this is simply good business. It helps children and avoids the threat of lawsuits. But sometimes, recalls seem to run amuck. In the summer of 2001, Burger King decided to recall over two million "Space Sprout" and "Bumblebee" toys. It had discovered that some of these toys could break, releasing small beads which might be a safety hazard for toddlers. And this was only the latest in a series of Burger King recalls. In March, the company had recalled almost a half million "Riverboat" toys. Although there were no reports of trouble, small pins might come off the toy's paddle wheel and could choke a child. In December 1999, Burger King had recalled Pokemon Balls after a choking incident. Other fast-food companies such as McDonald's and Chic-Fil-A have also joined what almost seems to be a recall mania.[32]

All this is well-meant, but it does raise a question. Are these fast-food toy recalls just the beginning of a strange "half-life" world in which toys can expect to live only a few months before being recalled to oblivion? Is there not a better way to try to control toy hazards?

THE PARENT'S ROLE

In our discussion thus far, emphasis has been placed on the toy maker and the government as safety watchdogs for toys. What about parents? Might they also be responsible for toy safety? If so, how might we make parents players in the toy safety game? One way could be to label especially worrisome toys, warning parents of their dangers, so that a parent could act accordingly. In 1995, Congress passed a law which required that small toys or toys with removable small parts be labeled. Marbles were an example.

Typically, the label says, "Warning. Choking Hazard. Small Parts. Not For Children Under 3." How effective are warning labels? The Consumer Product Safety Commission has some doubts. It has found that only a small percentage of buyers are really influenced by labels. This seems to be so because consumers are already familiar with these toys, and feel they know how to teach their children to handle them safely.[33] Even when the labels are clearly printed, many parents don't bother to read them. As one parent who was shopping at Toys-R-Us put it, "You are so busy monitoring the kids ... that you can't always stop to read the labels." And many parents, particularly foreign speaking ones, don't understand labels.[34] Finally, what does one do about a "toy" such as a lawn dart? They have been labeled as dangerous for children, and have even been banned from toy stores. But there is no way to ban human indifference. Lawn darts can be purchased in sporting goods stores, then given to children. And most people don't bother to read the label on the lawn dart box.[35]

Should parents do more than merely watch for labels? Might that be only a first step, part of a much wider responsibility? What if most toy accidents were due to careless play rather than to faulty toys? If so, should not a parent be responsible for safe play on the part of a child? Many years ago, this was simply taken for granted. I remember when I was a boy of four, playing with a small metal airplane. My brother and I were upstairs in the family's summer cottage, while the rest of our family was way down on the beach. As I swung the toy around, it bounced off my twin brother's head. I thought no more of it until I saw blood streaming (or so it seemed to a four-year-old) down my brother's face. Terrified, I ran down to the steps, shouting, "Bloody murder! Bloody murder!" Needless to say, my family raced upstairs, saw what had happened (not much really), put a Band-Aid on my brother's head, and gave me a stern lecture on toy play, accompanied with removal of the offending toy from my possession. Today, the end result would probably be anger against the toy company for selling a dangerous toy.

But just how important is careless play as a creator of toy accidents? Not everyone agrees about this. Back in 1986, the *Washington Post* ran an article titled "Deadly Serious Over Toys." The article centered on differences of opinion between lawyer Edward Swartz and toy company executives. One of their disagreements concerned the "Tyke Bike," which was made by Playskool. It was designed for young children, and could be used both in and out of doors. To Swartz, it was an unsafe toy, because it lacked a warning flag, and so would be invisible to parents backing out of driveways. But Stephen Schwartz of Hasbro (Playskools' parent company), said, "That's the most ridiculous thing I've ever heard in my life. We've been making the product for 22 years, and have yet to have a complaint." He thought Edward Swartz was way out of line regarding what toy safety meant. "The truth of the matter is, he hasn't been able to find dangerous toys. What he's been able to find are ways of abusing a product to make it dangerous, and there's no toy in the world that cannot become dangerous if misused." The Fisher-Price "Tag Along Turtle" was another toddler toy on Swartz' list of dangerous toys. He felt that its 36-inch pull string violated the industry rule that all crib or playpen toys should have a string less than 12 inches in length to avoid strangling an infant. Since this toy was marketed for children as young as one year, it would inevitably find its way into playpens or cribs and cause trouble, said Swartz. But Carol Blackley, who was director of public relations for Fisher-Price, said, "We've sold millions and millions and millions of them and we've never had any problem! The 12-inch standard that he is citing, I believe, is for toys that hang in the crib." And, she added, a parent will use common sense and not put the toy in a crib. "It's not common sense," said Swartz. "No parent is going to associate a flexible string with death or injury unless they've thought about it."[36]

How does one define a "dangerous toy"? The toy industry feels a toy is only unacceptably dangerous if it is capable of hurting a child who is using it properly. Or is a toy unacceptably dangerous if it is open to misuse, as Swartz seemed to feel (Fig. 6.4)?

The trouble with the Swartz view is that there may be no way to design a toy that is entirely safe from danger. As Stephen Swartz, a Hasbro senior vice president has said, "There is no toy in the world that cannot become dangerous if misused."[37] In one of his books, Swartz talked about the "death trap lurking in the toy box," but this death trap may not be a result of bad toy design, as he felt. Instead, the greatest danger in the toy box just may be lax supervision by parents or caregivers.

Interestingly, the Consumer Product Safety Commission, which was set up to monitor the toy industry, now spends much of its time and energy trying to make the American public more aware and responsible regarding toy safety. And it extends the idea of responsibility down to the child's level. In a coloring book called *Think Toy Safety*, there are pages to color with topics such as, "I put my toys away so that nobody will trip and fall," "We read the directions together," and "I help Mommy by keeping baby away from toys that he might swallow." The last two pages in the book are particularly interesting. One is "Draw your own unsafe toy." The other is even more thoughtful, for it says "Draw your own safe toy." Perhaps we all need to take a good look at this book![38]

It may well be that parents and even

Fig. 6.4. Could this be a hazardous toy of today? According to Edward Swartz, a pull toy such as this might end up in a crib, and strangle an infant.

children should learn to be more responsible and learn to use toys in a way that is safe. And yet, they can never be solely responsible for avoiding toy hazards. A recent finding shows how this is so. Most pesticide labels warn users to be careful when using the pesticide. But recent studies have found that even after they have dried, pesticides can move about a room. And as they do so, pesticides are particularly attracted to plastic and plush toys. What to do about this problem? It would seem to be a matter of joint responsibility. The government should monitor pesticides carefully. Pesticide makers should work to make them less hazardous. And parents should try to spray pesticides only in places where toys won't be used.[39]

How Safe Are Today's Toys?

As we have seen, there are toy safeguards in the form of design, testing, labels, and, ultimately, litigation. How effective have they been? In the late 1960s, the U. S. Public Health Service said that every year, 700,000 American children were injured by toys. In 1973, *Consumer's Research Magazine* said these figures were crude at best, and hazard in use of most toys is in reality at a low level. But in 1982, Edward Swartz accepted the public health service figure, and even enlarged it to 750,000.[40]

But what did the 700,000 and 750,000 figures include? And where did the data originate? One way to obtain more reliable data is to check emergency rooms, to see how many children visit them with toy-related injuries. For example, in 1994, 133,000 children visited emergency rooms with toy-related injuries. By 1996, the figure had gone down to 116,800 nonfatal toy injuries. Most patients were children under five, and most were boys.[41]

How worrisome are these numbers? Writing in a 1997 issue of *Consumer's Research*, Larry Laudan pondered that question. He noted that the harm done to children by toys "pales by comparison with other items around the house, which parents, ironically, are less apt to worry about." The safety commission notes that the probability that a child under five will be seriously injured by a toy in one year is about one in two hundred fifty. Seems high? Yet a child is eight times more likely to be seriously injured by other household items such as stairs or chairs, and one hears little about these dangers in the media.

As Laudan says, "The fact is that parental preoccupation with toy safety—aided and abetted by media fixation with toy dangers—displaces attention from many of the factors that are most likely to do harm to little Johnny or Susie."[42] And David Ropcik, a Harvard risk expert, is of the same opinion. As he has put it, "We may be too afraid of lesser risks and not concerned (enough) about the bigger ones."[43] What are some of these bigger risks? Children who engage in strenuous exercise in polluted cities triple their risk of developing breathing problems.[44] And it may be that our modern obsession with cleanliness has reduced our children's resistance to health problems such as asthma and diabetes.[45] But health problems such as these are much harder to solve, for doing that would involve lifestyle changes, both for us and for our children. Thus, it is easier to focus on the relatively minor problems of toy hazards.

A NEW VIEW OF RESPONSIBILITY

A hundred years ago, it was taken for granted that toy safety should be a parent's responsibility. Today, this notion can still be found. For example, *Parent's Magazine* and other family magazines feature articles telling parents to be more responsible in recognizing and avoiding dangerous toys. But for many of us, this message no longer seems to hit home. Six out of ten Americans seem to think toy safety is the toy maker's responsibility, that companies should make sure that their products are safe, regardless of cost. And if there is trouble, we are quick to blame the toy company. Apparently more and more of us think we should sue the toymaker, for product liability suits increased almost eight-fold from 1975 to 1993.[46]

7

Racist Toys

If we could watch children at play on a southern plantation of the 1850s, all would seem innocent and happy, at least at first glance. Some of these children would be the sons and daughters of the white plantation owner, or of the white overseer, whose job it was to manage the plantation and its slaves. But most of those we watched would be the children of slaves.

It was still a time of homemade toys and outdoor play. Boys would play with marbles, girls jumped rope and played house with dolls. Both girls and boys played the ball game called anty over, which was found all over America. But in the South it was Haley over. Children would divide into two teams, one on each side of a barn or other building. Each team would be a mix of African-American and white children. A player on one team would toss the ball over the roof, and someone on the other team would try to catch it. If that happened, he or she would race around the barn and try to hit someone on the other team. If hit, the victim had to join the thrower's team. The game ended when one team ran out of players.

As was so everywhere in America, southern children used nature's things to make toys. They might play with cane whistles, carve horses from tree limbs, or, as Candis Goodwin remembered, gather brown pine needles to build a playhouse. Candis and her friends (who were both African-American and white), used green needles to make the grass that surrounded the house.[1]

Sometimes, children would take many things, and put them together to create a play, which might replicate everyday life. On a Louisiana plantation, children made a hearse of fig branches, which was pulled by fig branch horses. Then they took a dead chicken, tied a black ribbon about its neck, covered the chicken with a white rag, and put it in the hearse. All the children, both African-American and white, marched along, singing hymns until they reached a grave, where a white girl preached a sermon called "we all must die."[2]

While African-American and white children did play together in ways such as these, a closer inspection of plantation play would uncover disturbing things. First of all, the toys of African-American and white children were not really equal. Launcelot Minor Blackford, the son of a plantation owner, used paper, paint brushes, molds and other equipment to make toy cannons, balloons, and kites, but these were materials that the poor African-American children on the plantation could not afford.[3]

By the 1850s, machine-made toys were beginning to appear in catalogs and stores, and here again, slave children were at a disadvantage. For example, white boys could now buy their marbles, but African-American boys had to make theirs out of clay.[4] And at a time when the daughters of plantation owners were beginning to play with porcelain dolls and miniature tea sets, African-American girls had to do with homemades. Emma Watson, who grew up as a slave, remembered that "Miss Lee have a china doll with a wreath of roses round its head. We take turns playin' with it. I had a rag doll, and it jes' a bundle of rags with strings tied round it to give it shape."[5]

Ironically, the very toys that slaves made could be used in ways that were racist. Topsy-turvy dolls, with a white head on one end and a black head on the other, were made by African-American children. When a slave girl played with one of these dolls, she would have the white head up, but when a white adult appeared, the slave girl would turn the doll so its black head was seen.[6]

In other and less obvious ways, slave play was diminished compared to that of white children. Slave quarters were often very uncomfortable, and so the slave children would play outdoors regardless of the weather, whereas the white plantation children could go indoors. And African-American children had to leave the innocence and playfulness of childhood at a much earlier time than did white children. By the time they were ten to twelve years old, slave children were full-time members of the plantation work force.

Most disturbing of all was the way in which white children sometimes treated African-American children in their play. One white boy hitched two African-American "friends," Jack and Peter, to a small wagon he had received as a present. He then cracked his whip "over their backs, and sometimes *on* the backs of [his] two legged horses." Jack and Peter played their parts, kicking and snorting like real horses.[7]

White children learned to play this way from white adults. For example, Sarah Alston, who was the widow of a plantation owner, talked of a new toy carriage that had been built for a grandson. "I reckon it will take all your little waiting men [she meant African-American boys] to pull it," Sarah said.[8]

While most plantation owners did not object to their children playing with African-Americans, some did. Mary Chapin, wife of a South Carolina cotton grower, worried that "the little Negroes are ruining the children by teaching them 'badness.'"[9] And when they did let African-Americans play with their children, the African-Americans were sometimes seen as more of a pet than a child. Tryphrena Fox let her daughter, Fanny, play with little Adelaide, who was a "bright little Negress." But Tryphrena called Adelaide a "house pet," and complained that Fanny sometimes got lonesome because there were no playmates for her.[10]

Very early on, white children learned to treat African-American children as inferior, and so they tended to look upon them in a patronizing way. In plantation daughter Letita Burwell's words, we "learned that happiness consisted in dispensing it," and so, we "found no greater pleasure than saving our old doll toys...for the cabin children."[11]

But sometimes African-American children got even. Southern children often played marbles for money. Sella Martin, who was a slave boy, became an expert marble player, and Martin remembered how he used this skill to good advantage. "There was a white boy who proposed to go into partnership with me....I knew that this boy only wished my partnership that he might have a banker upon whom to draw as he was constantly getting broke....I insisted on his putting in an equivalent in the way of service...to teach me the alphabet."[12] In later life, Martin became a noted writer and abolitionist.

With the abolition of slavery, the old habits of slave racism faded away, but America was not done with racist toys, for a new kind, born of the Industrial Revolution, would arise.

"A Very Funny Action Toy That Will Delight the Kiddies"

Mechanical banks were immensely popular in the late 1800s. Parents loved these toys, for they taught children to save their pennies. Children found these banks to be lots of fun, for they did all sorts of neat things. In one, you could place your coin in an eagle's beak, press a lever, and eaglets would rise from the eagle's nest, actually crying for food. Then the eagle would bend forward and drop the coin into its nest. Some banks extolled American heroes. When you put a coin in the slot of the Columbus Bank and pressed a lever, a Native American leapt out from his place of concealment within a log, and extended a pipe of peace to Columbus, who saluted him (Fig. 7.1).

Fig. 7.1. The Columbus Bank. By the 1890s, Native Americans had become part of our Wild West mythology. And so, this Native American was noble and commanding as he offered Columbus a peace pipe.

But the bank in Figure 7.2 was different, for it made fun of African-Americans. A touch on the knob at the bank's base made the mule kick and throw the rider overboard. As he went down, a coin popped into his mouth. There were many racist toys that made fun of African-Americans, and most were much more insulting than the Kicking Mule Bank. Sometimes, facial or anatomical characteristics thought to be unique to African-Americans became part of the fun. The Tango Picture toy consisted of a thin rubber sheet on which an African-American lady was painted. By stretching the rubber, you could change her face into "the most grotesque and laughable shapes," as one ad for the toy put it (Fig. 7.3).

In the toy world of the late 1800s and early 1900s, African-Americans were depicted as comical and grotesque, but they were also seen as childlike, without the moral sense of an adult. The Chicken Snatcher toy was an example. When its spring-driven motor was wound up, the frightened-looking African-American would stumble along, with a chicken dangling from his hand and a dog hanging on the seat of his pants. "Very funny action toy that will delight the kiddies," said a Sears Roebuck catalog of this toy.[13]

Chapter 7—Racist Toys

In the toy world, African-Americans might have been lazy, comical and irresponsible; but there was one thing they could do well: sing and dance. They did this on banks, as wind-up toys, and even as toys which were designed as noisemakers (Fig. 7.4).

Back before the Civil War, the African-American slave children of southern plantations had felt racial discrimination. But these new racist toys were different. After all, African-Americans were no longer slaves. Why then should they still be discriminated against in the toy world? The war's goal had been to free

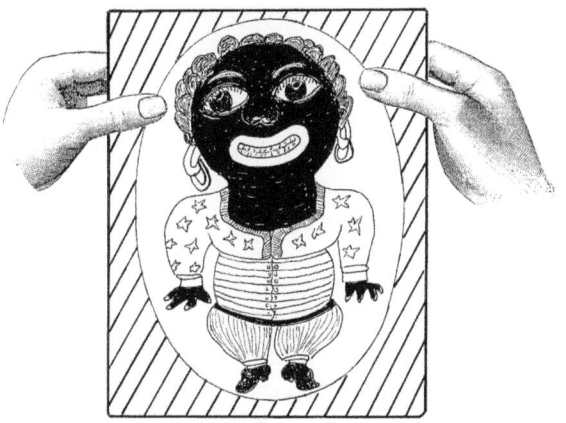

Top: Fig. 7.2. The Kicking Mule Bank. The legend on its front says "I always did 'spise a mule." *Bottom:* Fig. 7.3. The Tango Toy.

slaves and make them equals in American society. If this was an American goal, why did American families buy and enjoy these toys? To understand why, we need to go back to the antebellum South and take another look at the view that plantation owners and their families had of slaves. To begin with, how did these well-educated and presumably civilized people justify the institution of slavery? To plantation owners, freeing slaves would have been unthinkable. For one thing, slavery was an economic necessity. The rice and cotton plantations of the South could not survive without it. Plantations were labor-intensive, and a paid labor force would have meant the end of the luxurious life that plantation owners and their families enjoyed. But it was more than an economic matter. To southern whites, slavery also had a moral basis, for African-Americans were naturally inferior to whites, and thus destined to be subservient to them. As a southern governor put it, African-Americans were "destined by providence" for slavery.[14] In a famous speech before the United States Senate, John C. Calhoun put it this way: "I hold that in the present state of civilization, when two races of different origin, and distinguished by color, and other physical differences, as well as intellectual, are brought together, the relation now existing in the slave-holding states between the two, is, instead of an evil, a good — a positive good."[15]

African-Americans were seen as an inferior race. And, so thought southerners, they had childlike, even animal characteristics. As one southern lawyer said, "The negro is constitutionally indolent, voluptuous, and prone to vice...his mind is heavy, dull and unambitious...."[16]

But the African-Americans did have some good characteristics, southerners felt. In his African home, the African-American was a cannibal, destined to eat his fellows or be eaten by them. With better food and security as a slave, it was no wonder that African-Americans had developed a happy disposition. And so they were gentle, docile, affectionate, and given to song and dance.[17]

The Civil War was fought to abolish slavery and its abuses. But the Reconstruction that followed its end merely intensified southern racism. One reason for this was that southern whites were fearful of and concerned about the political power that southern African-Americans now had. How could they vote intelligently or hold office successfully if they were inferior? And if they gained economic power, particularly in the form of the right to own land, what would this lead to? And so, the old view — that African-Americans were inferior — remained in place as a way of justifying white resistance to the threat of emerging African-American power.

Frustrated at the way they were being excluded by southern whites, southern African-Americans began to move north in increasing numbers. And just as was so in the South, free African-Americans were seen by many white northerners as an economic threat. In the North, however, it was the white laborer, rather than the white plantation owner, who felt threatened. And there was another worry. What if the two races intermarried? Would mixed marriages dilute, even destroy the quality of the old-line American stock?

Plagued by these economic and racial worries, northern whites reacted in much the same way as southern whites had. African-Americans were not only different, they were also inferior. The happy-go-lucky, childlike, song-and dance stereotype of the southern black found its way into the thinking of the northern white, and into his popular culture. Postcards, song sheets, children's books, advertisements, valentines, yard ornaments, movies, radio shows — all contained racist images. Seen in this light, racist toys were inevitable; just another aspect of a racism that existed throughout America's popular culture.

Protest against this racism began in the early 1900s. The 1905 Niagara Movement and, later, the National Association for the Advancement of Colored People, the Urban League, and activists such as Martin Luther King Jr. and Jessie Jackson have aroused white Americans to the injustice of racism, and have led to political action such as desegregation laws and affirmative action.

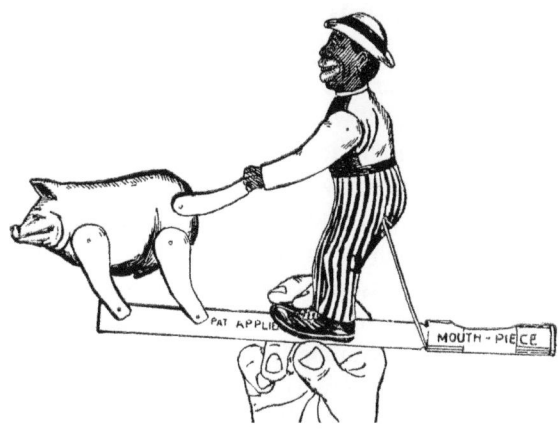

Fig. 7.4. A musical racist toy. To make the comical figure sing, you blow on the mouth-piece.

In tandem with these actions, the African-American stereotypes once so common in popular culture have declined. The notion of the happy-go-lucky African-American lingered on into the 1940s, but the public has become less and less tolerant of images such as this. Sometimes, this meant taking action. Back in the 1970s, a "Black Jockey Liberation Army" stole at least a dozen black-faced lawn jockies from Connecticut lawns.[18] The commercial world has joined the movement to get rid of degrading African-American images. Aunt Jemima, the buxom African-American slave with a head bandanna who once appeared on food packages, is now just a generic cook. Today, racist icons such as lawn jockies or Sambo toys are treasured collectibles, and about eighty percent of their collectors are African-Americans.[19]

The Changing World of African-American Dolls

Sometimes, it is hard to decide whether or not a toy is racist. In 1895, dolls called Golliwogs appeared in a children's book called *The Adventures of Two Dutch Dolls and a Golliwog*. Golliwog soon became a popular personality, and ended up as a toy. Was Golliwog an unseemly caricature of African-Americans? One writer has argued that its pop-eyes, large open lips, and fur-like hair were insulting, and backs up her view by noting that a dictionary of the English language calls Golliwog "a Black male doll of grotesque appearance."[20] On the other hand, another writer, who apparently collects Golliwogs, has said that his big eyes and wide smile make him whimsical and lovable, and so, he is surely no more offensive than, for example, Raggedy Andy.[21]

A doll named Addy Walker presented another sort of problem. Since 1985, the Pleasant Company of Middleton, Wisconsin, has created dolls with a special mission — that of providing children with positive models of early American girls. The first four dolls in their series were white. Addy Walker was doll number five, and she was African-American. Writing in *Ebony*, an African-American magazine, Lisa Jones called Addy a doll that "celebrates the courage of African-American pioneers...she bats her eyes, walks and coyly swings her brown hair."[22] In short, she was a doll that was sure to please young African-American girls. But others were not so sure about Addy, for she had begun her life as a slave. "[African-American] kids don't want to be the descendants of quote-unquote 'Slaves,'" said Carmen N'Namdi, who heads a private African-American school in Detroit. "They want to be the descendants of Africans, and there's a big difference."[23]

In spite of issues such as these, African-American dolls have moved steadily toward equality with white ones. When they were first manufactured, African-American dolls were used by whites. The idea was that white children could play with these dolls as a way of learning proper behavior toward African-American family servants.

But what about African-American dolls for African-American, not white, children? An African-American-owned company, the National Negro Doll Company of Nashville, Tennessee, tried doing this in the early 1900s. But it faced strong opposition from white toy merchants, who were afraid that African-American children would buy African-American dolls rather than the white ones supplied by these merchants.

But it was inevitable that African-American dolls would enter stores because of the growing power of the African-American consumer. By 1986, African-Americans were spending more than $1 billion a year on toys, many of which were dolls. Today, both African-American and white-owned companies produce dolls such as the Kenya Cousin, the Little African Princess doll, Huggy Bean, Shana and Kids of Color.

All of these dolls were designed to have African-American features and skin color. But what about dolls such as Cabbage Patch or Barbie, which were designed to have white features and skin color? Shouldn't they also come in an African-American version? This has begun to happen, but it's been an uphill battle.

The Cabbage Patch doll has been an example of this. There are African-American Cabbage Patch dolls, but in the past at least, the Hasbro Company, the doll's maker, would require a store to have and sell a minimum number of white Cabbage Patch dolls before it would ship the store any African-American ones.

By the early 1960s, millions of Barbie dolls were flooding the pre-teen market, and none of them were African-American. Every Barbie was exactly like every other Barbie — slim, blond and white. Mattel did respond to this problem, but the company's answer just got it into more trouble. It created an African-American Barbie, and called her Colored Francie. Besides her awful name, Francie was not really African-American, for she had Caucasian features and straight hair. Ironically, Colored Francie appeared right in the middle of the 1960s Civil Rights Movement. Colored Francie was a failure, and Mattel replaced her with another African-American doll, "Christie," and later added several more. But no Barbie doll was African-American. Finally, in 1980, Mattel made one of the Barbie series an African-American doll.[24]

What Kind of Doll Do You Want?

It seems only logical that an African-American child would want to have an African-American doll. But surprisingly, past research has produced contradictory and somewhat confusing answers to the question of choice. One early study found that African-American children had no obvious preference — it seemed to be simply a matter of chance as to whether an African-American girl chose an African-American or a white doll, when given the opportunity to do so under laboratory conditions.[25] Later studies contradicted this finding, but in the late 1980s, an American Psychological Association study concluded again that African-American children preferred white dolls over African-American ones.[26] If so, why would an African-American child make such a choice? Yla Eason, the president of Ilmec Corporation, an African-American-owned toy making company, thinks she has the answer to this question. "Whatever a child wants in a toy is inspired by what that child saw on television," says Eason, and what they see are mostly white children playing with white toys. "It's still a big struggle," says Eason, "The big test is, what is the black customer going to do? Are they going to buy African-American or not?"[27]

What should an African-American doll *look* like? In the early years of African-American doll-making, the head cast of a white doll was simply colored brown. But by the 1990s, African-American mothers wanted their daughters to have dolls that looked like them. And so, as one *Ebony* writer put it, "with full lips and noses and a variety of skin tones, the Shani doll by Mattel exhibits the strength, beauty and attributes of her Swahili name, which mean 'marvelous.'" Other companies have followed Mattel's example. For example, Tyco's Kenya doll has hair that can be braided, curled, or straightened.[28]

Today, African-American dolls are more than just dark skinned. Now, African-American children can choose beautiful bouncy baby dolls with "a range of spicy skin tones from mustard and cinnamon to deep persimmon and sweet chocolate."[29] Obviously, this is good, for there are indeed a variety of skin tones within the African-American community. But it also raises an interesting possibility. African-Americans are not the only people with diverse skin tones. This is also true for white people, who actually have skin tones that range from pinkish to swarthy. As more and more marriages take place between different ethnic groups, the diversity of skin color among Americans will surely increase. Thus, it just may be that fifty years from now American children will be buying dolls with a far wider range of skin tones than are available in toy stores today.

OTHER AFRICAN-AMERICAN TOYS

African-American dolls have entered the mainstream of the toy world. There are also many toys that are aimed especially toward African-American children. For example, Fisher-Price's Little People Garage features African-American figures. Also there are action figures such as Olmec's Sun Man, that are aimed at boys. Sun Man uses his magical melanin skin to combat evil.

But just as for dolls, other African-American toys have been subject to discrimination. Until recently, newspaper ads showed many more white than African-American children playing with toys. Ironically, when basketball was featured, the ads would show a white boy making a basket while an African-American boy watched from below.

AFRICAN-AMERICAN PRIDE

When she plays with her doll, a white girl does not say, "I feel good about this doll because she is one of my own," but it can be different with African-American girls and their dolls. As Dr. Janice Hals, a professor of childhood education, wrote, when African-American girls pick up an

African-American doll, "They are learning to love themselves."³⁰ In earlier times, the message that African-American girls received from their white dolls was quite different. As an *Ebony* writer said, "No longer do parents have to send their African-American daughters mixed messages by telling them they are beautiful on the one hand, yet buying them blond, blue-eyed dolls on the other."³¹

African-American oriented magazines such as *Ebony* have long argued that toys should have a major role in raising African-American children. For example, one writer speaks of toys that promote "healthy racial attitudes." And African-American toy makers agree. Yla Eason of Olmec feels that African-American children need toys which can give them the imagination "to live in places they may not live in today."³² Toys can also be role models. As one manufacturer says, "We hope that our learning toys have a positive impact so that children can see themselves as pilots, doctors and graduates at an extremely early age."³³ Some toys even help familiarize young African-Americans with their heritage. The On Your Mark toy company makes African animals. Olmec has introduced a Malcom X figure as a part of its Powerful Past series, and Briarpatch makes a West African activity kit.³⁴

Today's African-American toys have indeed come full cycle. Once, whether the cast-offs of a white plantation owner's daughter, or a dancing Sambo of the 1890s, they were instruments of oppression. But today, African-American toys are vehicles for play, power, and pride.

Toy Racism in a Nation of Immigrants

African-Americans have had to face a history of racist toys that demeaned them. But African-Americans have not been alone, for other Americans have also had to face this problem.

Driven from their homeland by the great potato famine of the 1840s, penniless Irish immigrants settled in the poorest parts of our cities. Undernourished and badly educated, they were seen as troublemakers, roughs who committed all sorts of crimes, and spread diseases such as cholera. Just as was so for African-Americans, these Irish newcomers were ridiculed in America's popular culture. Stereotyped images of them appeared in dime novels, postcards, and in racist toys, which had names such as "Paddy and the Pig."

Forced out of their homeland by famine, thousands of Chinese settled in western states in the 1800s. After gold was discovered, many located in mining camps. Some westerners liked the Chinese. For example, Mark

Twain said, "They are quiet, peaceable, tractable, free from drunkenness, and they are as industrious as the day is long. A disorderly Chinaman is rare, and a lazy one does not exist."[35] But others hated the Chinese. They had odd customs and were different in appearance. Even worse, the Chinese were willing to work for a fraction of what others demanded in wages. As an editor of the *Idaho World* put it, "The Chinamen are coming. Lord, deliver us from the locusts of Egypt, they devour all men before them."[36] And just as was so for the Irish, prejudice against these newcomers gave rise to toys such as "A Sin and the Heathen Chinese" that made fun of them.

Although they have become one of the most successful of our newcomers, today's Asian-Americans still face toy racism. Barbie is an example. The Mattel company has made African-American and Hispanic Barbies, but where are the Asian Barbies? It is true that Mattel does have a friend of Barbie called "Kira." But she is a stereotype in herself, for Kira wears a Japanese kimono. "It's just an outrage," says U.S. Representative Patsy Mink, a Hawaiian Democrat of Japanese descent. "How are these girls supposed to buy Asian dolls if there are none to buy?"[37] Mattel's explanation for the missing Barbie has been a bit lame. Asian girls tend to choose white dolls instead of Asian ones, says the company.

The movement of ethnic groups into America continues, and just as was so in the past, this movement can produce racist toys. The Homies of California were an example. They were tiny Chicano figures sold in gumball machines. Over a million were sold after they appeared in early 1999. Homies wore white T-shirts, bandannas, and knit caps, just as do the Chicano gang members of California's cities. Los Angeles Police Department members were not happy about these toys, for they stigmatized Chicanos as violent. "It's scary that kids are playing with (them)," said one officer. "We're trying to fight and teach the kids to stay away from gangs, and we have to contend with this as well?" But the maker of Homies disagreed. "Kids love them. They think they're great," he said. But media pressure can be very effective, for just one week later, he withdrew the Homies from gumball machines.[38]

NATIVE AMERICANS: A DIFFERENT KIND OF TOY RACISM

For many years, civil rights activists have complained about the images of Native Americans that appear in the movies or on television and then trickle down into dolls. These stereotypes often annoy people because they make Native Americans into bigger-than-life heroes or heroines, rather than ordinary people. For example, when Disney made its *Poca-*

hontas movie, it created a heroine that in the words of one writer, had the body of Demi Moore and the soul of Gloria Steinem.[39] And the same unreal image has appeared in all the doll spinoffs from the movie. Similarly, Native American men have suffered from images that are unreal. They are fearless, brave, always stand erect, and always wear a headdress (Fig.1). It is ironic that Native Americans still have to fight a positive image of them in the doll world.

CHILDREN AND RACISM

Are children racist about their dolls? Allister Byrd and Samantha Arvin are two young Chicago girls. One is African-American; the other is white. But both say the same thing about their dolls. They love them in any color.

Allister and Samantha are not unique in their views of a doll's race, and toy makers are taking note of this. In the American International Toy Fair of 2002, Mattel introduced the first multiracial doll. As a Mattel spokeswoman said, the new Barbie was a "mix of cultures in one doll."[40]

Adults may worry about mixing races in the doll world, but children think it's great. Samantha, who is white, asked at Christmas for her third African-American Barbie, so she could re-create a favorite music group, Destiny's Child. "It would be really boring if there were all white people," said Samantha. And Allister agrees. "Having different races is a lot funner," she said.[41]

Do Samantha and Allister represent a trend in the making? Probably, for toy makers are creating doll lines that are more racially diverse than ever.[42]

8

Gender Toys

The Changing Workplace

Work was very different in the world that preceded the Industrial Revolution. Many, perhaps most people, worked in a "home economy." Both men and women participated in the tasks that kept a family supplied with its daily needs. Women washed, cleaned, made the family clothes, tended animals, collected and grew vegetables, and prepared foods for the family. Men hunted and worked the fields, lumbered, and built houses and other shelters. Men and women shared in many tasks such as harvesting crops and butchering animals.

Before the Industrial Revolution and its new way of doing things, boys and girls made most of their toys. Girls would sew rag dolls, or make them from plant materials. Boys would use their jackknives to whittle everything from tops to water wheels. The skills each gained from their toy making served them well in later years when sewing, planting, and working with wood were skills needed for survival.

But all this changed with the Industrial Revolution. Some women worked in factories, but most remained at home, doing household tasks. Men also left home to work in factories, but increasing numbers entered one of the many new technical professions that grew out of the Industrial Revolution. Earlier, both men and women had been responsible for the creation of wealth and the development of new products. Now men, not women, were mostly responsible, for they, not women, worked in the technical professions such as engineering and chemistry that were reshaping society.

Techno-Toys for Boys

How did men come to have such power? In the view of many feminists, our society trains them to do this. And this training begins at an early age, when boys learn to use what have been called "techno-toys." These toys, like so many other things in our society, are a product of the Industrial Revolution. Four of these techno-toys are particularly important to the feminist argument. The first is the scale model, which is a realistic replica in miniature of a transport technology, such as an airplane or automobile. The second techno-toy is a miniature powered version of one of these scale models, such as a plane that flies or a car that races. The third is a construction toy such as an Erector Set. And the fourth techno-toy is the science kit. All of these techno-toys have been aimed at boys. And in the eyes of many feminists they have been sexist, for they have helped to give boys a head start in the race to a power career in one of the new technological professions that grew out of the Industrial Revolution. To see how they may have done this, we will examine each of these technological toys in depth.

THE SCALE MODEL

Model making, constructing an accurate but small-scale replica of something, has a long history. For many years before the advent of computers, naval architects made scale models of ships to guide them in designing the real thing. But what of model making as a pastime for boys? The idea that this could be an enjoyable and instructive thing for boys to do goes back well over a hundred years. For instance, in 1866, E. Landells published the *Boy's Own Toymaker*, which included ways to make a variety of model boats. The "Boy's" in his title foretold a view that was to continue: model making should be for boys, not girls. To Landells, model making was to be much more than mere fun, for the making of models could lead a boy into a successful career in one of the new technological professions that was just emerging. Citing the inventor of the steam engine, Landells wrote: "George Stephenson, who in our day has done such great things for human progress, was in boyhood always making Lilliputian mills and clay engines in a small stream that ran by his father's cottage."[1]

Does model making really lead boys into a successful career in technology? There is at least one instance in which this was very much the case. In 1931, an advertisement in the *National Geographic Magazine* invited boys to enter a very special kind of model-making contest. The Fisher Body Company, which supplied General Motors with car bodies, had created a guild whose mission was to prepare young boys for a career in the auto industry. Boys would join the guild, and then would build small replicas of the Napoleonic coach which was the logo of the Fisher Body Company. Each year, the company would award about a thousand boys who were judged to have made the best models. The top award would be a $1,000 scholarship (big money in those days) to a top engineering school. Local business leaders, including General Motors management officials and engineers, helped in the guild's contests, meeting and encouraging the boys who were participating. And GM officials encouraged guild winners to seek jobs with General Motors after graduation. All of this paid off handsomely for GM. By 1968, over half of the creative design staff at GM had been members of the Fisher Body Guild. As one designer put it, the guild "was very much a part of my teenage years." And another said "The guild got me started on the road to being an industrial designer."[2] There was only one limitation to those who were applying to the guild: they had to be boys (Fig. 8.1). Fisher Body Guild modelers were not alone in their expertise. In the 1930s, other institutions, including magazines such as *Popular Science*, held contests, rewarding boys who made the best models.

All of these models were scratch-built. You had to find the needed materials and work them into the model you were building. However, by the early 1900s, a new and easier way of making models had already appeared: the commercial model kit. To make this kind of model, you went to a store and bought a kit which had all of the parts you needed for a specific model, such as a particular kind of airplane, car, or ship. This was much easier than the old scratch-built method, but it still was difficult. Often, the parts needed further work before they could be put together, and that could take skill and patience. L. E. Sissman, who made models in the 1930s, remembered the challenge of putting a model plane together. "You had to cut several ... parts out of a printed balsa sheet with an X-acto knife, a chore guaranteed to make strong boys weep."[3]

Frustrating or not, model making was every boy's challenge. By 1941, it was one of the five top hobbies for American boys. And by 1961, nine out of every ten boys between the ages of eight and fifteen were making models as their prime hobby.[4]

Besides the fun it provided, model making had other benefits. High school teachers began to incorporate model making into their shop classes, for they believed model making taught creativity and self-reliance, and helped to teach American history. They also felt model making aided boys who wished to enter some technical career. It helped them to understand mathematics and physics. As one teacher said, "You never saw such an eager physics class when our project was assembling an atomic power plant." By actually building the unit, the students "quickly grasped the basic scientific fundamentals of this complex subject and discussed material which ordinarily belonged in college level courses."[5] However, there

Chapter 8 — Gender Toys

THOUSANDS of boys all over America are completing miniature model Napoleonic coaches in the first year's activity of the Fisher Body Craftsman's Guild. These models they will shortly submit in a nationwide competition for four university scholarships of four years each, 98 trips to Detroit, and 882 other valuable awards.

The Fisher Body Corporation sponsored this inspiring movement, believing that this exercise of creative talent, this quickening of the hand of youth, are essential steps toward the development of high ideals—that only by training the coming generation can fine craftsmanship be perpetuated and superior coachcraft be assured.

CADILLAC · LA SALLE · BUICK · OAKLAND · OLDSMOBILE · PONTIAC · CHEVROLET

Fig. 8.1. This advertisement shows a young man offering a girl the Napoleonic Coach he has made for the Fisher Body contest. Presumably, she's delighted to have such a talented young boyfriend.

is no firm data to show that model making did give boys a head start toward careers in science or engineering. But model making did have a more mundane value, at least in the eye of one writer, who happened to be a woman: The men and boys, she said, think this is a great hobby, "because it leaves them a masculine realm yet uninvaded by females."[6]

Powered Models

Scale models were powerless and went nowhere. But they just might give a boy some of those skills that were needed for a career in science or technology. Even more challenging to build was a tiny model airplane that was powered and could fly up into the air, or a small model automobile that could race along a roadway, just as their real counterparts did. This kind of model would be great fun to play with, and in their playing boys could imagine themselves as designers or commanders of the real thing. Soon after the Wright brothers' epochal triumph at Kitty Hawk in 1903, magazines and books began to tell boys how to make their own "flying machines." They were difficult to build and hard to fly. They could soar into the air and then land safely, but as often as not these little planes would go up, take a nose dive, and crash into the ground. But that made this new hobby just that much more exciting. Furthermore, the designs of real airplanes were continually improving. Model planes kept right up with these changes, and so, the model maker was more than a pretend flyer, he could also imagine himself as an airplane designer, building and testing new and experimental airplanes.

World War I helped to make model airplane building a popular boy's sport. The boys and their planes in Figure 8.2 are from a 1915 advertisement which said in part, "Exact 3-ft model war aeroplanes just like the ones now used in the European war."

The excitement of building and flying model planes hit its peak soon after Charles Lindbergh's trans-Atlantic flight of 1927. This excitement was just one part of a much larger national love affair with flying. As one writer put it, "Nothing in aviation, no single achievement, no combination of aerial events since the Wright brothers made their first mechanical flight twenty-four years ago has had such influence on the public mind as Charles A. Lindbergh's lone dash from New York to Paris." Thousands of college students besieged the aeronautics industry, seeking jobs that would give them a career in the air, and every school boy dreamed of flying.[7]

It was not surprising, really, that the making of model planes which

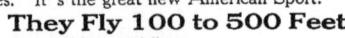

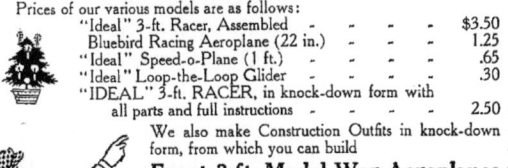

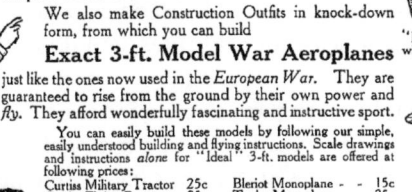
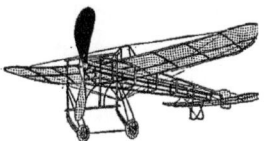

Fig. 8.2. Model airplanes of World War I. They were rubberband powered, and as the advertisement said, could fly up to 500 feet. Where are the girls?

actually flew soon became a major hobby for boys. Merrill Hamburg, a manual training teacher in the Detroit schools, decided to organize the sport. He wrote a short notice announcing a model plane contest, and put it in a magazine, the *American Boy*. Contestants would vie with each other to build the best flying model. Hamburg would help them by sending each entrant plans for building a plane. The response was huge. "I've got five hundred letters at home," he said. "I'm swamped. I've worked way past midnight for two weeks. They're coming in from every part of the country." And that's how the Airplane Model League of America started. The *American Boy*, newspapers, the Boy Scouts, even the American Legion came to his rescue, and soon the league was holding national contests.[8]

Within a few years, other organizations were formed which also encouraged boys to make and fly model airplanes. One of these, the Playground and Recreation Association of America, which was in the business of giving boys and girls interesting things to do, set up its own program which featured contests in over a hundred cities and a national contest for finalists.⁹

What did boys do in these contests? First of all, they had to join a local flying club. The Philadelphia Model Airplane Association was a typical example. By the early 1930s, it had become quite sophisticated. The association was organized into chapters of ten to fifteen members, each led by an adult. Classes taught boys how to build and fly their planes. As he became more adept, a boy could progress from being a "Grease Monkey" to a "Pilot," and finally to an "Ace." To become an Ace, a boy had to keep his plane in the air for at least four minutes, and do well in distance and control contests.¹⁰

Most model plane clubs were part of a national organization, and sometimes, this fun could lead to really exciting national events. Merrill Hamburg's Airplane Model League of America had a "Flying Squadron" made up of really expert flyers, who went about the country demonstrating their planes so as to arouse interest in the hobby. Once, the squadron flew its planes on the White House lawn while president Coolidge watched. And some boys even went to Europe as part of an international flying contest.¹¹ The hobby of building and flying model airplanes kept growing and growing. By 1981, it was estimated that there were twelve million model airplane builders in America.¹²

Boys saw this hobby as an entry into a career of designing or flying real airplanes. In doing this, they could use the Wright brothers themselves as a kind of model. When they were boys of eight and eleven, their father had given Wilbur and Orville Wright a toy flying machine. They played with it, broke it, and then spent hours trying to remake larger versions of the toy. In later years, Orville would say that it was this little toy that had started them on the road to Kitty Hawk.¹³ L. E. Sissman, who built model planes in the early 1930s, remembered how a career in aeronautics had become the dream of every American boy. "My whole generation was brainwashed to think of flying as America's ... last frontier. To us lads of ten or twelve ... flying a plane for a living seemed both a suitable and an admirable lifework."¹⁴ Great pilots of the time felt the same way about the potential of the hobby for a career in aviation. One of these, Admiral Byrd, the famous polar explorer, predicted that boys who followed this hobby would become the designers, manufacturers, and flyers of the future aviation world.¹⁵

Although airplanes were the most popular powered toys, boys also played with other models. In the early 1900s, city recreation departments began to organize "yacht regattas." Boys would build small sail-powered boats, and race them about on a local lake or stream. At first, these models were yachts in the true sense of the word. That is, they were replicas of the grand sailing yachts used by wealthy people. But by the 1940s, more and more boys were racing boats that were gasoline powered. At first, these were tethered. The boat sped around in great circles, held by a long line. Later, remote control became the rule.

But this was the age of the automobile, and so racing tiny model cars became popular. By 1920, boys were building their own racing cars. Some were called "spindizzies," because they whizzed around at the end of a tether. Others were "slot cars," which ran on a special race track. By 1965, six million enthusiasts were racing slot cars. Miniature car racing was great fun. As one ad for these cars put it, "There's no greater gift for a boy ... a car he can race on his own.... Especially if he is at that impatient age: Old enough to want a car, but too young to drive one.. He can slam through curves, ... brake hard for turns, go flat out down the straightaway."[16]

It depends on one's version of what a toy is, but the Soap Box Derby should at least be mentioned here. It began in 1933, when a newspaper photographer saw some children with homemade racing cars and took a picture of them. Then he thought, why not organize an event? Nineteen kids showed up for the first race, but later in the same year, 362 kids and forty thousand spectators turned out, and the Soap Box Derby was on its way. Just like the little cars, the fun is in the making and the passion boys have for speed. Anything that goes downhill is great, even if it's only run by gravity, as are the Derby cars.[17]

Construction Toys

Building blocks have a long history. But the construction toys that came out of the Industrial Revolution were very different from simple blocks, for they were true techno-toys. The Erector Set was the best example of these new toys. It was invented by A.C. Gilbert. And it was no accident that he thought of it as a boy's toy, for Gilbert himself was a boy's boy, and later a man's man. Self-confident, aggressive, a super achiever, and a fine athlete, Gilbert's autobiography, *The Man Who Lives in Paradise*, said it all. One day in 1913, Gilbert was riding the train to New York, when he looked out the window and noticed rows of steel girders which were being erected to carry new power lines. As Gilbert put it in his autobiography, an inspiration hit him — would a construction kit for boys that used toy girders be a success? Gilbert went home and began to experiment with cardboard girders. He found that flat pieces would not stay together. So he added a groove to them, and the basic unit of the Erector Set was born.

Fig. 8.3. A 1920 advertisement for Gilbert's Mysto Erector set.

Introduced at the 1913 New York Toy Fair, Gilbert's Erector Set was an instant success. By his death in 1961, his company had sold over ten million of them (Fig. 8.3).[18]

Gilbert used a variety of strategies to sell boys on the fun of using his new toy. For instance, he had a Sunday evening radio program that advertised Erector Sets. It was called "Engineering Thrills," and featured "True stories about real engineers and their hair-raising adventures in digging the Panama Canal, building bridges and skyscrapers."[19]

Sometimes, Gilbert reached a boy indirectly, by working through his mother. In one advertisement for the Erector Set, he included "A word with the Mothers of American boys." It told mothers that Erector Sets solved the "Boy Problem," which was presumably the difficulties mom had in controlling and guiding her rambunctious sons. The Erector Set, said Gilbert, appealed to their imagination and awakened and developed the *constructive* side of their nature. Also, said Gilbert, it helped to prepare them for the business world by developing ambition.[20]

Gilbert was a master of promotion. As he put it in his magazine *Gilbert Thrills*, "the highest honor a boy engineer can win is membership in the Gilbert Institute for Boys." All this selling worked. By the 1930s, boys were writing 250,000 letters a year, telling Gilbert about all the things they had made with the Erector Set.[21]

SCIENCE KITS

In the late 1920s, Yale University was puzzled by the growing number of young men who had decided to study chemistry. One professor surveyed his classes, asking why these students had become so interested in a subject usually considered difficult. The answer was completely unexpected. Neither money nor fame drew them to chemistry. Instead, it was a toy they had played with as a boy.

The 1920s was a time of tremendous growth in the American chemical industry, and in response toymakers designed chemistry kits for boys. The idea that fun with chemistry could lead to a career in chemistry was used as a way of increasing sales. For example, the Porter Chemical Company, which made Chemcraft play sets, said "today, boys play at chemistry, tomorrow, men hold scientific posts with industry."[22]

TECHNO-TOYS FOR GIRLS

What about girls? Did they have any new techno-toys to play with? Yes, they did, but their new techno-toys were completely different from those of boys.

No airplanes, cars or chemistry sets for them! In the decade after 1920, more and more women were using electric stoves, refrigerators, and sewing machines. And so, toy makers saw an opportunity. As one 1928 writer put it, what about "Grown-up accessories for small housekeepers? Mothers

Fig. 8.4. A Sears, Roebuck advertisement of the 1920s. From *Collectible Toys and Games of the Twenties and Thirties from Sears, Roebuck and Co. Catalogs.* By permission of Dover Publications, 1988.

would welcome a new and interesting development in toys to gladden the heart of the little girl."[23]

Soon, toymakers such as F.A.O. Schwarz were offering toy electric ranges and small electric-powered sewing machines and irons for girls to play housekeeper with. As a writer said, these toys would "satisfy the little girl's natural love of home activities."[24]

Sometimes, girls did try to cross the line by breaking into the boy's world of techno-toys. One woman recalled those "terrible Christmases when I didn't get my chemistry set.... For two years in a row, I desperately wanted that chemistry set and for months before each Christmas I dropped huge hints to my parents and every aunt and uncle in the area. Both years, I was bitterly disappointed."[25]

Besides their new electric toys, girls continued to play with traditional housekeeper toys. For example, the 1926 Sears, Roebuck Catalog had the advertisement shown in Figure 8.4. It featured a clothes wringer and dryer which a girl could use to do her dolly's laundry. The ad said, "Girls! When mama does her washing, you can do yours."[26]

Techno-Toys Today

Scale models, power models, Erector Sets, and chemistry kits, all seemed to direct boys, rather than girls, toward a career in science or tech-

Fig. 8.5. Just as did boys, men liked to experiment with new kinds of airplanes. Here was an early example. It's a "pusher" airplane that is rubber-band powered.

nology. However, in the past few decades, some of the old barriers to girls have fallen. For instance, the 1994 Soap Box Derby winner was 13-year old Danielle Ferraro. And she was the first two-time winner in the derby's history, for she had won the Kit Car championship the year before.[27]

While scale model making is still a boy's domain, it may not be as effective in training boys for a technological career as was so in the past. Today, many so-called scale models come as plastic snap-together kits, which have only a few parts. They are aimed at little boys, and it's hard to see how they could really prepare a boy for a career in technology. And the making of powered toys such as airplanes and boats has also changed. Just as in scale model making, this hobby may be less of a benefit to boys than it was in the glory days of Lindbergh. Today, the making of powered toys is a very sophisticated and expensive hobby. And it has left most boys behind, for the average age of today's power modeler is twenty-five (Fig. 8.5).[28]

The picture respecting construction toys is mixed. On the positive side, there are many new kinds of construction toys, and this provides more options for girls who want to use them. "Construction toys are not perceived as just a boy's category any longer," says Joel Ciesielski, a toy store owner.[29] On the negative side, it seems hard to entice girls into using construction toys. Lego, the best-known construction toy maker today, has worked hard at breaking the sex barrier that seems to exist for these toys. Its Belville and Paradisa lines are aimed at girls, and in 1999 Lego introduced another line called Lego Scala that is oriented toward girls.[30]

Children still play with construction kits and other traditional techno-toys. But today's electronics have opened up a new world of play. For example, a huge number of computer games are now on the market — games that appeal to boys.[31]

What about girls? Here, there is a problem. Very young girls actually spend more time at a computer than do boys, but this has changed by fourth grade, when more boys are playing their computer games. As Patricia Greenfield, a psychology professor at UCLA, has put it, video games "provide socialization and learning in computer literacy. If girls don't have that exposure, they won't have the skills needed for computer use as adults. They will be behind the eight-ball economically and socially."[32] Computer companies have been working to even this playing field. "Computer games have been a gateway to the technology for boys," says Laure Groppe, who runs a company called Girl Games. "We want to develop games that will do the same for girls."[33] And Mattel has worked hard to develop computer accessories for Barbie.[34]

But computer games are only a part of the new toy technology. Today, children can play with all sorts of hand-held electronic toys. Some, like the Barbie Shop with Me Cash Register, or the Sing Along with Me Karaoke Machine are for girls. But most of these toys are aimed at boys. Cross-Fire, a rapid-fire shoot-out game, and Backyard Football are examples. Yet girls are gaining more and more entry into this new world of techno-toys. For example, a new company called Girl Tech has been hard at work trying to even the playing field by inventing techno-toys aimed at girls. Bug-Em, a ladybug toy with a spy-like listening feature, is one of these. Interestingly, says Janese Swanson, who is the founder of Girl Tech, "The boys want to play with [it] too, which is cool — and a very big switch for the industry."[35]

Girls may be gaining more and more of an entry into this high-tech toy world, but their tech toys are still seen as different. "Girls are interested in technology as it relates to them socially," says Susan Mackey, a clinical psychologist. In contrast, she notes, "Boys are interested in the technology itself, and how many things they can kill off."[36] And Tech Toy founder Swanson agrees. "They don't like the same kinds of toys that boys like," she says.[37]

Even if a toy inventor wants his or her toy to be unisexual, others may have different ideas. When Janese Swanson designs a new toy for girls, she tries to escape the usual stereotypes that go with girl toys. But that can bother those who work in the toy business. "Can't you make it pink?" they will ask.[38]

And so, gender differences continue to persist in the world of toys. Why is this so?

Two Toy Worlds

Obviously, many toys are shared by girls and boys. And sometimes, toys can even cross the gender gap. After Russell Wenkstern, maker of Tonka Trucks, died, a woman wrote the *New York Times*, telling readers about the Tonka Truck her daughter had loved. Her father had bought it for her when she was two years old, and the little girl had loved it. "I am grateful to my parents for being willing to look beyond gender stereotypes when choosing toys for a grandchild," she said.[39]

But many toys seem to remain obstinately sexist. Girls like their dolls, toy vanities, and Trolls. Boys prefer action men, racing cars and basketball toys. Why is this? Those who do research on toys have given us many answers.

Children

Researchers have found that girls seem to prefer their own toys, and the same is true for boys. They know this because they have heard it from children. How do researchers obtain this information? One way is to ask children what they want for Christmas. You can do this by pretending you are one of Santa's helpers, and ask groups of preschool children what they want for Christmas. Studies of this sort show that a boy wants things like construction toys and toy vehicles, while girls want art equipment and dolls.[40]

Another way to acquire information about toy wants is to look at children's letters to Santa. Many children write Santa, and obliging parents mail these letters, which end up in the dead letter department of a post office. Once again, these letters show gender preferences in toy choice.[41]

An additional method of gaining data about their toy preferences is to watch children at play. Research of this sort has produced some interesting and unexpected results. Very little girls will play with hammers and other "boy toys." And little boys will play with dolls. But by preschool this changes. Now, the hammers belong to boys and the dolls to girls.

Why is this so? A part of the answer, as one research team found, is this: children tend to choose toys based on what the toy can do. Is it action oriented? That will appeal to boys. Is it a socializing toy? Then it tends to be a girl's choice.[42]

But where do children get their ideas about how to play?

Parents

As might be expected, parents are their children's most important teachers. Very early in a child's life, parents begin to teach the child how to *act* like a boy or a girl. This then sets the stage for the toys they will choose in play. This teaching is often subtle, but nevertheless very effective. A father may roughhouse with his infant son, teaching him simple acrobatics. On the other hand, he will cuddle his infant daughter. Dad will even talk differently to his children. He will say things like "little footsie" or "little beddie" to his infant daughter, but not to his little boy. Instead, dad is already at work, training his boy to be masculine. When 21-month-old Scott began to cry, his father punched him playfully on the arm, saying "C'mon, Scotty, be a big boy!"[43]

Besides speaking or acting differently when they are with a boy or a girl, parents teach a child to be boyish or girlish through the things the parents buy. A little girl's room is furnished very differently from a boy's: pink bedding for girls and blue for boys. Color differences extend to clothing and other accessories. Girls have more pink and multicolored clothes than do boys. And the same color differences can be found in their pacifiers. When they go shopping, parents choose room furnishings, clothes, and other accessories according to sex. And parents also make sex-typed selections when they buy fun things for their children. Often, coloring books aimed at girls tend to differ in content and color from those aimed at boys.[44]

Sometimes, parents will directly intervene in a child's play. Research has shown that some parents will punish a daughter for playing with soldiers, or a boy for playing with dolls. Fathers seem more likely then mothers to do this.[45]

Finally, parents are normally very sexist when they choose toys at a store. It is true that they will sometimes "cross over," buying a toy stove for a boy, or a toy gun for a girl. But this seems to happen rather rarely. One study showed that only one in fifty shoppers bought a girl toy for a boy. The opposite was a bit more common. More girls got boy toys.[46] What happens if a family has four boys and only one girl? Will this change a parent's buying habits? Do gender buying habits differ between mom and dad? What if a male shopper had received girl toys when he was a child? Does this influence his later buying habits? There seems to be little information about situations such as these.

SIBLINGS AND PEERS

Obviously, parents are not the only ones who teach children to want boy toys or girl toys. Once a child begins to play with other children, the members of his play group will exert powerful pressures to conform. Both boys and girls will play with gender-neutral toys such as large rubber balls or bubble blowers. But what about toy guns, baseballs, and dolls? Many children seem to feel that it's all right for a girl to be a tomboy and play with boy toys. But it's not acceptable for a boy to play with girl toys. That would make him a sissy. As one observer wrote, boys won't touch a Barbie doll with a ten-foot pole.[47] Finally, siblings send sexist messages to their younger brothers or sisters. An older girl will teach a younger sister how to play with a toy stove or a doll, and the same sort of educational training will take place between two brothers.

TOY COMPANIES AND TOY STORES

Besides parents, peers, and siblings, other people send powerful messages about "correct" toy use. In a somewhat circular process, toy makers will use research to determine which of their toys are used by girls and which are used by boys. Then, they will advertise these as appropriate for one sex or the other. Sometimes, toy makers will make use of a market segmentation strategy to turn gender- neutral toys into toys that are gender specific. For example, they will take a toy wagon, which is essentially a gender neutral toy, and make it either a girl toy or a boy toy by painting one set black for boys and a second set pink for girls.

In toy stores, aisles will be segregated. A pink aisle will be full of toys like Barbies, doll cradles, and toy dressers. But black and brown aisles will have Water Craft toys, Ultimate soldiers, and space weapons. The toy advertisements of a Sunday newspaper are also divided: a pink section for girl toys and a darker section for boy toys.

Newspaper and catalog ads for toys show still another variety of sexism. In a 1996 study, Debra Haffner coded 566 catalog pictures which showed children with toys to see what the children were doing. Only one boy was shown with a doll. Cars, trucks, and trains were shown with boys. The only toys used equally by girls and boys were musical instruments.[48]

Salespeople also help to keep gender alive in the toy world. Nancy Kutner and Richard Levinson had their students go to department stores and ask clerks for advice in buying birthday gifts for twins, one a boy, the other a girl. As most of us might expect, over half of the sales people made sex-stereotyped suggestions—a doll for the girl, a dump truck for the boy.[49]

TELEVISION

And finally, television is a powerful conditioner of toy choice. Because it is animated, TV does far more than just show a boy or a girl with a toy. By words, action, and music, TV will associate a toy with boyhood or girlhood. Thus, boyhood and its toys are accompanied by staccato music, bright colors, and abrupt camera shifts, while girl toys are accompanied by flowing movement, soft music, and slow camera fades. Television is also an especially powerful conditioner of toy choice because its message is so simple. As Joanne Oppenheim has put it, "Children tend to sort out the world into simple and absolute terms of right or wrong, hard or easy, boy or girl." What about toys that can't be put into TV's boy or girl format? They tend to be avoided by television.[50]

ASKING CHILDREN

What do children think about toy sexism? There are many studies of children's behavior respecting toy sexism. But not many ask children whether toy sexism is a good idea. However, one reporter did ask two children, a girl and a boy, what they thought of the girl and boy aisles in Toys-R-Us stores. Here is what each said: Kellen Calinger, age twelve: "Toys shouldn't be sequestered into boy's and girl's sections ... neither boys nor girls should be limited to certain types of toys." David Bryan, age eleven: "I think stores should separate girl's toys from boy's toys because sometimes it makes it easier to find your toys. I wouldn't want to walk through a section of toys I'm not interested in just to find what I need."[51]

TWO VIEWS OF TOY SEXISM

The idea that girls and boys are taught to play with different toys is part of a larger view which is sometimes called cultural determinism. It argues that sexism, whether in clothing, jobs, toys, or anything else, is a result of cultural conditioning, for there is nothing innate about sexist attitudes or practices. As the famous anthropologist Margaret Mead, who was a cultural determinist, put it, "Many, if not all, of the personality traits which we have called masculine or feminine ... are almost entirely to be laid to differences in conditioning, especially during childhood."[52] According to this view, sexism is learned, not innate. In support of cultural determinism, some anthropologists claim to have found societies where sex roles are reversed, and women, not men, hold the key positions of power in the society. It is true that as it was in country America, early societies typically divided the responsibilities of maintaining a home-based economy. Some of these societies were matriarchal; that is, the mother was head of her family. But there is no evidence for the existence of a technologically advanced society such as ours in which women have held most of the key power positions in that technology.

In recent years, cultural determinism has come under increasing criticism by those who call themselves sociobiologists. The sociobiological view argues that sexism exists in the workplace and in play because there are innate biological differences between the two sexes which act to create different roles for males and females. Sociobiologists note that males are more aggressive, more likely to be violent, to pursue women more than they are pursued, and tend to do work that is more physical than that done by women. They argue that behavioral differences such as these are biologically based, for they are found in all human societies. Much sociobiological work has centered on the role of hormones in eliciting behavioral differences, and some of this work tends to show that differences between girls and boys respecting their play and toys may have a hormonal base. For example, one study found that girls who had an abnormally high level of male hormones during their gestation were much more likely to play with boy toys in their early childhood than was so for other girls.[53]

There is a vast literature that explores the views of cultural determinists and sociobiologists. Two books, *Male/Female Roles*, edited by Jonathan Petrikin, and *Sex on The Brain*, by Deborah Blum, provide valuable insights respecting these opposing views, and are cited in the bibliography. And the landmark article by Carroll Pursell provides an overview of boy's techno-toys as sexist.[54]

Could it be possible that there is merit in both views? Surely, as cultural determinists would argue, each society will develop its unique concepts of what aptitudes its leaders should have. Yet at the same time, there may be male-female differences that are innate, and make either males or females fitter for these leadership positions. There is good evidence that boys tend to excel in spatial perception and perhaps mathematics, and that this is innate. Both of these skills could lead them toward using techno-toys which could then prepare them for later careers in some technologically oriented profession. But there may be skills that will become even more important for those who seek a power career in the future. We are rapidly becoming an information-centered society. Girls excel in spelling and verbalizing, and both of these aptitudes are important in dealing successfully with information. Perhaps one day we will have girl toys which develop and encourage these aptitudes, and which lead girls, rather than boys, into the most important career positions in the world of the future.[55]

II. Toys Past, Present, and Future

9

Toys of the World We Have Lost

THE OUTDOOR PLAY OF LONG AGO

A hundred years ago, Americans were predominantly country people, for only a third of us lived in urban areas of 8,000 or more.¹

What was it like to be a country child a hundred years ago? Since we were not there, we have to try to understand that lost world from the autobiographies of those who grew up in that time.

One of these, *Dorothy's World*, was written by Dorothy Howard, a well-known folklorist. In her book, Howard recalled her early life in Sabine Bottom, which was on the Texas frontier of a hundred years ago. Then, she was Dorothy Mills, a six-year-old who was awed and a bit frightened by the strange new world she had entered. The Mills family had come to Texas at a time when Sabine Bottom was sparsely settled. Point, the nearest town, was only five miles from the Mills farm, but it might as well have been in another world as far as Dorothy was concerned. The Millses did go to town on occasion, but it was a major effort to drive all that way in their buggy.

Hands, not machines, did most of the Millses' work and so, there were lots of chores for Dorothy to do. Some were indoors, like cleaning oil lamps, dumping ashes from the stove, and building morning fires. But most of her chores were done outdoors. Weeding the vegetable garden, gathering fruit, and feeding the farm animals were examples.²

Dorothy was not alone with her chores, for all across country America, children had chores to do. Some of these seemed to take forever. Allie Wallace, who grew up in rural Oklahoma, remembered how she hated churning cream into butter. She would try everything, including making up churning songs, to cut the monotony. If Allie got careless and spilled some cream, an irritated ma might switch her.³ Some indoor chores were unusual. Ed Dale, who also lived in the Cross Timbers country of Oklahoma a hundred years ago, remembered fly duty. On those rare occasions when the family had supper guests, Ed had to stand by the table switching a leafy branch back and forth to keep the flies away.⁴ Although most chores were boring, some could be fun. One girl in Nebraska remembered how much she enjoyed helping her parents set fire-breaks about the homestead. "In those days, [we] felt needed," she said.⁵

Chores may seem a peripheral topic in a book dedicated to toys, but that's not so. In Dorothy's time, children had to make most of their toys, and with all their chores, country children had little time for toy making. Furthermore, as partners in the family's work, children grew up at an earlier age than they do today. For both of these reasons, toys were less important to early American children. For example, Dorothy had around a dozen toys, mostly homemade, in her "pretty box." In contrast, an average middle class American child of today owns over ninety toys.⁶

Where were toys used in that lost world? Early American children knew and loved the out-of-doors, and that's where they used most of their toys. Ed Dale of Oklahoma put it this way: "the house ... was only more or less incidental.... In good weather [we] stayed indoors just as little as possible."⁷ It was easy to see why Ed felt this way. Most country houses of Ed's time were small, hot in summer, cold in winter, and generally uncomfortable. The worst were the sod houses of the western plains, which were made of bricks cut from the soil. The frame shanties built on other parts of the frontier were a bit better, as were the more permanent homes that would come later. But all were crowded, with little privacy, and everything from dust to animals such as mice, centipedes, spiders, and snakes came into houses through the cracks in walls and ceilings. There was no running water, and no electricity.

When they played outdoors, what toys did children use? Girls might take a store-bought porcelain doll outside, but more often, it would be a rag doll. These had been made of old cloth from the family's rag bag. The cloth would be cut into a doll shape, stuffed with cotton, and sewn together. Yarn would be added for hair, and buttons for eyes. Working in the woodshed, a boy might fashion a walnut collecting wagon out of pine board, which was soft enough to saw and whittle. Its wheels were never quite round, but the wagon would work well enough to help a boy gather the walnuts which fell to the ground in autumn (Fig. 9.1).

But most of the time, country children made ephemeral toys that did not last very long, such as the doll hammocks of Figure 9.2.

Many things in the nature that surrounded them could be turned into

Chapter 9—The World We Have Lost

Fig. 9.1. Boys foraging for walnuts. Country children knew all about nature. Many of today's children would not even know where walnuts grow.

toys. Miriam Coffin of Maine discovered that lady-slippers made fine ducks. They had a bill and eyes, and you could float them and feed them chickweed through the openings on each side of their bills. Boys also used plant parts in their play. Miriam Coffin's brother, Peter, took large peapods, wedged them open with match sticks, and floated them down a stream as

Fig. 9.2. Girls making an ephemeral toy. They are making a doll hammock out of leaf blades.

tiny canoes.[8] Ed Dale remembered how he and his brother discovered that winter onions called shallots made great noisemakers. They pinched off the top end of a shallot and blew through its hollow stem. And boys everywhere made willow whistles in springtime, when a willow tree was full of sap. They would cut six inches off a willow branch, slip its bark off, cut airways around the wood and slip the bark back on. Leaves also made fine noisemakers (Fig. 9.3).

Many children played with animals. Chickens were a favorite, for they were on every homestead. Like most little girls of her time, Dorothy Howard had been taught the Bible. Dorothy and her little brother would sneak up on a chicken and shout a biblical name like Thessalonians at a chicken, which would cackle angrily and hop away.[9] One girl whose family had homesteaded in Sonoma County, California, was an only child and had no playmates. So she talked with the chickens. Her mother gave the child some dolls to use as friends. "Pretend you're keeping house," she said. So the daughter took the dolls out to the shed, sat them in chairs and tried to talk to them, but they didn't talk back. "The chickens were lots more fun," said the girl. Chickens were fine, but many children preferred to tame wild animals, such as infant antelopes, prairie dogs, owls, possums, or baby badgers.[10]

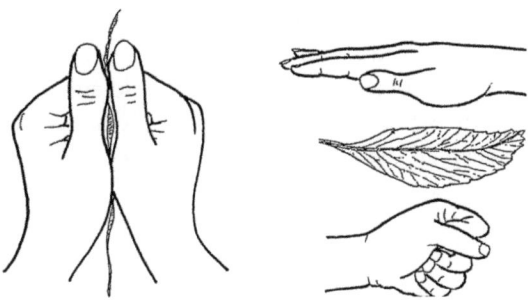

Fig. 9.3. Leaf noisemakers. Hold a leaf between your thumbs and blow, or place a leaf on one hand and hit it with the other.

Large animals made fine pets, but children also used insects and other small animals in their play. They would watch dung beetles roll a ball of dung, and then hide the dung to see if the beetle could find its lost treasure. Fireflies were everywhere in summer, and children delighted in gathering them to see whose insect bottle glowed the most. Butterflies were used as toys. Dorothy Howard and her friends had butterfly races, trying to be the first to chase their butterfly from one flower to the next. Even in death, animals became toys. Country children would find a dead animal, such as a bird, and hold elaborate funerals. They knew just how to do this, for death was a part of everyday life on the frontier, and by the time a child was only a few years old, he or she had attended a real funeral.

Many girls made animals of one kind or another into dolls. One of the strangest of all animal dolls must have been one owned by Lettie Teeple, who grew up in Michigan during the 1830s. She captured a frog, dressed it in doll clothes, and put it in her baby sister's cradle. When her mother found the frog, she laughed but told Lettie to put the frog back in the brook.[11]

As they grew older, more and more of a child's play centered on sport toys, such as tops, jump ropes, hoops, or baseballs. There were no coaches, no playing fields, no printed rules to obey, or special uniforms to wear. In short, the one most striking thing about these games was the absence of adults who decided when, where, and how the games should be played. One result of this was that each sport toy was used in many different ways. There were endless hoop games, from follow-the-leader to a new version of the old Indian hoop and pole game. Thomas Alford, a Shawnee Indian who grew up in the mid-1800s, remembered the "hat game." A round hoop was made of a wild grape vine. The boys would choose sides and stand in two lines, facing each other. Then, they would roll the hoop between the two lines, and try to shoot an arrow through it. When a boy did this, the game would stop. All the boys would stick their arrows into the ground, and the winning boy would sling the hoop into the arrows. He would get to keep all the arrows he had knocked down.[12]

In spring and summer, many children played tops by casting their top against those of other children, trying to knock their tops out of a ring. But Charles Eastman, a Sioux Indian, remembered a winter version of tops. He and his friends would play a kind of follow-the-leader, whipping their tops over snowdrifts and aiming them so that they would land in patches of ice.[13] In New Mexico, Hispanic children played a game called Arriada. It was a team game. Two goals were set up, and a ball placed between them. Each team would try to hit the ball with their tops, driving it into their opponent's goal.[14]

If you played baseball, you usually made your own equipment. Ed Dale remembered how a good baseball could be made from yarn unraveled from old hand-knitted socks. You rolled the yarn up, sewed it tightly together, and covered it with some old leather from a shoe.[15] Then you searched for a good place to play. Jump rope, marbles, tops, and even baseball—they all could be played in almost any patch of dirt.

Children often made up their own rules when they played a game. Bruce Catton, of Benzonia, Michigan, remembered how he played baseball in the early 1900s."We had no one to teach us how to play." We had to pick it up as we went along, and we did not learn much ... the chief thing we took to heart was that all fielders must keep up a steady flow of chatter, to encourage the pitcher and discourage the batter. None of our pitchers could throw a curve. Mostly, they just lobbed the ball in and trusted to luck. We had no umpire, and there were no bases on balls."[16]

Just as so for those who lived in the countryside, town children made most of their own toys and used them outdoors. Lucy Larcom and her friends in Beverly, Massachusetts, held buttercups under their chins, to help them decide who was fondest of butter. As everyone knew, the more a buttercup reflected its yellow on your chin, the more butter you had eaten. Dandelions could also tell secrets. The girls would blow fuzz from a dandelion head to make it answer the question, "Does my mother want me to come home?"[17]

Max Miller, a town boy, found some string and bits of paper. He put the paper on the end of the string, and whirled it around below a street light, trying to capture the bats that were flying there. Town children would use pins as fishhooks. They would tie them to a piece of string, and fish down through gutter grates, trying to hook the mysterious things that lived in the sewer.[18]

In North Minneapolis, Minnesota, Melvin Frank and his friends would have hoop races around the block.[19] Don Gardner remembered stomping on discarded Pet Milk cans, so that their ends would fasten around the soles of his shoes. Then, he would clip-clop noisily along the sidewalk.[20] Caroline Creevy always played with her hoop or jump rope when she was sent on errands to the store.[21]

And even if they lived in larger towns, children would play with animals. Flannery O'Connor, of Savannah, Georgia, dressed a gray bantam chicken in a white pique coat with a lace collar and called it Colonel Egbert.[22]

Sometimes, children were very ingenious in thinking of ways to make new toys. Anne Johnson, who grew up in an Iowa town during the early 1900s, took two straight pins, crossed them, and placed the crossed pins on a railroad track. After a train went over, she had a pair of little scissors, just right for her dolls.[23]

Just as country and town children did, those who lived in cities spent most of their free time outdoors. As Catherine Brody, who grew up in New York City a hundred years ago, remembered: "There was no such thing as playing in the house."[24]

Why did city children go outdoors? The late comedian George Burns, who also grew up in New York City a hundred years ago, gave us this answer: The Burns family were immigrants, and like so many families of that time, were very poor. Here is the way Burns described the family apartment, which consisted of four small rooms on the third floor of a tenement house: "There was a coal-burning stove in the kitchen, which was used for cooking and for heating the rooms, and we had cold running water except in the winter, when the pipes froze. If you had to go to the bathroom, you went down three flights and out into the yard where there were just three toilets for the whole building. We had gaslight, but very little of it...." Not a fun place for play, especially as there were twelve children in the Burns family![25]

What kinds of toys did city children make? Sometimes, they used nature's things. Jimmy Savo, who lived in New York in the early 1900s, remembered pulling hairs, one at a time, from the tails of city horses. "They came out easily. The horse just turned around and looked reproachfully," said Jimmy. The hairs were made into rings and other playthings. Just as Dorothy Howard did, he would use junk to make toys. But his was city junk. For example, Jimmy took lumps of coal from ash cans, and used them to make the eyes and coat buttons of snowmen.[26] Sam Levinson, also a New Yorker, made old oatmeal cereal boxes into telephones.[27]

Cities lacked woods and fields, but they had other places to play. The sidewalks were fine for many kinds of toys. You could find an old crate, put some wheels on it, and have a sidewalk scooter (Fig. 9.4).

But sports were a problem. Where could you play baseball? It was dangerous to play in the streets, and if you played on sidewalks you would get in the way of adults. One answer was to play stickball, a defused version of the game. George Burns remembered how he and his friends did this: "A manhole cover was home plate, a fire hydrant was first base, second base was a lamp post, and Mr. Gitlitz, who used to bring a kitchen chair to sit and watch us play, he was third base."[28]

Besides sidewalks and streets, city children had other special places for play. Fire escapes, rooftops, and even fountains were used. The stoop, or entrance platform at the front of tenements, had a special meaning. It was where children gathered. The older ones took the top steps, while younger children had to make do with the bottom steps. The stoop was a city playroom, used for endless games of skully, patsee, spauldeen, hopscotch, and marbles. And the stoop itself could be made into all kinds of imagined places—a battleship, a stagecoach, or a fort.[29]

THE INDOOR PLAY OF LONG AGO

Although country children played outdoors whenever they could, there were times when this was not possible. Then, they would have to make do with household play. When inside, Dorothy Howard would place two chairs together and throw a sheet over them to make a covered wagon. Then she and her little brother would talk about horses, Indians, and how to get food for supper. Her brother would have to climb down with his shotgun (a broom) to bring back a rabbit, which was really a door stop. Dorothy's family took the Sears, Roebuck catalog, and she would spend long winter hours cutting people out of old catalogs and making them into paper dolls. Then Dorothy would add stoves, chairs, and beds, all made from old boxes, spools, or scraps of paper. If her ma had a free moment, she might play games with Dorothy. For example, she would hang a sheet on the wall, light a candle, and use her fingers and the candle's light to throw animals on the sheet. Dorothy would guess what each animal was.[30]

In Oklahoma, Ed Dale and his brother, George, played checkers when indoors. Their board was an old wooden lid, while lima beans or corn kernels became checker pieces. They did many other things with food. Ed remembered playing "ranching." Big white grains of popcorn became

Fig. 9.4. A city scooter made out of a shoe box. What is going on in the background?

sheep, peanuts became cattle, and marbles were horses. "We bought and sold livestock, traded cattle for sheep or vice versa, and swapped a horse for more cows, pausing sometimes to 'kill a beef' or a couple of sheep."[31] And Allie Wallace of Oklahoma remembered how she and her friends would find some melon rinds, cut them to the right shape, and play "false teeth."[32]

Just as did their country relatives, children in towns and cities would play indoors in bad weather. Vera Osborne, who grew up in Charlotte, Michigan, early in the last century, made use of the stairway in her house. She tore up bits of paper and threw them over the banister in handfuls, pretending they were butterflies as they flitted down to the first floor. "Then I would go down, gather them into a shoe box, and return for another flight."[33]

The New World of Machine-Made Toys

They could not have known it, but the handmade toys of Dorothy Howard, Catherine Brody, Ed Dale, Jimmy Savo, George Burns, and Vera Osborne were soon to be replaced by a new sort of toy, a product of the

Industrial Revolution. Beginning in England during the 1700s, the Industrial Revolution quickly spread throughout the Western World. It created sweeping changes in people's lives—new occupations, a new level of luxury, and a new world of machine-made objects, including toys. At first, only wealthy families could afford to buy these new toys, but by the late 1800s, almost every child had at least one machine-made toy.

What did children of the time think of these new toys? Many of the autobiographies which recall child life in early America speak fondly of old-time toy making. But these memories of toy making may be colored a bit by nostalgia, for the truth seems to be that children of that time actually thought more of the new machine-made toys than of the ones they had to make. Some of this was more a matter of desire than anything else. These new toys were beyond the reach of most children, and so they had a romance that everyday homemade toys could never equal. Edwin Way Teal of Michigan felt that way about the wonderful machine-made toys he saw in the family Sears catalog. "It was a farm-boy's book of dreams, a doorway into magical realms," he said. And Dorothy Howard, in Sabine Bottom, Texas, seems to have felt the same way. She would cut the toy pages from her family Sears catalog, and carry them around in her pocket.[34] At Christmas, Dorothy would get something special—a store-bought toy. She particularly remembered china dolls. They were small—from five to eight inches tall—with china heads and hands.[35] Ed Dale remembered how his older sister, Fannie, who lived up in Nebraska, sent the Dales a Christmas box. In it were store-bought toys for Ed—a bag of beautiful marbles and a harmonica.[36]

Sometimes, children had a first-hand glimpse of the new toy world that was to come. Jimmy Savo was a poor boy, but he was friends with the son of a minister who was well-off. When Jimmy first went to his friend's house, he entered this new world. His friend "had all the toys in the world—a rocking horse, a football, a train with an engine on tracks.... I had never seen such things. It was like paradise to step into his home."[37] And this paradise was soon to be the norm for more and more American children. Like the minister's son, they too would own many toys. And like him, they would mostly use their toys indoors, rather than outdoors.

The Outdoor Play of Today

Although most of their play time is indoors, today's children do use toys in the out-of-doors. If they live in the country, they may play in the fields and woods. Just as did the children of early America, they may roam far and wide as they play. But outdoor play is very different for most of America's children, who live in urban areas.

Lack of wild spaces confines them to play in parks, and on sidewalks, driveways, and patios. There is another factor in addition to the loss of natural environments which keeps young children near home when they play outdoors. It is the worry that small children can be kidnapped or abused by strangers if they play outdoors. For seventy percent of today's parents, the greatest fear respecting the safety of their children is that kidnappers or child abusers might be lurking about, waiting for a child who ventures too far from home.[38]

When they do play outdoors, today's children will sometimes make ephemeral toys, just as their country ancestors did. Once in awhile, they will even use material taken from nature. In her fine book, *Dramatic Play in Childhood,* Virginia Koste cites two boys playing in a mud puddle near a driveway who used empty pea pods to make boats, just as Peter Coffin did back in early America. She also mentioned two girls who were raking leaves and decided to play house. They turned their leaf pile into separate rooms. But more often, today's children make their ephemeral toys from urban trash. The author remembers moving to a new home, where his children were joined by new friends. Working together, they turned empty cartons that were standing about in the driveway into a town. Koste cites a little girl named Dianne and her friends Dennis and Steven, who took an oil drum and turned it into a boat. "'Batten down the hatches! Lower the sails!' yells Dennis. He rocks the drum so hard that Steven falls off. Man overboard! Get a rope! cries Dennis. Tracy, another boy, runs to get a rope, but the troubles have only begun. 'Sharks!' screams Dennis. They manage to rescue Steven, and everything is once again under control."[39]

But most of today's outdoor toys are not ephemeral. Instead, they are machine-made and store-bought. Many of these urban outdoor toys have been designed for use on grass or concrete. Slides and playhouses are fine for backyards. Ever since sidewalks appeared, toys have been designed for use on them. Some of these, such as the handmobile are long forgotten (Fig. 9.5). Others, like tricycles, roller skates, and scooters are still with us.

The children of early America used their homemade baseballs or hoops in open spaces such as fallow fields. But today's children use their sport toys on city playgrounds, streets, or driveways, or other man-made places. And much of today's sport play is organized. Little League and the many town and city soccer leagues are examples of this.

But outdoor play is becoming less and less common. One study has shown that in 1997, American children of twelve and under spent thirty minutes less per day in outdoor play than they did in 1981.[40]

Ironically, school recess, one of the few remaining outdoor playtimes treasured by young children, is also dying away. School recess has always been a time for innovative play. At PS 87 in New York, Kaitlin, age six, sketches steam engines on the blacktop, while Bettine, age five, is turned into a human wheelbarrow by friends who hold her ankles. But many educators seem to feel that there is no need for innocent fun of this kind. Today, more than forty percent of American school districts have done away with recess or are considering doing so. But as Anthony Pellegrini, professor of educational psychology at the University of Minnesota, notes, studies suggest that recess breaks actually help children learn.[41]

Fig. 9.5. A handmobile of the early 1920s.

THE INDOOR PLAY OF TODAY

Back in Dorothy's world, children played with their toys in the outdoors unless bad weather forced them to go indoors. But today, this is reversed. Given a choice, most children will use their toys indoors. Why is this? Because today's houses are a world apart from those of Dorothy's world. By 1900, most of them had running water. By the early 1900s, a third of America's houses had electricity, and by the 1930s, two-thirds did. By the 1960s, central heating and air conditioning had become common.[42] And so, today's houses are fine places in which to play.

This new indoor play environment led to a boom in the toy industry, which has grown tremendously since 1900. Most of today's toys have been invented specifically for indoor use. Often, these indoor toys were miniature versions of some new invention that was sweeping across America (Fig. 9.6). And grand old sports such as baseball became indoor table games (Fig. 9.7).

No one, least of all the children who had lived in the uncomfortable houses of early country America, would question the many advantages that came when children moved indoors with their toys; today's toys pro-

Fig. 9.6. Indoor toys of the 1920s. Houses and railroads have both moved indoors.

vide children with a wealth of play that is far beyond anything the children of early America could have imagined. But this new indoor play has created problems.

The Isolation Problem

Sometimes, country America could be a lonely place. But more often, the children of country America played in groups. In contrast, today's

Fig. 9.7. This was an indoor baseball game of ninety years ago. The company that sold this toy called it "Baseball at Home." It said you could make "Sensational one-hand stops, pick-ups, and line drives."

housebound children are much more likely to play alone. One study has found that today's children spend about eighty percent of their time alone, often in their rooms, when they play in the house. In part at least, it may be parents who are responsible for this. Often separated from their children because of divorce or jobs, today's parents shower toys on their children as a form of guilt giving. But as Brian Sutton-Smith has noted, what they are also saying is "we give you these toys in order to bond you to us, now go and play with them yourselves."[43] In his book, *Toys as Culture*, Sutton-Smith lists over fifty kinds of toys that encourage isolation. Coloring books and handicraft kits are examples. Some people would say that playing in isolation is bad, arguing that it deprives children of the give-and-take play that helps them to become responsible community members when they are adults. Yet, as Sutton-Smith has noted, this isolation of children as they play with their toys may not be entirely bad. Increasingly, adult Americans work in isolation, whether on an assembly line or in an office cubicle. Also, solitary play with toys can help to develop the ability to depend on one's self.[44]

Although indoor play can lead to isolation, and that may be a problem, there is another aspect of this indoor play that is much more worrisome.

Indoor Play and Exercise

The children of early America had to clamber about the countryside, looking for things that they could make into toys. Once found, it took them still more energy to make a toy. But it's very different with today's housebound children, for all they have to do is to sit quietly on the house floor, watching their toys move about. And when not watching their toys, today's housebound children will spend much of their remaining time sitting passively at a computer or watching TV. Finally, while sitting quietly, today's child is as likely as not to be snacking on a wide variety of fast foods.[45]

All this leads to an inevitable result: the prevalence of overweight children in America has more than doubled in the last 25 years. And this is so for children of all ages, ethnicities, and social backgrounds.[46]

What are the long-term effects of being overweight as a child? There is an unexpected link between a child's inactivity and his health. Adults who don't exercise are twice as likely to get heart trouble as those who do. And there is good evidence that once children get into the habit of being inactive, they will stay inactive as adults.[47]

Could toys and television cooperate in making housebound children more active? Robin Wes, a musician turned entrepreneur, has developed Little Gym music cassettes. These are to be used in the house. Children watch them and do exercises in tune with the music. Recently, another researcher, Dr. David Allison of St. Luke-Roosevelt Hospital in New York, has come up with another idea. He has built a TV cycle, which must be pedaled to turn on a television set. Allison tried his cycle out on four overweight children, saying, "Here you go. For the TV to work, you have to pedal. See ya." There was a bit of cheating, but Dr. Allison did find that after ten weeks of pedal work, the children had lost a significant amount of weight. Could the same idea be used with specially designed activity toys? These might be accompanied by a cassette which challenges a child to use the activity toy in difficult (yet safe) workouts.[48]

The ideas of Wes and Allison might have merit, as does another possibility. Today's children are accustomed to being a part of many planned activities. What about enlisting young children in fitness programs, which are tailored to young interests? A YMCA near Boston has tried doing this. Nine- and ten-year-olds come in several times a week to use fitness machines designed for children. One, called the Duck-Duck-Quack-Quack gives children a thorough workout. Another, the Star Wars Fighter Pilot, does the same thing. And schools are also starting physical fitness programs.[49]

All of these are good ideas. But another seems the most promising of all: getting children back outdoors which they have all but abandoned. Done properly, programs that take children out into nature would have two merits. First, they would be a fine way to exercise sedentary young bodies. And secondly, they would help end what many observers see as a dismaying trend among today's children: most have lost any real understanding of nature. But is it really important for a child to know nature?

Knowing Nature

When they played outdoors, the children of early America were surrounded by nature. But today's children spend most of their time indoors. Does their loss of contact with nature hurt today's children? In his book, The *Geography of Childhood*, Gary Nabhan says yes in romantic, almost mystical terms: "Wildness—even in its simplest forms—can nourish a lasting attachment to the earth, and, in turn, nurture self-esteem." It is clear, he says, that "we need to find ways to let children roam beyond the pavement, to gain access to vegetation and earth."[50] In her book, *The Children Speak*, Mary Rivkin worries about how rapid our change away from nature has been. As she notes, this change from knowledge to ignorance about nature "has happened so fast, along with everything else in this speed-ridden [twentieth] century, that we have not coped with it. If someone had said to our grandmothers, 'your great-grandchildren won't know how to find worms,' they would not have believed it."[51]

What of those who lived in the country America of our past? What did they have to say about nature? Many said that they came to know nature in a way that would astound today's children. Within four months after the Warners had moved to western Kansas, daughter Luna had collected and catalogued 117 plants she had found around the Warner homestead. Out in Nebraska, Grace Snyder soon came to know every hill and canyon, every plum thicket, current patch, and buffalo trail within a half mile of her new home.[52] And it was the same for the famous naturalist Edwin Way Teale, who grew up on a farm near Lake Michigan: "Inch by inch, I knew our farm.... I knew its vast mow where I jumped from beams into the hay, sending up multitudes of glinting motes of dust.... I knew its north woods, a mysterious realm of little trails and piles of yellow sand dug from burrows, and its even more mysterious marshlands."[53]

But it was much more than just coming to know nature. Often, the children of America's country past recalled their time in words that were almost wistful, as they tell of play in a lost Eden that today's housebound children will never know. In his landmark book, *Growing Up with the Country,* Elliott West gives many examples of this. He cites Owen McWhorter, who remembered the Texas high plains this way: "In those days, the grass, especially in wet years, was knee-high to a horse — beautiful, actually, a beautiful, beautiful scene.... There was something about it a kid loved, the country, I mean. It was good earth."[54] And Hamlin Garland, who wrote of prairie life in his book, *A Son of the Middle Border,* put it this way: "Sometimes ... Harriet (his sister) and I wandered away to the meadows along Dry Run, gathering bouquets of pinks, sweet-williams, tiger-lilies and lady-slippers.... The sun flamed across the splendid serial waves of the grasses and the perfumes of a hundred spicy plants rose in the shimmering mid-day air. At such times, the mere joy of living filled our young hearts with wordless satisfaction."[55] Others felt the same way. Bruce Catton, who grew up in northern Michigan, said, "Childhood then mirrored a peace of mind that is not to be found today.... We had all outdoors at our disposal. All we needed was a trace of imagination, and every child has that. The place to experience the imagination lay all about us."[56]

Many country children found private places where they could settle down and play. Henry Conklin, who lived in upstate New York in the 1840s, had a special place he called the "little play house in the grove." When he was nine, Henry fell in love with Ann, a schoolmate. Together, they would go to the grove to make dishes and saucers of acorns and acorn cups. Henry recalled those "happy golden hours," when he and Ann would sit in the playhouse and talk of years to come, when they would build a real house of their own.[57]

Anne Sneller also had a secret place which she called the "King's Palace." It was a "perfect circle of hemlock trees standing on a knoll and overlooking the rest of the scattered woods," and that was where Anne and her friends went to play. But as so for many country children, Anne's memories end with a sense of loss: "The King's Palace is gone. Many years later when a new highway was put through, moving and destroying the Known World, the walls of the Palace crumbled."[58]

One does have to realize that people who write memoirs of their childhood can be carried away by nostalgia, or be tempted to romanticize what was actually a rather humdrum time in their life. Even so, early experiences of nature do seem to give some children special advantages. In a landmark study called *The Ecology of Imagination in Childhood,* Edith Cobb both quantified the view that nature is important for a child's development and gave it added weight. She reviewed the autobiographies of several hundred creative thinkers and found that they felt their childhood experiences of nature helped them toward their later creativity.[59]

Reinventing Country America

Thus, it does seem possible that children lost two things when they went indoors. First, the kind of physical tone that comes from outdoor play. And second, an ill-understood but probably real sense of peace and even creativity that can grow out of a oneness with nature.

How can today's children become once more a part of nature? Most of them can't go out into the countryside and play with toys, because nature has been turned into developments and shopping centers. What about creating nature parks, modern versions of our lost country world?

What would such a park be like? There are a number of these parks in the Chicago area. At Kline's Creek Farm, children can learn about bats, watching them swoop down on mosquitoes. At the Grove Forest Preserve near Libertyville, children learn about aquatic plants and animals.

In the Washington, D.C., area, the Brookside Center brings children face to face with nature. There's a Discovery Room, where kids can feel animal pelts and discover the difference between rose, lemon, and peppermint plants. They also can handle live turtles. Do turtles sometimes poop when they get scared? asks a six-year-old. No, says the resident naturalist, that's never happened.

At Franklin Canyon Ranch in Beverly Hills, California, children can explore "night crawlers."[60]

These parks are fun, provide some exercise for children, and help to teach them about nature. But they feature planned activities, led by park naturalists. And children do not come alone, for they are brought by parents who see these parks as a fine educational experience for their children.

What about children who are on their own? Do they really want to go out and muck about in nature? In a pioneer 1955 study, Alvin Lukashok and Kevin Lynch, both of the Massachusetts Institute of Technology, asked students what they did in the outdoors when they were children. The students had grown up in a wide variety of places. Many had lived in towns or cities, and they remembered back alleys, or places with rocks, broken bottles, and holes to fall into. Greenery was very important: "You could invent things. Bushes sort of formed a clump surrounding an open square, and this can begin to mean something to you, such as a house." Even though an assortment of places was mentioned, one thing stood out: they had preferred to play anywhere but on a playground. Instead, the students had favored messy places, full of disorder and surprise.[61] In a later study, perhaps the most exhaustive ever made on the outdoor play of children, Roger Hart found the same thing. As he said, "The freedom to make one's own play environment is important to children."[62] In a 1980s research project, Kimberly Dovey asked students of environmental design about places they remembered from their childhoods. One interesting finding was this: although they had spent most of their time indoors, the majority of their memories were of outdoor play. And once again, they remembered unplanned places. Trees were favorites. "The willow tree in our backyard was our favorite thing.... It was the center of my childhood fantasies. The branches served as whips for horses, swords for duels, hair for mermaids."[63]

Besides autobiographical memory, another and perhaps more reliable way of answering the question of where children like to play when outdoors is to watch them. For example, Mary Ann Kirkby watched children in a half-acre playground. It had things to play on, such as a pile of tires, an H-bar, and a balance beam. In addition, there were two small unplanned sections of the playground which Kirkby called "refuge areas." These had vines and bushes, with patches of bare ground. The unplanned spaces took up less than a fourth of the playground, but children seemed to prefer them, for they played there half of the time. When in the refuges, they talked, made branches into horses, jumped in the bushes, and made plant parts into magic wands, food, and other toys.[64]

What about creating an unplanned nature park, full of plants and perhaps animals, where children could fashion their own toys? These are more common in Europe, but they do occur in the United States. The Environmental Yard of Berkeley, California, is an example. It contains a variety of plants that could be used in play. And it has been a success, for children seem to love it. "Whatever's there, you can make something out of it," said one child. "That's what's neat. If I see a branch that broke off a tree and has a few leaves on it, I use it for a broom," said a girl. Other girls made an old stump into a doll's house, adding man-made junk such as aluminum foil and Popsicle sticks as well as leaves and flowers to furnish the house. Boys were more likely to play combat games, or recreate TV shows. "We use sticks for phasers and pieces of rock for communicators," explained one.[65]

The Environmental Yard at Berkeley has been highly successful. And so, this question inevitably arises: Why not broaden the Berkeley concept, making it a way of life for all children? In that way, they could regain the physical tone that so many have lost, and also come to understand nature in a way that most of today's children do not.

In an eloquent, sometimes impassioned book titled *Noah's Children: Restoring the Ecology of Childhood*, Sara Stein argues that this must be done. To Stein, oneness with nature is more than just a matter of making nature familiar to children. Instead, it is a biologically built-in necessity that we deny children when we build the sterile environments that surround our towns and cities.[66] If so, what could we do about this loss? Stein's solution would be to "wild the land," surrounding our living spaces with wild brush, weeds, and a variety of small animals, all of which would recreate that nature that children once enjoyed.[67]

Could we do this, in effect bringing natural environments into our towns and cities? Perhaps, but how many children would actually use these natural areas? Unfortunately, the Lukeshok-Lynch, Hart, and Kirby studies cited earlier may have become somewhat dated, for there is some evidence that fewer and fewer of today's children are really that interested in nature, particularly if they have grown up in the city. The sights, sounds, even the smells of nature seem to mean less to children of today than those of the past. Mary Rivkin cites a study that asked this question: "What smells cause you to become nostalgic?" People who were born seventy years ago cited lilies, honeysuckle, hay, and fresh air. But those born in 1960 cited crayons, airplane fuel, nail polish, and tacos.[68] And a recent study asked urban teens to rate a number of things along a continuum from "not disgusting" to "extremely disgusting." Stepping on mud by a pond and sitting on a log in the woods were both seen as disgusting.[69]

There is another problem with Stein's solution. The children of an earlier America felt at home with nature, but that did not mean they always respected it. In fact, they could be cruel to nature in their play. Peter Coffin once skinned an eel alive, and during a locust plague, Maggie Deland hung twelve hapless locusts by their necks, side by side. And boys would roam across the countryside, randomly shooting small animals, from frogs to birds.[70]

When they played outdoors, the children of country America would break branches and pull up flowers to make their toys. But the damage they did would soon heal, for they played over many acres, giving nature a chance to mend its wounds. But it would be different if children played in small wild areas that surrounded our houses. How soon would these areas become barren, stripped of their plants and animals?

Introducing natural areas into suburbia and cities could help children understand the nature they have lost. But there is still another place where this might be done — at home. In recent years, a whole family of "ecological toys" has appeared on the toy market. Some of these toys help children understand the dynamics of nature by having them to do things such as measuring acid rain or pollution. Others, like the Ant Ranch or Butterfly Garden, help children understand how animals live in nature. Most of these toys tend to be heavy on fun, and light on sophisticated ecological themes. But they are in their infancy, and it just might be that someday they will become an important part of ecological education, a way of bringing country America to the children of today, but doing it in a way that earlier American children could never have imagined.

10

The Commercialization of Toys

MERGER MANIA

Although you don't hear much about them, there are still many small toy companies in America. A recent estimate says about a thousand of them.¹ Often, they make niche toys, things like wooden tops and whistles that the big companies don't want to take a chance on. Don Olney owned one of these small toy companies. His company, which he called the Toycrafter, employed about a dozen people, including Olney's father and mother. The company lacked the large and cumbersome bureaucracy typical of large companies. It was small enough so that everyone knew everyone else. No endless staff meetings, no specialists in production, marketing, and advertising. Olney's tiny toy company was almost a relic of the past, for most of today's toys are made by companies that are far, far larger. Mattel and Hasbro, the two largest toy companies in America, operate in a world that is light years away from that of Olney's Toycrafter. By the late 1980s, Hasbro had nearly $3 billion in annual sales, and had eleven thousand employees.² Mattel, the other giant, had annual sales of over $3 billion. Its best seller, Barbie, has brought the company over a billion dollars a year in revenues.

A company with sales of over $3 billion a year may seem large enough to most of us, but Mattel has worked hard at becoming even larger. One way to do this is to increase sales by inventing another winner like Barbie. But another strategy, which has been pursued relentlessly by Mattel, is to grow by swallowing up smaller companies. In 1992, Mattel bought Wham-O, a smallish company which had a reputation for inventing winners such as the Super Ball, the Frisbee, and the Hula Hoop. In 1993, Mattel bought Fisher-Price, an old-line American company. In 1994, Mattel went abroad and gobbled up J.W. Spear, an English company that makes the game Scrabble. In 1995, Mattel added the Cabbage Patch Kids to its assemblage, and in 1996 it took over Tyco, which made Matchbox cars. Why did Mattel take over these companies? One reason for doing all this was to reduce its dependence on Barbie. But implicit in these mergers was the assumption that size means success and security.

These acquisitions gave Mattel worldwide sales of almost $4 billion a year. But Mattel's merger mania had not ended. In 1996, Mattel offered to buy Hasbro, its biggest rival. If successful, this merger would have put Barbie, G.I. Joe, Mr. Potato Head, and the Cabbage Patch Kids all under one roof. But the merger did not happen, for Hasbro fought back, and Mattel gave up its takeover attempt. Mattel's merger mania made other members of the toy making community unhappy. "No one is comfortable when members of the family fight," said David Miller, who was president of the Toy Manufacturers of America, the industry's trade group.[3]

Oddly, some other people were also unhappy about all of this. Some small toy companies wished that the merger had succeeded. Why was this? "That's because the merged company would have dropped some toy lines," said Frank Reysen Jr., editor of *Playthings*, the industry trade publication. This would have given the small companies a chance to make the toys that were dropped; to pick up the pieces so the speak.[4] Small toy makers were not the only ones who were sorry that the merger failed. Some Hasbro stockholders sued their own company, saying that Hasbro's refusal to accept the merger denied them stock profits that they would have realized from such a deal.[5]

Does larger size really mean increasing success, and thus increasing profits? Is corporate gigantism a good thing? Some would say so—that it makes production more efficient, and even helps America's competitiveness in a global economy. But others disagree, arguing that all mergers do is to shift ownership, while the weaknesses within the merged companies remain. According to Peter Drucker, a well-known management consultant, out of every five mergers two are disasters, two merely hold the line, and only one improves company performance.[6]

If not mergers, what else is it that makes a toy company a success? In other words, what makes a toy sell? Don Olney, with his small toy company, has no idea what a "successful" toy really is. And so, he makes toys that he likes, hoping they will sell. But it's different with the giant toy companies, for they are owned by big institutional investors, who manage the money of many people. And as Al Verrecchia, a Hasbro executive, put it, "Those institutions are brutal ... they want profitability."[7] But just how does a toy company meet the pressures imposed by big investors? It's a hard question to answer, for toy making is a very iffy business. As Frank Reyson Jr. said, "The ever-changing nature of toy sales is a source of endless fascination and frustration to even the most seasoned industry analysts."⁸ How does a toy company go about becoming a money maker, thus satisfying its owners?

"The Tragedy of Child Labor is of Global Proportions"

Besides mergers, a toy company can maximize its profits by making toys more cheaply than does its competitors. One way to do this is to make toys abroad, where labor is cheaper.

But this can lead to ethical problems. Tom Harkin, United States senator from Iowa, opened a 1994 newspaper article this way: "On Christmas morning, millions of American children will play with the latest toys and the hottest sports equipment and dress up in new clothes to celebrate the season's festivities. But for many of the World's children, the true spirit of Christmas will have long been buried in the drive for increasing corporate profits and the search for cheap labor."⁹

Harkin went on to say that we must look at trade issues from a moral, not just a money-making, perspective. After all, he said, we prohibit imports made of endangered species. Why can't we also prohibit imports made by child slaves? Harkin is not alone, for others are equally concerned about child labor. Religious and student groups have complained about the brutalizing of Third World children by American companies. And so have labor groups. But, of course, the latter have a second reason for concern — Third World labor undercuts American jobs. These groups are not alone, for a 1996 survey indicates that more than six in ten Americans are also concerned about companies that use Third World child labor.¹⁰

What do Third World children make for us? How many of them make toys? To read the media, one would think that they spend most of their time making toys. For example, Harkin's article is titled "No Cheer from Toys Made with Child Labor." Other articles about child labor have similar headers: "Toys Made with Child Labor are Targeted in New Campaign," and "Did Child Labor Make That Toy?" are examples.¹¹ But these headers reflect a media bias. After all, there is something particularly gross about children who slave away, making toys for American children to play with. Toys are indeed a part of the child labor problem, but a close look at articles on the subject indicates that most of these children are actually making things such as clothes, rugs, and athletic gear, rather than toys.

What about toys? A half century ago, most were made here, but that has changed dramatically. Today, over two-thirds of our toys are made abroad. Who makes these toys? Not all of these workers are children. Many of our imported toys are made in Europe by skilled labor. Examples are the Brio toys of Sweden, and the Ambi toys of Holland. These toys are aimed at affluent, educated parents, who are willing to spend a bit more for a "quality" toy. As one somewhat cynical market analyst put it, these are "parents whose kids are taking ballet lessons at age four. They all want their kids to go to Harvard."[12]

What about everyday toys such as Barbie? Do children make Barbie, and do they work under bad conditions? The answer is mixed. Mattel makes most of its Barbies in China, Indonesia, and Malaysia. A visit to a Chinese factory near Hong Kong results in some surprises. It's a well-managed factory, better than most in the area. The workers live in adjacent dorms, which are quite comfortable. And the workers are not children, but young women. Their wages are horrendous by our standards—less than $2 a day. But in China, this is a good wage, and women come from all over China to work at Mattel's factory. The secret of Mattel's success is simple: it owns, and therefore can supervise, its China factory.[13] Disney also makes its toys abroad. But this company, which has such a peachy-clean image, does not own or supervise its toy factories. Instead, it subcontracts to locals. The company has about four thousand contracts with factories in countries such as Sri Lanka and Indonesia, where low-cost labor is available. What are labor conditions in these factories? The evidence is at best indirect, because factory owners are understandably reluctant to have Americans inspecting their operations. But some investigators have been able to look at locally managed Third World toy factories. Ironically, one recent investigation centered on a Mattel factory in Thailand. There, ownership was local, and conditions seemed to be very different from those in Mattel's China factory. Anton Foek, the investigator, saw hundreds of women and children stuffing, cutting dressing, and assembling Barbie dolls. "Many of the workers have respiratory infections, their lungs filled with dust from fabrics, said Foek. "And not only dust," he said. "Others work with lead and other chemicals and suffer from chronic lead poisoning."[14]

All the evidence says that American companies do use Third World children to make toys, and these children sometimes work under conditions that we would never tolerate in our own country. And the problem will not go away easily, for it is complicated by the economic realities of our time. In an increasingly global economy, we are sure to become more, not less, dependent on foreign labor.

If there is any bright spot in the child labor problem, it comes from a look at the past, for the use of children to make toys is not new. Writing in a 1913 issue of *Survey Magazine*, Florence Kelly talked of the "sweating system" in which thousands of German children of kindergarten age worked along with their families to produce toys for Americans. "Sleep, play and school attendance all suffer ... when orders pour in," she said.[15]

Another visitor found this in an 1880 visit to German children who were making marbles for American use: "I shall never again watch a lot of happy, intelligent, bright, well-fed, and well-clothed American boys playing at marbles but I shall think of the poorly clad German children munching away on a piece of bread (for that is all they get to eat), as they work on their weary tasks for a few cents a week."[16] Although foreign "slave labor" still exists in the making of American toys, at least the glass may be half full, not half empty.

"Everybody Played, Including President Harrison"

Third World children can help a toy maker become more profitable. But the surest way to be successful is for a toy maker to create a fad toy. It's every toymaker's dream — to invent a toy that becomes a national fad, the kind of toy that people fight for, a toy that sells by the millions, and makes him rich. What was the first American toy fad? It may have been Pigs in Clover, which was invented in 1889 by Charles Crandall. It was one of those toys that look so easy to use but which turn out to be a real challenge. All you had to do was to move the four marbles or pigs from the outer clover ring, and roll them into the pen. Everybody played, including the prime minister of England (Fig. 10.1). Merchants had fun with the game as they worked to

Fig. 10.1. This cartoon shows William Gladstone, who was prime minister of England in the 1880s, when Pigs in Clover was at its height of popularity. It was in *Punch*, a popular English magazine of the time. The cartoon's caption said, "I think I shall get all of 'em in," which expressed the PM's desire to capture his opponent's votes.

publicize Pigs in Clover. In Cleveland, one merchant put a huge version of the toy in his store window, and hired a boy to drive real pigs into a pen.[17]

How Toys Become Fads

No one really knows what makes a toy become a fad, although some things can be said about the conditions under which toy fads appear. Gene Del Vecchio, president of Cool Works, a consulting company that helps toy makers design toys, said that fad toys such as Pokemon "touched timeless emotional needs" within children. For example, part of Pokemon's appeal stemmed from its story line of good vanquishing evil, a story in which children participate by capturing monsters, which they train to fight for the child. Change is also important, and so the fall of the year 2000 witnessed a brand-new Pokemon series with new adventures. But child psychologist Christine Wekerle saw Pokemon differently. It's all in the numbers, she said. Kids loved to memorize the names, spellings, and characteristics of the 151 Pokemons. "This is where kids are at," said Wekerle, "They like ordering, computing and categorizing."[18]

Sometimes, it's as simple as a matter of climate. The Crazy Daisy, a flexible flower that can be attached to a garden hose, was a big winter fad in California, but did not become a fad in the colder Midwest until springtime.

Sometimes, the "Hula Hoop factor" plays a part in creating a fad. In its first year as a fad, 25 million Hula Hoops were sold. Sales then dropped off, but kept bouncing back every few years. As a new crop of parents comes along, they remember all of the fun they had with a Hula Hoop and buy one for their children, thus restarting the fad.

And sometimes, it's a result of some kind of improvement in a toy that already exists. The Wave Hoop, a new and improved version of the Hula, seemed destined to become a fad. Wave Hoops contain a non-toxic liquid that creates a centrifugal force when the hoop is spun. The result was that the Wave Hoop would twirl five times longer than the Hula. By the summer of 2000, two million had already been sold.[19]

The same thing has happened with scooters. Years ago, these toys were heavy and clumsy. But today's scooters are very different. Designed for use in Europe, where clogged streets made them a practical form of transportation, today's scooters have foldable lightweight aluminum frames and durable urethane wheels.[20]

How does a fad spread? Two economists, one at the University of

Michigan, the other at the University of California, have given us some insights about this. According to their theory, a fad will spread when a few people like some new object, such as a toy. They tell others about it, and as more and more people hear about the new toy, a kind of follow-the-leader psychology develops. These later buyers get the toy simply because they have heard from friends or the media that many others have done so, and not because they really want it[21]

The Razor scooter was an example of this. Walker Baron was an eleven-year-old at Palisades Elementary School in Los Angeles. In 1999, Walker bought a Razor scooter. When he rode it to school, students gathered to watch this new toy in action. "The scooters started to reproduce," said Palisades principal Terry Arnold. Word of its wonders spread from student to student and classroom to classroom. Finally, Arnold had to ban them from school, holding firm in the face of student protests, which included a petition from fifth graders.

Some parents had reservations about the toy, but others loved it. "They're so much fun," said Diana Baron, Walker's mother. "They're greased lightning." And many parents saw the fad as a way of applying some sorely needed leverage with their children: It was all right to have a scooter if they promised to mow and take out the garbage.[22]

Once they have a fad, toy makers try to keep it alive. One way is to create shortages of a toy, hoping that this might lead to a "run-on-the-bank" psychology, as parents rush to buy the toy before it disappears. After Tickle-Me-Elmo became a fad in late 1996, shortages of the doll soon developed. This sent shoppers rushing to the stores to get an Elmo before they disappeared, which made him just that much more of a fad toy.

Sometimes, toy makers try to extend the life of a fad toy by producing clones of it. When Tickle-Me-Elmo began to fade, Tyco Toys came out with a Sing-And-Snore Elmo. Remembering how they were caught short when they went to a store and found Tickle-Me-Elmo was sold out, mothers rushed to buy Sing-And-Snore Elmo before it was also gone.

The Beanie Babies have been one of the most successful toys ever invented. Ty, the company that makes Beanie Babies, hit upon an ingenious way to keep the Beanie Baby fad going. There were around 125 different kinds of Beanie Babies on the market, and they were all fated to die. Every six months or so, Ty introduced a new Beanie Baby, and as the company put it, an older one was "retired." Because they became increasingly rare, retired Beanie Babies were much sought after by adult collectors.[23]

In spite of all the efforts of toy makers, most toy fads don't last very long. Tickle-Me-Elmo was born in 1996. Early in that year, more than a million of these toys were sold. But by Christmas 1996, Elmo was fading fast. The Tamagotchi Virtual Pets came to America from Japan in 1997. The demand for these toys was so huge that three hundred million were produced in each month of that year. By 2000, they were still selling, but demand was way down. Furbys were born in 1998. By Christmas of that year, black marketers were selling $20 Furbys for $200.

Why are fads so mercurial? One reason, as suggested by A.O. Scott, who is a film critic for the *New York Times*, is this: we live in a culture which idealizes youth, he says. And to be young, says Scott, is to be in a hurry—"chasing fads, trashing last month's enthusiasm, changing tastes as fast as you change your clothes."[24]

How to keep up with the ever-changing tastes of kids? Perhaps the best a toy maker can do is to go directly to children, show them a new toy, and see what they have to say.

Asking the Children

One way to obtain information about toys that might be winners is to watch children at play with these toys. Many things can be learned this way. For example, when first developed, Fisher-Price's Sportcar was tested in a parking lot, with unexpected results. Fisher-Price had assumed that it was important to have a Sportcar with variable speeds, but this turned out to be wrong. "They all had them set on high," said Bernie Schauf, the project engineer. "Kids don't want to go slow."[25]

Still another way to explore a child's mind is to use a focus group. Children are placed on the floor in a circle, and loosened up with games. Then an adult leader begins to ask them questions about toys. It takes a skilled leader to do this successfully, for children, particularly young ones, live in a world that is largely foreign to adults. They have short attention spans and little patience with difficult things. This can influence the way in which a child will respond to questions posed by a focus group leader. For example, children may give any old answer to a question, hoping that the focus group will then move on to a more interesting topic.

Additionally, very young children have a limited vocabulary. Most three-year-olds have command of no more than a thousand words. Thus, when a leader describes an ad that reads "some assembly required," a child may not know what he or she is talking about. Finally, there is the interfering parent. One researcher recalled how a ten-year-old boy's parent came into the room, sat behind the child, and proceeded to answer all of the researcher's questions that were directed at her child.

Many young children feel uncomfortable about talking in a focus group, so there are other ways of getting at their feelings about toys. Sometimes, researchers will ask children to draw a picture. They might ask the children to "draw the toys you would like to buy when you go shopping." Sometimes, children will draw a rainbow around a particular toy, which is a sure sign that they would like to have it.

Watching children at play with a new toy or asking them about it in a focus group can give toy researchers much information. But toddlers are just too young to give toy researchers much helpful information when placed in groups of this sort. To help get around this problem, toy researchers go to malls, and watch little toddlers as they wander along with their parents. Does the toddler point at a particular toy, or try to grab it? How does the parent react to the toy and the toddler's wants?

Is market research on children, whether in a focus group or in a mall, an invasion of privacy? In his book *Kids as Customers*, James McNeal said "Kids are the most unsophisticated of consumers.... Consequently, they are in a perfect position to be taken."[26] With this in mind, it does seem wise to keep an eye on what market research on children is doing today, and on what it might do in the future. Already, some market researchers have used the Internet to offer prizes if children are willing to fill out survey forms which tell the researchers about the child's purchasing habits. As one offering put it, children would do this "as good citizens of the Web." The Center for Media Education sees this as unwarranted intrusion into a child's privacy. It's a problem that will become much worse if not stopped now, says Jeffery Chester, director of the center.[27]

THE CHANGING TOY ADVERTISEMENT

Toy makers can try to sell their toys by gaining some idea of a child's wants through focus groups and mall watching. Yet another tried and true strategy is to sell the child or parent on the merits of a toy through advertising. At first, most advertisements for toys were in written form, but by the mid-1800s, the familiar pictorial toy advertisement was appearing in newspapers and magazines. Some magazines, such as the *Ladies' Home Journal*, were aimed at middle class housewives. Others, such as the *Youth's Companion*, or *St. Nicholas*, were for children. Ads for toys sometimes appeared in unlikely places. The *American Agriculturalist* may seem a strange magazine to have toy advertisements. But it really made good sense, for the *American Agriculturalist* was a family magazine, with stories of interest for everyone who lived in rural America. There was also another

Chapter 10—Commercialization

RABBIT TRANSIT.

This has a most lifelike movement very like that of the animal itself. It has three wheels, which prevent its being easily knocked over, and it can be used by any child old enough to walk. It is neatly gotten up, and is appropriate for an *out-door* as well as an in-door toy.

Price, 50 Cents.
Expressage to be paid by the Recipient.

Fig. 10.2. The Rabbit Transit advertisement of 1880.

reason for toy advertisements in this magazine. The *American Agriculturalist* was owned by Charles Crandall, one of the most successful of early American toy makers.

The Rabbit Transit toy was an early example of a Crandall advertisement. It appeared in an 1880 issue of the *American Agriculturalist* (Fig. 10.2). The Lively Horseman (Fig. 10.3), was another example. It said that "The horse and rider are of wood, finely painted. Can be taken apart and packed in the box on which it performs." Early toy advertisements, such as that for Crandall's Rabbit Transit, would simply describe a toy. But by the early 1950s, toy makers had begun to do more than this, for the emerging disciplines of sociology and psychology were giving toy makers valuable insights about ways in which they could appeal to the inner wishes of their customers. The idea of fun morality was one of these insights. In 1900, the primary mission of a parent was to train a child, and that often meant refusing something, such as a toy, that the child wanted. By mid-century, however, fun morality had taken over. Now, something was wrong if a child was not having fun, and giving children fun things to make them happy had become a major mission of parenthood.[28] The idea of fun morality became a part of social science lore and soon toy advertisements reflected this new notion of parenting. A good toy was one that made children happy; therefore, toy makers began to design ads which were very different from the Rabbit Transit advertisement of Charles Crandall.

A hundred years ago, toy advertisements such as that of Figures 2 and 3 had no children in them. But by the 1920s, that had begun to change. Instead of simply describing a toy, advertisements now showed children who are telling their young readers (or parents, for that matter), how much fun a toy was. The toys of figures 10.4 and 10.5 are examples.

Fun morality is still with us. Try this simple experiment: Look at a page in the toy advertisements of a Sunday newspaper. Somehow, those few toys without children look lost!

Advertisements in newspapers and magazines help to sell toys. However today, television has become the most effective salesperson of all. In TV ads, a toy seems to come alive, showing the viewer all the wonderful things it can do.

Besides showing a toy in newspapers and magazines and on television, toy makers have found yet another way to keep a toy's image in the public's eye. This is the arrangement called licensing. When a toy is licensed, its maker sells the toy's image to other companies, who now have the right to use it to help sell their own product.

Sometimes, a toy is only one player in a family of goodies. For example, Pokemon showed up on collector cards, T-shirts, watches, bed sheets, athletic shoes, school binders, skateboards, a Monopoly game, Japan Air Lines Planes, and in comic books, movies, and TV shows, to name a few places.[29]

Besides licensing, another way to increase a toy's visibility is to make it into a giveaway. Burger King, for example, offered Poke-

Fig. 10.3. The Lively Horseman advertisement of 1879.

Top left: Fig. 10.4. An early fun morality advertisement. It was in a Sears, Roebuck catalog of the 1920s. *Top right:* Fig. 10.5. Another Sears advertisement of the same era.

mon toys as a part of its Kids Meals. Until this caused a tragedy (see Chapter 6, Hazardous Toys), this promotion was highly successful for both Pokemon and Burger King. In New Jersey, for example, Yvette Jain was taking her two sons, Aris, 5, and Alex, 3, once or twice a week to Burger King. And she was thinking of using the two dozen Pokemon balls her kids had collected as Christmas decorations.

But some of those who work in the food industry are not very happy about using toys to hype food. This trains customers to think more about the quality of the toy than of the food, said one marketing professor.[30]

Santa's Toys

Many Americans don't really like Christmas. Those who are not Christians may dislike the religious nature of the holiday. Yet others are equally offended because they don't think that Christmas is Christian enough. To some of us, there is simply too much stress at Christmas time. Gary Cross, who has written a history of toys called *Kid's Stuff*, put it this way: "This is the time of year I dread. Soon I will hardly be able to walk in our walk-in closet — so full will it be of toys and other gifts to be wrapped for the holidays. In the next month, most of us will be contributing to the $17.5 billion in sales expected by the toy industry this year."[31]

James Henry, an economist and journalist, has a much darker view of Christmas. It uses up vast resources, increases congestion, and destroys the environment, he says. And if that were not enough, we sit around at our parties eating and drinking too much, while ignoring the poor who so badly need help.[32]

But lots of people are very much in favor of Christmas. Kids love it, and so do the toy makers and merchants who depend on the holiday for much of their yearly sales. Far from trying to change the holiday, toy makers and toy retailers work away at expanding its scope. One way to do this is to have the right toys on hand at Christmas. As one toy watcher put it, "Having the hot toy of the season can make or break a manufacturer." Scooters, PlayStations and Harry Potter were some picks for Christmas 2000.[33] Were they good guesses?

Still another strategy is to look for new markets. Baby boomers might be one of these. "Remember that boomers are very self-oriented," says one toy watcher. "What that means at the checkout counter is both gift giving and self giving."[34]

Toy merchants have begun to look at another potential market. Those with deep religious convictions sometimes feel left out of our commercial Christmas. But Family Christian Stores do have Christmas toys, such as Jesus dolls, Nativity sets, and Scripture bears.[35]

CELEBRATING CHRISTMAS

Studies have shown that most Americans follow similar rituals at Christmas time. Santa is supposed to bring children their gifts, but it's mom who actually does most of the shopping. Toys and other gifts are almost always wrapped (which is a fairly recent habit), and then hidden away. Often, children try to outsmart mom and dad by finding where gifts are hidden. At least the older ones do. In contrast, most younger American children believe that there really is a Santa who will come down the chimney on Christmas Eve with a bag full of toys. Decorating the tree (which is more and more likely to be artificial today) is most commonly done on Christmas Eve. The Christmas stocking is a long-standing tradition. Some families hang their stockings in front of the fireplace. Others hang them on beds so that children can open them before the main event,

Chapter 10—Commercialization   161

a way to let mom and dad sleep a bit longer. Some families open their presents on Christmas Eve, but for most it's Christmas morning. Each family has its own opening ritual. Some families put all of the gifts together in a pile under the tree, but other families give each family member his or her own spot, such as a chair or sofa. There are all kinds of little variants to these rituals. In some families, each person makes a short thank-you speech when opening his or her first present.

Santa is in the middle of all this, but how many children really believe that there is a Santa? On the face of it, one might think he doesn't have a chance. After all, Santas are everywhere, which should not make any sense to kids. Besides the ads, the stores, and the malls, Santa shows up in school and at private parties. How does all this affect a child's belief in Santa Claus? What if a small child who is sitting on Santa's lap says, "I saw you in another mall"? This does bother some children. "My mom would always make me behave by telling me Santa Claus wouldn't come if I wasn't good. I was always doubtful about Santa Claus, though, because I just couldn't imagine how he could get around the whole world in just one night. My friend suggested he went in a fast helicopter, but that just sounded dumb."[36] And then there is the package problem. One mother had problems when her daughter asked why her presents from Santa had the same wrapping as those from her mom and dad. What about the returns? How do they get back to Santa? she asked.

Christmas can be tough on kids, but it can be even tougher on parents, who have all those presents to buy, which can be expensive. One study found that two-thirds of 1990s parents spend $100 or more each year on Christmas toys.[37]

Today's Santa has two faces. He has long been seen as a fat, genial person, with values we all want our children to have. These are best expressed in the famous article Francis Church wrote in response to a little girl who asked if there really was a Santa: "Yes, Virginia, there is a Santa Claus. He exists as certainly as love and generosity and devotion exist.... Alas! How dreary would be the world if there were no Santa Claus."[38]

But Santa has another face. Very early on, merchants saw how Santa could be a good salesman. After all, everyone knew he was a giver of gifts. Why not have him help sell all those Christmas toys? And so, more and more Santas began to appear in Christmas advertisements. At first, Santa was a somewhat reluctant salesman, but as time passed, he became happier with his new job. Two magazines, the *Ladies' Home Journal* and *The Saturday Evening Post*, were examples of this. In 1906, only one in ten of their Christmas ads featured Santa. But by 1920, one in four did. One trade journal writer of that year went so far as to say that a Christmas gift "has to be approved by Santa Claus before it is acceptable."[39]

At Christmas time, Santa is everywhere. He shows up in advertisements, out on the streets, and in the malls. What about truth in advertising? Are mall Santas, who often suggest toys that their little customers might buy, engaged in deceptive advertising? Common knowledge has it that mall Santas are physical fakes. It is true that temporary Santas do go to Santa training schools where they learn how to be kid-friendly, to use a deodorant, and to avoid saying "Ho-ho-ho," because it will frighten a small child. And some schools even show their students how to look like a Santa. But mostly, mall Santas are real, at least in a physical sense. A recent study has found that 95 percent of mall Santas have real beards and a round tummy. And they are no dummies. About two-thirds have gone to college.[40] What will Santa look like tomorrow? (Fig. 10.6)

What do small children think about mall Santas? Greta Pennell, who was working on her Ph.D. in developmental psychology, disguised herself as an elf and listened to 1,722 conversations that little children had with mall Santas. Most seemed naive about Santa, for they thought he was real. But when it came to ordering toys, they were much more sophisticated. One child blurted out that he had already mailed a letter, so what should he do? The mall Santa said he would check in his computer, and there would not be any problem. Another child who wanted a teddy bear told Santa, "It's on layaway at Kmart. You can get it there." And far from being a deceptive meanie, Santa often did good things beyond his toy work. One mother marched up with her two children and told Santa that her children were not sharing their toys. "What do you think?" she asked him. Santa gave the children a stern look and said, "Christmas is all about sharing." Awestruck, both kids nodded in agreement.[41]

Another child, Karen Cohen, aged seven, probably spoke for many when she said, "It's hard to know what you want because there's like tons of toys out there."[42] Yet at the same time, other children know what they do want—whatever is currently cool. Not surprisingly, most of these are TV toys. And today's children are not content to ask by toy type. Instead of "doll" or "train," they ask by brand name. In one study of 344 letters to Santa, over half of all requests were for brand names such as Barbie, Batman, or Lego.[43]

Is Christmas Too Commercial?

Has our children's Christmas become too commercial, too greedy? Many people think children are inundated with toys and are targeted by

Chapter 10—Commercialization

Fig. 10.6. This is what a *Punch* magazine cartoonist of 1905 thought Santa would soon look like.

all kinds of sophisticated marketing techniques. As one critic says, "The modern Christmas ritual is more than a celebration of the family.... It is also a celebration of consumption, materialism, and hedonism."[44]

Many parents agree. But why, then, do they overindulge at Christmas? And parents do just that, for one study has found that preschoolers asked for an average of about three toys during the holidays, but actually received over eleven.⁴⁵ Some parents may over-give because they remember a childhood of poverty with few presents, and somehow wish to make up for their own lean past. But the makeup of today's American family has more to do with this over-giving. Well over half of today's mothers work, and many of today's children grow up with single or remarried parents. In both cases, parents will often give their children more gifts than other parents do, which has been called a kind of guilt giving.⁴⁶

But all is not lost, for our Santa is two-faced. He has his commercial and materialistic face, but his kinder, gentler face remains. As one counseling professor has put it, "When you ask adults what they remember about the holidays when they were children, they'll usually tell you about the special time their family spent together. Only rarely will they tell you about the gifts. And he adds, "What your children really love is your presence, not your presents."⁴⁷ And many children seem to agree. When asked what Christmas meant to her, Libby, aged nine, said, "I like the presents the best, but I don't think Christmas is about getting presents. It's about giving and sharing stuff with our family." And Dan, aged eight, said: "What is the true meaning of Christmas? I would tell people that it's a loving celebration — plus, school's out."⁴⁸

HAS CHRISTMAS BECOME YEAR-ROUND?

Children love Christmas and all its toys. But parents are not so sure about Christmas, for they see it as a symptom of a much larger problem. Somehow, they feel, it has turned into a year-long battle against a toy industry that has taken toy choice out of their hands. What is this industry like? In his 1998 book, *Toy Wars*, G. Wayne Miller gives us an insider's view of two toy industry giants.⁴⁹ Miller describes the battle between the two largest American toy companies, Hasbro and Mattel, as they struggle to dominate the toy market. A "well-developed, suspenseful narrative that will appeal to marketing enthusiasts," says one reviewer of the book.⁵⁰ "A case study in market domination by mega-conglomerates, which in this case are given virtually free reign over [the] young, reporting only to shareholders," says another reviewer.⁵¹

Another book, Stephen Kline's 1993 *Out of the Garden: Toys, TV and Children's Culture in the Age of Marketing,* shows us how television has become the primary way of advertising today's toys. In the process of doing this, says Kline, television has shaped a children's culture that craves poor-taste toys.⁵²

Gary Cross' book, *Kid's Stuff*, makes essentially the same argument.⁵³

His book can be heavy reading. "Make no mistake, the man has read every trade journal, toy press release, Erector Set ad and obscure article from or on American toy history," said one reviewer. And he adds, "I doubt anybody has ever put together so much fascinating, sometimes horrifying information about American toys."[54] What does Cross tell us? He shows how our toys have evolved from a time when they were under parental control to a time when a consumer culture, powered by mass advertising, especially that on television, is shaping a children's culture that has broken free of parental control. Today's toy companies pander to this culture. One way they do this is to create poor-taste toys that appeal to today's TV-addicted, fad-driven children who watch poor-taste TV shows.

What to do about all of this? Phil Phillips has one answer. He sees the problem as a moral, even a religious one. In his 1986 book, *Turmoil in the Toybox*, Phillips argues that the "vast majority of toys on the market deal with violence and the occult." His answer to this problem would be a return to Christian homes where such toys would be prohibited.[55]

The Challenge of Change

It's easy to castigate today's toy companies. But it's not easy to be a toy maker. For one thing, the toy maker's world is one of constant and often unpredictable change. Today, admission to top-level colleges has become very, very difficult. Therefore, more and more parents want to put their toddlers on a fast track that might gain them entry to Harvard. "I told my husband, 'Enough with dinosaurs,' I want educational toys," said one mother. And so, educational toys, which have long had moderate sales, are suddenly popular items in the toy market.[56]

Toys that have been gone for years can suddenly be reborn. Sarah Zelenka is only twenty, but she is already full of nostalgia for her childhood. "I don't think I'll ever get old," she said.[57] One way for Sarah to recapture her childhood was to return to the toys she had as a child. And so, Sarah has almost 400 of the toy called "My Little Pony."[58] Back in the 1980s, it was a top toy, made famous by a TV show and movie of that time. Zelenka is not the only young person who is recapturing their childhood through forgotten toys, for it has become something of a fad.

Finally, as we saw in the chapter on Fashion Dolls and Action Figures, major cultural events such as wars can affect toys and their sales. G.I. Joe languished during times of anti-war sentiment, but was reborn when war once again became respectable.

11

The John Burroughs Toy

In early America, children spent most of their free time in the outdoors. And most of their toys were crafted of nature's things: of leaves, sticks, flowers, stones, mud, and even insects.

Some people lament the loss of this earlier lifestyle. And as we saw in an earlier chapter, educators have tried various ways of luring children back into this lost world, but with little success.

What about those handmade toys of early America? Were they really better than today's machine-made toy? Many educators have thought so. Writing almost a hundred years ago, the great naturalist John Burroughs said this: "I doubt if I had one boughten toy when I was a child.... I earned my playthings and they never surfeited me. They each meant something." Speaking of the new machine-made toys that were moving into his world, Burroughs had this to say: "They corrupt (children's) simplicity, stimulate their destructiveness and bloat their curiosity."[1]

Perhaps, but why not have the best of both worlds? What about a machine-made toy that had the advantages of a handmade one? This is hardly a new idea. Large alphabet blocks have been a part of childhood for hundreds of years. But blocks such as these do have their limitations. Children cannot build complex structures with them. That problem was partially solved in 1866 with the invention of Crandall's Interlocking Blocks (Fig. 11.1). A creative genius, Crandall even added a human element with his Interlocking Figures, for they could be put together in all sorts of interesting ways and added to his blocks (Fig. 11.2).

Over the years, many other building blocks have been invented. Lincoln Logs, TinkerToys, and the Erector Set are examples. But a new age of construction toys really began in 1907. In that year, six-year-old Ole Christiansen was working as a shepherd on the moors of Denmark. It was a lonely job, and Ole whiled his time away by whittling small objects, including toys. By the time Ole was a teenager, he had become an expert

Top left: Fig. 11.1. Crandall's Interlocking Blocks, 1866. *Top right:* Fig. 11.2. Crandall also invented these put-together figures. They could be fastened to each other or to his blocks.

woodworker. In 1916, Ole had become a professional wood worker with his own carpentry shop. In the summers, Ole built houses, and winter saw him building chests and wardrobes.

Ole was the father of two boys, so it was only natural for him to make toys, first for his boys, and later as a sideline in his shop. These proved so popular that Ole switched to full-time toy making. Ole and his seven helpers made toys in the tradition of the Danish toy makers of the past; toys that were partly machine-made and partly handmade. Ole took great pride in making toys that encouraged creative play, and so he took the Danish for "play well," which is "leg godt," and shortened it to Lego, which became his company's name.

At first, Christiansen's company made simple, high-quality toys such as boats. But for years, his company had also made building blocks, which he liked to call "bricks." In the beginning, these bricks were of wood, but something happened in 1949 which would change Lego products forever. As was so for many toy companies, Lego was changing from wood to plastic toys. When his company began to make plastic bricks, they seemed to offer opportunities that had not been possible with the wooden ones. In his book on the Lego company, Henry Wiencek recalled what happened. Ole's son Godtfred thought that the bricks would become an even better toy if they could somehow be locked together.² And so, the Lego brick was born.

The Lego Company has grown into a multimillion-dollar international giant, but Christiansen's goal of making creative toys has not changed. The secret of the company's creativity lies in these simple bricks, for just six of them can be fitted together in 102,981,500 ways.

Today, the Lego Company has diversified its offerings. A small child can use a small Lego kit to build one kind of toy. When he or she is older the child can choose a Bob The Builder, Explorer, or Creator kit and design a variety of different toys (Fig. 11.3).

And the Lego Company has taken yet a further step toward a new way of toy making. What about using computer power when designing a toy? The first step in this direction was taken by the Lego Company in the 1980s. Seymour Papart, a mathematician and learning theorist at the Massachusetts Institute of Technology, had devised Logo, a computer language for children. Kjeld Kristiansen, president of the Lego Company, learned of Papert's work, and it occurred to him that Logo might be somehow linked to Lego's bricks. Thus, Lego-Logo was born. A child begins his work with this toy by building a simple robot out of Lego bricks. Some of the bricks he uses are of the traditional kind, but others are new to the Lego family. These new bricks are mini-brains or units that can direct the robot to do things such as moving to the right or left, or turning a light on. After he has finished making a robot, a child uses the Logo language devised by Papert. He writes a program that tells the robot how to act. The robot is then connected to a computer so that it can receive commands.³

Fig. 11.3. For 25 years, the Lego system of play has encouraged creativity and stimulated imagination in America's children. Lego, the Lego logo and brick configuration are trademarks of the Lego Group, copyright 2003. The Lego trademarks and products are used with permission. The Lego Group does not sponsor or endorse this publication.

The Logo program for controlling robots was designed for use in schools, where it has been very successful. But what about a unit for home use? Working at M.I.T.'s media laboratory, Mitchel Resnick and others have developed more sophisticated versions of the unit. Their work has been supported by Hasbro, Mattel, Disney and the Lego Company, all of whom have a stake in the development of increasingly sophisticated interactive robots.[4] By 1998, Resnick and his co-workers had developed a new version of the "smart" brick called the Rex, which is a part of the Lego Mindstorms building kit. As its user guide says, Mindstorms lets kids "design and program real robots that move, act and think on their own." Just as so for the robots programmed by Logo, these robots are fashioned from a variety of bricks.[5]

Could Lego-Mindstorms be the first step toward achieving John Burroughs' dream of returning to handmade toys? Could there be a handmade toy that would look just like those machine-made toys that children buy in stores?

What would such a toy be like? Following the concept used by the Lego Company of designing a toy by using a computer, a future program might begin by asking children to imagine a toy that she or he would like to have. Once the child has decided, the computer would ask for details. If, for example, the child had chosen a doll, what kind of hair would it have? What would its features be like? And what kind of behavior would it have? These decisions would be up to the child, not the computer. Once the doll had become more clearly defined, the computer would provide the child with a list of parts needed to make a completed doll. These could be purchased at a "toy parts store." When the child came home with the needed parts, the computer would show the child how to assemble the doll.

Interestingly, a first step toward this new age homemade toy has already been taken. Dimitri Gurevich of Boston has a Web site called iDolls, which lets a girl design her doll's clothes, facial features, and accessories. According to Gurevich, his dolls can be configured in any of sixty-nine billion possible combinations. A girl's request is sent to China, where it is turned into a doll and shipped back to her within two weeks.[6]

The children of an earlier America made toys for fun. In doing so, they learned manual skills, such as sewing and carving. Skills such as these were important to have. When children became adults, these skills would be useful, for the everyday needs of an earlier America were met by hand work. In our society, machines and computers have replaced the hand labor of an earlier America. Thus, it seems only appropriate that today's handmade toy should be a product of the computer, for today it is skill with a computer, not hand skill, that children need to succeed in the world.

If they ever do come to be, these computer-driven toys would awe John Burroughs, for they would be more sophisticated and perhaps more imaginative than anything the children of country America could ever have made.

And best of all, these toys could be a way of using the power of machines, coupled with computers, to create toys that are under the control of children, rather than adults. After all, many of today's toy problems are not the work of children. Instead, they are the work of adults who are lax in their watchfulness over children's play, and who use toys as a way of furthering their own interests, whether it's the maintaining of sexism or the making of money.

III. Afterthoughts

12

The Special Problem of Media Bias

We have looked at toy problems in some depth. But we have not addressed a central question: why is it that for many years, media writers have been questioning the quality of our toys?

Of course, one answer might be that America's toys are in trouble. But there may be a different answer, which we shall now explore.

Homemade toys did have their problems. Suppose a toy was faulty or, even worse, had injured a child. What could be done about this? Obviously, since the toy had been made by a family member, there was no one else to blame for the mishap.

But once toys became machine made, this changed. Now, neither parents nor their children were responsible for the toy's quality. Some unknown toy maker had created and produced the toy for profit. And so, when a toy caused trouble, you pointed your finger at the maker. But suppose you lived in Illinois, and a toy had killed a child who lived in Texas? You might be about to buy the same toy, but would not know about the Texas tragedy. What might be done about this?

To help answer that question, toy watchers began to use our mass media, telling families across the nation about troublesome toys.

Soon, articles attacking toys as dangerous, mindless, even vulgar, began to appear in newspapers and magazines. As toys became more common, more a part of childhood, these articles increased.

Could it be that these worries about toys are part of a larger media tendency to color the news, to emphasize worry topics as a way of gaining readership? Could it be that those popular sayings, "coloring the news," "slanting the news," and "if it bleeds, it leads" are really true? Let's see what one media watcher has to say about the bleeds-leads syndrome. Writing in *USA Today*, Gerald Kreyche argues that the media does focus "undue attention on almost every worrisome aspect of life." He notes that an almost endless variety of scares, from infectious mouse droppings to flesh-eating bacteria to flying saucers, have been subjected to media hype.[1]

What about toys? Does this bleeds-leads syndrome exist in the world of toy watchers? The answer seems to be yes. The media's urge to highlight scare topics has led it to magnify toy problems that may be titillating, but are really of no national concern. Furby's tilt with the National Security Agency, which was described in the chapter on toys that come alive, was an example. It was more laughable than alarming, but no matter, it still became national media fare.

But Furby was not alone, for other dolls that come alive have done crazy things, and have also come under the media spotlight. As described in the chapter on toy hazards, the Cabbage Patch Doll called the Snacktime Kid was guilty of pulling a child's hair. That is, a few dozen of the thousands of Snacktime dolls sold did so. These children were not seriously hurt, and the guilty dolls became a collector's item. But to judge from media coverage of the event, one would have thought that half of the doll world was in trouble, for dozens of hair-pulling articles appeared in newspapers across the country. Why did this happen? Hair pulling was hardly a serious problem, but it was bizarre, and that was enough for the media to turn hair pulling into a major issue, which, of course, distorted the public's image of these dolls, and gained readership.

Bleeds-leads topics make fine "grabber" material for the media. And so do all the toy issues raised by activists, who love the way the media will publicize their concerns.

From the 1850s until the 1970s, the *New York Times* contained only a handful of articles about toy dangers. But then the number rose dramatically. In 1972, the *Times* published about fifty articles about toys, and twenty of them dealt with toy dangers.[2] Why the sudden increase in danger articles? Had a large number of toys suddenly become unsafe? Not at all: if anything, toys had become safer. But something else had happened: activists had become interested in the issue of toy safety. Edward Swartz, who was cited in our chapter on toy hazards, was the best known of these activists. Two of his books, *Toys That Kill* and *Toys That Don't Care*, were written to attract attention to dangerous toys. And so they did, for his charismatic attack on toys drew all kinds of media attention. Swartz appeared on national TV, gave talks to huge audiences, and was largely responsible for the 1970s surge in media articles about toy dangers, which attracted many readers.

Others also helped publicize the problem. Ralph Nader believed the government was not doing enough about toy safety, it should be much harder on toy makers. And citizens who were pressing for safer toys joined to form a Public Action Coalition. Finally, activist Peggy Charon brought her TV program, *Action for Children's TV*, into the fray.

Activist concern over dangerous toys continued beyond the 1970s, but then it began to decline. And so did media interest in the issue. In 1999, out of approximately one hundred toy articles cited in the *Times*, only three dealt with dangerous toys.[3] Why this decline? Perhaps toys had become so safe that there was nothing for toy watchers to report. But something else was happening. Without the activists to give it drama, danger no longer seemed a grabber topic to the media, one that was sure to increase readership, and so it simply stopped writing about this problem.

The media has been accused of paying too much attention to some topics. Yet its most serious bias lies not in what it hypes, but in what it chooses not to talk about. Stephan Klaidman, a senior research fellow at the Kennedy School of Ethics at Georgetown University, puts it this way: "Although investigative reporting is a much-discussed form of journalism, in practice, it is relatively rare ... much of what passes for investigative journalism is really secondhand reporting of the investigation of others."[4]

Bernard Goldberg has yet another concern about the media.[5] Writing in his book *Bias*, Goldberg notes that the media avoids using the scientific method, which is what we must do if we are to understand cause-effect issues. The Columbine shootings, which were described in the chapter on toy weapons, were an example of this. Does cops and robbers play really train children to be killers? This is an extremely difficult question to explore, for so many variables are involved. For example, what is the role of parental lifestyle in creating killer children? What about family income, the climate, political beliefs of the family, television, and the myriad other variables that might influence a child to become a Columbine-style killer? It is hard to untangle all these variables, and so the media, which is always in a rush, prefers black and white answers to a complex issue such as what it is that makes children into killers.

The media often ignores history. After all, history can be rather boring to many readers. As we saw in the Fashion Dolls and Action Figures chapter, the many media writers who attacked Barbie ignored a very important point: fashion dolls were not new. Long before Barbie's time, French fashion dolls were on the market and, like Barbie, they were hedonists. As one museum curator has put it, they were meant to teach little girls the things they needed to know in the "most ostentatious era ever."[6]

These early fashion dolls were even worse than Barbie, for they were snobs. At least Barbie is egalitarian, for almost all children can afford her.

But only the rich and royal could afford to own those early fashion dolls. Impatient with history, media writers have ignored this point, even though it makes Barbie look much better.

Barbie also does something that earlier fashion dolls never did. She has helped a little girl's vision of the future by invading what were once all male roles. Pilot Barbie is an example. But the media would rather emphasize her faults, even if they are trivial, because they make more interesting reading. For example, as we saw in the Fashion Doll and Action Figures chapter, her unfortunate saying, "Math is tough," appeared in newspapers across the country.

The Homies, Chicano dolls that appeared in California during the late 1990s, and were cited in the chapter on racism, created a wave of media outrage. Yes, they were racist, but was the problem really that bad? Were they just one more example of a racism that continued to plague the doll world? One might have expected the media to explore this question, but it did not. And for the many readers who were unfamiliar with the toy racism of our past, the Homies could well have been seen as a real threat, rather than what they really were: merely a remnant of what was once a major problem.

Often, the media is suspicious of big business. Can bias of this sort distort the view that toy writers have of the toy industry? Three influential books—*Toy Wars*, by G. Wayne Miller, *Out of the Garden*, by Stephen Kline, and *Kid's Stuff*, by Gary Cross—tend to see today's toy industry as a mindless giant, depriving today's children of good toys.[7] They argue that through a clever and relentless use of the mass media, especially television, today's giant toy makers have stolen our children and their toys away from parental control. Today, our children listen to the endless "buy me, buy me" call of these giant toy companies, who urge them to clamor for more and more of their faddish, often poor-taste toys.

There is surely truth in this, but might something be missing from their argument? When our children crave the latest toy, might they be doing what their parents do? After all, we Americans are the world's most avid consumers. We covet the latest clothing styles, the newest SUV model, and the latest technology. And we go to the mall, shopping until we drop.

Might we become better models for our children, teaching them to be less consumer minded? And could we become wiser in our choice of toys? Unfortunately, these are not easy things to do. Our media does give us some advice about "good" toys. Yet, most of the time, it urges us to buy ever more toys, whether good or bad. How many toys should our children have, and what is a good toy anyway?

Parents face a plurality of problems as they try to answer these questions. More on the plight of the parent in the next chapter.

13

The Plight of the Parent

Helped by articles and books, today's parents sally forth to buy good toys. But this is not easy to do, for a number of things have weakened a parent's power to wisely choose toys. For one thing, parents now spend much less time in contact with their children. Forty years ago, three-quarters of our children had stay-at-home mothers. Now, the figure is almost reversed, for only a third of American preschoolers have mothers at home. Also, parental surveillance is further diminished by our climbing rates of divorce. Today, around half of all American children grow up in single-parent homes. One result of this is that a child may have two separated parents who disagree about which toys are proper for their children.

As they strive to take control of their children's toys, parents face a second challenge. Today, a child's peer group has an increasingly powerful role to play when it comes to decisions about things such as good or bad toys. As Kay Hymowitz, who has written a book on American childhood, expressed it, peer groups are "replacing simple friendships and are invading earlier grades, where they oversee dress and behavior more cruelly and exactingly than adults ever did."[1]

Christmas is the time when pressure from the children's culture is at its peak. Before Christmas 1999, one mother was doing whatever it took to get those highly coveted Pokemon cards under the Christmas tree for her children. To do this, she had to dispatch her husband, mother-in-law, and brother to stand in line at toy stores. But Christmas 2000 was better. "The pressure [was] off a bit," she said. "So I have time to think about what these kids really need."[2]

This pressure may be at its worst during the Christmas season, but it never goes away. "Parents always feel the pressure to buy [fad toys], otherwise they look like they are bad parents," said Marion Szymanski, president of Toytips.com, a toy research firm. For example, scooters had become big by the summer of 2000. The Razor scooters were particularly popular. "All the kids were bragging about their Razors," said one mother, who ran out to get one for her six-year-old daughter. "I just didn't want her to be made fun of," she said.[3]

Besides weakened families and pressure from the children's culture, there is a third challenge that parents face as they attempt to choose the right toy for their children. In an earlier America, most adults shared certain moral truths. Acts such as cheating or cruelty were bad. If it was to prosper, the members of a society had to learn to act responsibly, even altruistically. But little children had not as yet learned these truths. They were essentially amoral, and it was the duty of a parent to teach them to be moral. Today, as Kay Hymowitz has persuasively argued, we have largely abandoned the notion that moral education should be a part of childhood. Instead, children are today seen as born with an innate moral compass. "No you can't do that," or "No, that's a bad toy, and I won't allow you to have it," is largely passe. Instead, today's childhood education emphasizes the development of skills, not morals. Hence, today's parents endlessly seek educational toys, but avoid moral values when selecting toys for their children. This means that they will be loath to tell their child that a toy he or she has seen on television is somehow bad.

Even when parents do feel that their children need to be taught moral values, they face yet another challenge unknown to the parents of an earlier America. In the past, most parents had the same notions about what was good and what was bad behavior in children. Consequently, they also shared similar values about children's toys. If a child clamored for a toy that a parent thought was immoral, he or she could say "you can't have that toy," and feel sure that other parents would have responded in the same way.

But today's parents live in a diverse, pluralistic society. Some of us are born-again Christians, some atheists. Some are gay, others hate homosexuals. Some seek ways of going back to nature, others love city life. Some feel selfless civic duty should drive our behavior, but others would argue that self-expression is more important. This weakens parental decisiveness respecting toys. What, for example, should a parent do about the Teletubby toy called Tinky Winky? Here are two parents. They are trying to get their two-year-old ready for preschool (both parents work). But their child is wailing. "I want to see the Teletubbies!" The Teletubbies are on the tube, and under normal circumstances, would be a fine send-off for their child before she went to preschool. But both parents have just read Charles Lane's 1999 *New Republic* article called "Tubby Ache."[4] They now know that Jerry Falwell of the religious right thinks the Teletubby called Tinky Winky is gay. After all, he carries a purse, wears purple (the Gay

Chapter 13—The Plight of the Parent

Pride color), and has a triangle, supposedly a gay symbol, on his head. Is Tinky Winky gay? If so, that would not bother them. What does is the uncertainty. Is Falwell no more than a bigot, as Lane says? And what do other parents think? Faced with toy problems such as this, it's no wonder that today's parent often feels lost when it comes to making decisions about good toys.

Would it be possible to escape problems such as these by going back to some kind of reinvented country America, to a place where toys were fewer and easier to understand, a place where most everyone had the same views about "good" and "bad" toys? What would such a reinvented America be like? Perhaps the best model we have is the kibbutz of Israel. Started early in the last century by settlers who had come to the Near East, the kibbutz is a collective agricultural settlement. Central to the kibbutz movement is the conviction that physical, particularly agricultural, labor is the noblest means of making a living.

What is it like to be a child in a kibbutz? In the early 1950s, Melford Spiro carried out an intensive study of one kibbutz, and published his results in a book titled *Children of the Kibbutz*.[5] Children lived in small groups, each with its own dwelling. Parents could visit, but each group was under the supervision of a resident adult. All toys were the property of the kibbutz. They were kept in cabinets, and passed out by the resident adult, who also controlled the children's play. Many of these toys would be familiar to American children. Wagons, marbles, sand pails, and dolls were examples. But controversial toys such as toy weapons, Barbies, or action figures were absent. Rather than playing with toys that imitated movie or other media celebrities, children were encouraged by kibbutz leaders to play in creative or artistic ways, such as working with blocks or stringing beads. By high school age, children were given a modest allowance and could buy some toys of their own, such as marbles or roller skates.

Some of us would opt for life in a society such as the kibbutz described by Spiro. Gone would be the endless advice from experts who tell us what our children's toys should be like. Also gone would be the endless advertisements created by toy companies as they battle each other in an attempt to sell their wares.

The kibbutz that Spiro visited was a monolithic society. It had one set of values. All who lived there had to conform to the social order established by the kibbutz. As would be expected in a society of this sort, kibbutz toys were monolithic, for the kibbutz controlled their type, their number, and the way they were used. In sharp contrast to the kibbutz, we live in a pluralistic society, a society which places great value on the right of individuals to build the lifestyle they want. A society of this sort is one of choices. This is true for our religious beliefs, for our occupations, and for our toys. But choice always leads to opinion, and that means toy advisors with all their differing views. Choice also means toy merchants, who hype their competing wares.

Parents often complain about the ways that toy makers manipulate them. Yet in reality, parents are not the victims of evil toy makers. Instead, the store is indeed right: toys are us. If we wish our children to have mindless, poor-taste toys, toy makers will make them, knowing they will sell. And so, it is the parent, not the toy maker, who will ultimately decide the quality of our toys.

How might parents change their ways and once again gain control of their children's toys? Joanne Oppenheim, who is probably the leading expert of our time on issues of toy choice, has suggested a modest start. Her views about parental responsibility are worth quoting at some length.

"Much as we like to blame the toy companies and television for bombarding our children with messages to "Buy! Buy! Buy!" it may be that we as parents have played a part in fueling children's desires. Just visit a family with a new baby or young toddler and you'll see that long before children can form the words "Buy me!" the buying has begun.... Clearly, it seems that more and more buying leads to less and less satisfaction. Indeed, *buying* toys seems to be more interesting to many kids than actually playing with them!"[6]

Beyond the question of parental control lies yet another which has been a central issue in this book: are today's toys better or worse than those of the past? Our survey suggests that it has been more a matter of change than a simple gain or loss. The toys of our past provided children with more exercise and contact with nature than do those of today. And children had more control over their toys. They could imagine a toy they wished to make and how it might be used. But today's toys are less racist, safer, richer in their variety and more egalitarian than ever before. In spite of media hype to the contrary, it does seem that today's toys are better than those of the past.

We adults can evaluate the toys of today. But so can another group: our children. Yes, some would covet fad toys, or those of poor taste. But surely, most children of today would say that they like the challenge and excitement of the ever-changing toy world in which they live. And interestingly, that's exactly the decision that children such as Dorothy Howard and Jimmy Savo made back in Chapter 1. Having seen what the new toys of the machine age were like, they too yearned to become a part of this new age.

Chapter Notes

Chapter 1. The Changing World of Toys

1. Howard, Dorothy. *Dorthy's World*. Englewood Cliffs, NJ: Prentice-Hall, 1977. P. 11.
2. Rheingold, Harriett and Kaye Cook. "The Contents of Boys' and Girls' Rooms as an Index of Parents' Behavior." *Child Development* 46 (1975): 462.
3. *Reader's Guide to Periodical Literature.* H.W. Wilson Co., 950 University Ave., Bronx, NY 0452

Chapter 2. Toy Weapons

1. Eastman, Charles. *Indian Boyhood*. Rapid City, SD: Fenwyn Press, 1970. P. 66.
2. O'Kieffe, Charley. *Western Story: The Recollections of Charley O'Kieffe, 1884–1898*. Lincoln: University of Nebraska Press, 1960. P. 14.
3. Applegate, Jessie. *A Day with the Cow Column in 1843*. Chicago: The Caxton Club, 1934. P. 83, 84.
4. Conroy, Jack. "Boyhood in a Coal Town." *American Mercury* 23 (May 1931): 84.
5. Howells, William Dean. *A Boy's Town*. New York, Harper, 1918. P. 84.
6. Dargan, Amanda, and Steven Zeitlin. *City Play*. New Brunswick, NJ: Rutgers University Press, 1990. P. 149.
7. Savo, Jimmy. *I Bow to the Stones*. New York: Howard Frisch, 1963. P. 57.
8. Hale, Edward. *A New England Boyhood*. Boston: Little, Brown and Company, 1964. P. 34.
9. Wigginton, Eliot, Ed. *Foxfire 6*. Garden City, NY: Anchor, 1980. P. 215–6.
10. Smith, Dorothy. "School Days." *Reminisce* (Sept.–Oct. 1997): 54.
11. Beard, Dan. *Hardly A Man Is Now Alive* New York: Doubleday, 1939. P. 99–100.
12. Cox, Michael. "Little Soldiers." *New York Times Magazine* (Aug. 6, 1995): 26.
13. Sutton-Smith, Brian. *A History of Children's Play: New Zealand 1840–1950*. Philadelphia: University of Pennsylvania Press, 1981.
14. Hearst, James. "Young Poet on the Land." In *Growing Up In Iowa*. Ed. by Clarence A. Andrews. Ames: Iowa State University Press, 1978. P. 56.
15. O'Brien, Richard. *The Story of American Toys*. New York: Artebras, 1990. P. 25.
16. Brown, Joe David. "The Rifle Called Daisy." *Sports Illustrated* 18(17)(April 29, 1963): 58ff.
17. Abbott, Eleanor H. *Being Little in Cambridge*. New York: Appleton Century, 1936. P. 77–8.
18. Rutland, Robert. *A Boyhood in the Dust Bowl, 1926–1934*. Niwot: University Press of Colorado, 1995. P. 86.
19. Public Law 100–615. Nov. 5, 1988.
20. Howells, op. cit., 124.
21. Beard, op. cit., 151.
22. Garland, Hamlin. *A Son of the Middle Border*. New York: Macmillan, 1962. P. 11.
23. Catton, Bruce. *Waiting for the Morning Train. An American Boyhood*. Detroit, MI: Wayne State University Press, 1987. P. 46.
24. Sneller, Anne. *A Vanished World*. Syracuse, NY: Syracuse University Press, Detroit, 1987. P. 203.
25. Howells, op. cit., 149.
26. Holland, Barbara. "It Was a Wonderful Toy and a Glorious War." *Smithsonian* (July, 1992): 128.
27. Stivender, Ed. *Still Catholic After All These Years*. Little Rock, AK: August House, 1995. P. 15.
28. O'Dell, John. *The Great American Depression Book of Fun*. New York: Harpers, 1981. P. 9.
29. Kernan, Michael. "Buddy, Jean and Me,

Going Great Guns." *Smithsonian* (August, 1990): 142.
30. Stivender, op. cit., 41.
31. O'Dell. op. cit., 2.
32. Anon. "War Toys?" *The Rotarian*, 57(Dec., 1940): 19–21, 57.
33. Anon. "Children Should Not Be Encouraged in War Games." *Science News Letter* 45 (Feb., 12, 1944): 104.
34. O'Brien, op. cit., 163.
35. Andreas, Carol. "War Toys and the Peace Movement." *Journal of Social Issues* 25 (1)(1969): 83–99.
36. Hofstadter, Richard. America as a Gun Culture. *American Heritage* (October, 1970): 4–11, 82–5; Fuentes, Annette "The Crackdown on Kids." *The Nation* (June 15/22, 1998): 20–2.
37. Cockburn, Alexander. The War on Kids. *The Nation* (June 3, 1996): 7–8.
38. Johnson, Jeffery et. al. "Television Viewing and Aggressive Behavior During Adolescence and Adulthood." *Science* 295 (March 29, 2002): 2468–71.
39. Galyan, Gohar. "One Year Later." *Los Angeles Times* (April 16, 2000): E 1,9.
40. Levy, Bob. "At Turtle Park, a Volley of Toy Weapons." *Washington Post* (May 13, 1999): C 11.
41. Suhay, Lisa. "Boys Will Be Boys." *Family Circle* 112 (11)(Aug. 3, 1999): 120.
42. Meltz, Barbara. "Should Boys Have War Toys?" *Boston Globe* (May 29, 1999): F 1,3.
43. Kantrowitz, Barbara. "The New Age of Anxiety." *Newsweek* (Aug. 23, 1999): 40; Condor, Bob. "Violent Toys Aimed at Youngsters Aren't Child's Play." *Chicago Tribune* (April 6, 2000): Sect. 13:3.
44. Meltz. op. cit., F3.
45. Holmstrom, David. "Replacing Toy Guns with Soft and Squishies." *Christian Science Monitor* (Dec. 12, 1997): 10.
46. Anon. "Group Swaps Guns For Leftover Toys." *Lansing State Journal* (March 18, 2000): 2 B.
47. Struck, Doug. "Violent Toys? They're Not Playing." *Washington Post* (Feb. 17, 1997): D 1,2.
48. Kaminer, Wendy. "The War On High Schools." *The American Prospect* (Dec. 20, 1999): 11–12; Leo, John. "Will boys Be boys?" *US News & World Report* (July 17, 2000): 17.
49. Glod, Maria. Judge Reverses Suspension Over Boy's Toy Gun. *Washington Post* (May 14, 2000): 3.
50. Terlap, Sharon. "Teen's Future Hangs in Limbo." *Lansing State Journal* (July 12, 2001): 1,6 A.
51. Van Horn, Royal. "Violence and Video Games." *Phi Delta Kappan* 81 (2) (Oct., 1999): 173–4.

52. Van Horn, op. cit.; Jabs, Carolyn. "Child's Play?" *Family PC* (Oct. 1999): 66; Quiltner, Joshua. "Are Video Games Really So Bad?" *Time* 153 (18) (May 10, 1999): 50, 54, 56, 59.
53. Van Horn, op. cit.; Quiltner, op. cit.; Grossman, Dave. "We Are Training Our Kids To Kill." *Saturday Evening Post* (July/Aug. 1999): 65.

Chapter 3. Fashion Dolls and Action Figures

1. Stirn, Carl P. *Turn-of-the-Century Dolls, Toys and Games*. New York: Dover, 1990. P. 91.
2. McLaughlin, Patricia. "Doll Shows Women Have Gained Some Fashion Freedom." *Lansing State Journal* (Sept. 18, 1991): 3C.
3. Berg, Elizabeth. "Confessions of a Barbie Lover." *Parents* (Sept., 1999): 141, 142.
4. Brumberg, Joan Jacobs. *The Body Project*. New York: Random House, 1997. P. XVII; Jones, Wendy. "Barbie's Body Project." P. 91–109 in McDonough, Yona, Ed. "*The Barbie Chronicles*." New York: Touchstone, 1999.
5. Zeiger, Lisa, "A Doll's House." *New York Times Magazine* (Oct. 3, 1999): P. 22.
6. Attfield, Judy. "Barbie and Action Man: Adult Toys for Girls and Boys, 1959–93." P. 80–7 in Kirkham, Pat, *The Gendered Object*. New York: Manchester University Press, 1996.
7. Stewart, Douglas. "In the Cutthroat World of Toy Sales, Child's Play Is Serious Business." *Smithsonian* 20 (9) (Dec., 1989: 73–6,78, 80–3.
8. Anon. "Rah!" *Sports Illustrated* (Aug. 1997): 22.
9. Greenwald, John. "Barbie Boots Up." *Time* (Nov. 11, 1996): 48– 50; Mabry, Jennifer E. "Barbie Turns 40." *Lansing State Journal* (Dec. 24, 1998): 1D.
10. Lord, M.G. *Forever Barbie*. New York: William Morrow, 1994: 40.
11. Anon. "The Barbie Doll Set." *Nation* 148 (18) (April 27, 1964): 407.
12. Lord, *op. cit.*, 39.
13. Healy, Michelle. "Creator Looks Back at Inspiration for Barbie." *Lansing State Journal* (Mar. 12, 1994): 6 D.
14. Chamberlain, Kathy. "Idollatry." *Tikkun* 10 (2) (Mar.–April, 1995): 57–60
15. Rakistis, Ted. "Debate in the Doll's House." *Today's Health*. 42 (2) (Dec., 1970): 28, 31.
16. Cross, Gary. *Kid's Stuff: Toys and the*

Changing World of American Childhood. Cambridge, Mass: Harvard, 1997: 233.

17. K.B. "Way to Go, Ken!" *Fortune* 122 (5) (Aug. 27, 1990): 14.

18. Schroeder, Ken. "In Brief ... Barbie Doesn't Add Up." *The Education Digest* 58 (Dec., 1992): 72–5.

19. Firestone, David. "While Barbie Talks Tough, G.I. Joe Goes Shopping." *New York Times* (Dec. 31, 1993): A 12.

20. Abraham, Kitty G. and Evelyn Lieberman. "Should Barbie Go to Pre School?" *Young Children* 40 (Jan., 1985): 12–4.

21. Anon. "Barbie: In Shape and Dressed for Success." *Newsweek* 105 (Feb. 18, 1985): 12.

22. Greenwald, *op. cit.*, 49.

23. Brooks, Andree. "Barbie for President." *New York Times* (April 4, 2000): A 22.

24. Lewin, Tamar. "Flatter, Smarter and Socially Sensitive Think Tank." *New York Times* (Nov. 29, 1997): B 9.

25. Hobson, Katherine. "Meet Corporate Turnaround Barbie." *U.S. News & World Report* (Mar. 5, 2001): 43.

26. Shen, Fern. "Barbie's Style Not Holding Attention." *Lansing State Journal* (Feb. 21, 2002): 1 D.

27. Eltahawy, Mona. "Meet Barbie of Arabia." *U.S. News & World Report* 127 (9) (Sept. 6, 1999): 44.

28. Cox, Palmer. *The Brownies: Their Book.* New York: Dover, 1964.

29. Meyer, Michael, and Dody Tsiantar. "Ninja Turtles, Eat Our Dust." *Newsweek* (Aug. 8, 1994): 34–5.

30. Monaghan, John. "Parents Confront Violent Movies." *Lansing State Journal* (June 20, 2003): 1,3 D.

31. Carlsson-Paige, Nancy and Diane E. Levin. *The War Play Dilemma.* New York: Teacher's College Press, 1987. P. 13.

32. Sutton-Smith, Brian, John Gerstmyer and Alice Meckley. "Playfighting as Folkplay amongst Preschool Children." *Western Folklore* 47 (July, 1988): 161–76.

33. Cross, *op. cit.*, 204.

34. Barnes, John. "Heroic Rescue Figures May Top Holiday Wish Lists." *New York Times* (Sept. 26, 2001): C 6,7.

35. Wheeler, David L. "Could Boys Get Barbie Syndrome?" *Chronicle of Higher Education* (June 11, 1999): A 22.

Chapter 4. Toys That Come Alive

1. West, Elliott, *Growing Up in Twentieth-Century America.* Westport, CT: Greenwood Press, 1996: 183.

2. Kline, Stephen. *Out of The Garden: Toys, TV and Childrens Culture in the Age of Marketing.* New York: Verso Books, 1993. p. 208.

3. Bok, Sissela. *Mayhem. Violence as Public Entertainment.* Reading, MA: Addison-Wesley, 1998: p. 25.

4. Jackson, Kathy Merlock. "Targeting Baby-Boom Children as Consumers: Mattel Uses Television to Sell Talking Dolls." p. 187–97 in Eiss, Harry Ed., *Images of the Child.* Bowling Green, OH: Bowling Green State University Popular Press, 1994.

5. *Ibid*, p. 196.

6. Hickey, Mary. "How the Power Rangers Stole Christmas." *Ladies' Home Journal* CXII (Dec., 1995): 126–7, 167, 169.

7. Anon. "G.I. Joe Surrenders." *Consumer Reports* 58 (July, 1993): 413.

8. Anon. "Kids Ad Special Raises Some Eyebrows of Critics." *Advertising Age* 63 (6) (Feb. 10, 1992): 5–14.

9. Bowman, Karylin. "TV Ads: What's Appropriate, When." *The American Enterprise* 8 (2) (Mar.–April, 1997): 93.

10. Davies, Maire. *Fake, Fact and Fantasy. Children's Interpretation of Television Reality.* Mahwah, NJ: Erlbaum, 1997. P. 53.

11. Hickey, *op. cit.*, 166.

12. Kline, *op. cit.*, 328.

13. Englehardt. "Toys Are Us." *The Nation* (December 29, 1997): 38.

14. Kline, *op. cit.*, 318.

15. Kline, *ibid.*, 329–30.

16. Hickey, *op. cit.*, 169.

17. Anon., 1964, *op. cit.*, 62.

18. Phillips, Phil. *Turmoil in the Toybox.* Lancaster, PA: Stardust, 1986.

19. Hickey, *op. cit.*, 167.

20. Hillier, Mary. *Automatia & Mechanical Toys.* London: Bloomsbury, 1988. P. 96.

21. Miller, James P. "Techno-pets a whole new breed." *Chicago Tribune* (Mar. 19, 2001): B4.

22. Hamilton, Anita. "How 'Bout Them Bots?" *Time* 157 (8) (Feb. 26, 2001): 56.

23. Miller, *op. cit.*

24. Manning, Ric. "Robot Pets Racking Up Strong Holiday Sales." *Lansing State Journal:* (Dec. 4, 2001): 3 D.

25. Jailer, Mildred. "Autoperipatetikos: The Self-Walking Doll." *Antiques & Collecting* 91 (Feb., 1987): 32–4, 36.

26. Madigen, Pauline and Dick. "The SFBJ Walking-Kissing Doll. Why So Scarce? *Hobbies* (Jan., 1984): 36–40.

27. Wallace, Robert. "Look! Its Nose Runs!" *Life* 29 (Dec. 18, 1950): 55.

28. Langdon, Grace. "What's New in Dolls?" *Parents* 26 (Oct., 1951): 184–5.

29. Rakistis, Ted. "Debate in the Doll House." *Today's Health* 42 (2) (Dec., 1970): 28–31, 65–6.
30. Helmbreck, Valerie. "Living Dolls. These Babies May Be a Bit Too Human for Many a Mommy." *Lansing State Journal* (Dec. 18, 1993): 1D.
31. Anon. "Barney-Mania." *Popular Electronics* 15 (4) (April, 1998): 21.
32. Jackson, Maggie. "Parents Become Pet Sitters." *Lansing State Journal* (Sept. 29, 1997): 5D.
33. Tousignant, Marylou. "A Whining, Dining Doll." *Washington Post* (Jan. 19, 1999): A 11.
34. Flynn, Michael. "Spies R Us." *Bulletin of the Atomic Scientists* (May/June, 1999): 8, 9.
35. Meehan, Thomas. "Creative (And Mostly Upper-Middle-Class) Playthings." *Saturday Review* 55 (Dec. 16, 1972): 45.
36. Singer, Dorothy G., and Jerome L. Singer. *The House of Make-Believe*. Cambridge, MA: Harvard University Press, 1990. P. 86.
37. Brooks, Geraldine. "The Quarter Acre Universe." *New York Times Magazine* (Sept. 27, 1998): 108; Brunius, Harry. "Smart Toys Interact with Kids and TV." *Christian Science Monitor* (Feb. 24, 1999): 13; Rakistis, *op. cit.*, 65.
38. Oldenburg, Don. "Let the Toy Wars Begin." *Lansing State Journal* (Sept. 23, 1999): 1,2 D.
39. Kinnick, Katherine, and Sabrena Parton. "Gruesome Toy Sends Wrong Message to Kids." *Atlanta Journal Constitution* (Oct. 31, 1999): G 5; Hulbert, Dan. "Toying with Violence." *Atlanta Journal Constitution* (Nov 11, 1999): D 3.
40. Achenbach, Beth. "Hey Rosie, epilepsy is no laughing matter." *Lansing State Journal* (Dec. 23, 2001): 15 A.
41. Louderback, Jim. "Love & Robots." *USA Weekend* (Jan. 25–7, 2002): 4,5.
42. Pham, Alex. "Dog Bytes Man." *Los Angeles Times* (Mar. 22, 2001): T 1,7; Alpert, Mark. "Kibbles and Bytes." *Scientific American* (June, 2001): 102–4.
43. Pham, *ibid*, T1.
44. Louderback, *op. cit.* 4.
45. Hafner, Katie. "What Do You Mean, 'It's Just Like a Real Dog?'" *New York Times* (May 25, 2000): D, 7.
46. Porterfield, Deborah. "Fewer Tech Toys Emerge, But They Have Improved." *Lansing State Journal* (Feb. 19, 2002): 8C.

Chapter 5. Toys That Teach

1. Hewitt, Karen, and Louise Rommet. *Educational Toys in America: 1800 to the Present*. Burlington, VT: Queen City Printers, 1979. P. 1.
2. Locke, John. *Some Thoughts Concerning Education*. London: National Society's Depository, 1880. P. 273–4.
3. Edgeworth, Maria, and R.L. Edgeworth. *Practical Education*. New York: Woodstock Books, 1996.
4. Brosterman, Norman. *Inventing Kindergarten*. New York: Abrams, 1997.
5. Gibson, Janice, "Games That Teach." *Parents* 59 (Jan., 1984): 78; Cain, Joy D. "Toys That Teach." *Essence* (Aug., 1990): 102, 104; Heller, Linda J. "The Magic of Make-Believe." *Parents* (June, 1996): 76–8; Palar, Barbara. "Toys That Teach." *Better Homes & Gardens* (Nov., 1993): 36,38.
6. Quilitch, H. Robert. "Can Toys Really Teach?" *Saturday Review World* 2 (Nov.16, 1974): 60, 62.
7. Sutton-Smith, Brian. "Toys for Object and Role Mastery." P. 11–24 in Hewitt, *op. cit.*
8. Sutton-Smith, Brian. "The Role of Toys in the Instigation of Playful Creativity." *Creativity Research Journal* 5 (1992): 3–11; Schimpf, Shella. "Help Your Children Have Fun, Creative Play." *Lansing State Journal* (Jan. 6,1999): 6 D.
9. Harris, H.A. *Sport in Greece and Rome*. Ithaca, NY: Cornell University Press, 1972. P. 135.
10. Eastman, Mary. *The Biography of Dio Lewis*. New York: Fowler, 1891. P. 92.
11. Balch, Ernest. "A New System of Physical Training." *St. Nicholas* 43 (1) (Mar., 1916): 400.
12. Miller, Sue. "Make Them Feel Like a Somebody! A Hula Hoop Unit Did." *Teaching Exceptional Children* 11 (Summer, 1979): 149–52.
13. Zonglie, Chen. "Hula Hoop Craze in Beijing." *Beijing Review* 35 (Mar. 30, 1992): 40–1.
14. Turner, Ray. "100 Years of Physics and Toys: Balancing Toys." *The Physics Teacher* 30 (Dec., 1992); 542–3; Buckwash, Vincent. "Ways to demonstrate center of gravity." *The Physics Teacher* (Jan., 1976): 39–40.
15. Summers, Carolyn. "Science and Children." *Natural Science Teacher's Association* End Paper, 1994, P. 101.
16. Janes, Patricia. "Teach with Toys." *Scholastic Instructor*. (Nov./Dec., 2001): 40–1.
17. Anon. "New Breed of Toys." *Time* 84 (Dec. 4, 1964): 90.
18. Cobb, Viki. "How to Make a Science Lesson Out of Anything." *Instructor* 90 (April, 1981): 44.
19. Taubman, Bryna. "Playing Doctor with Gail Zayka's Lifelike Dolls Helps Kids Facing

Surgery Get Over Their Fears." *People Weekly.* (Sept. 14, 1987): 57.

20. Anon. "Thanks To a Texas Orthodontist, Cabbage Patch Kids Can Now Be Dressed to the Teeth — With Braces." *People Weekly* 23 (May 27, 1985): 107.

21. Singer, Patti. "Dentists Make Visits Easier on Children." *Lansing State Journal* (Jan. 3, 1997): 2 E.

22. Heekin, Shelly. "New Friends." *Children Today* 13 (5) (Sept.–Oct. 1984): 9–13.

23. Anon. "A Doll Made to Order." *Newsweek* (Dec. 9, 1985): 62.

24. Canedy, Dana. "More Toys Are Reflecting Children's Needs." *New York Times* (Dec. 25, 1997): A1, C4.

25. Ibid., 1A.

26. Lecesse, Donna. "Special Toys for Special Children. *Playthings* 94 (1) (Nov., 1996): 27.

27. Therrien, Lois. "These Baby Dolls Really Deliver." *Business Week* (June 8, 1992): 36.

28. Hill, Adeline. "What Toys mean to a Child." *Parents* (Nov., 1940): 28,68; Anon. "What Is a Good Toy?" *Good Housekeeping* 16 (Nov., 1965): 214; Clepper, Irene. "What Toys Teach." *Parents* 49 (Nov., 1974): 50–1, 62.

29. Levine, Susan. "A Cultural Approach to Toymaking." *School Arts* 84 (5) (Jan., 1985): 27.

30. Swinarski, Louise. "Toys: Universals for Teaching Global Education. *Childhood Education* 67 (Spring, 1991): 161–3.

31. Provenzo, Eugene F. Jr., and Asterie Provenzo. *The Historian's Toybox.* Englewood, NJ: Prentice-Hall, 1980.

32. Englehardt, Tom. "The Morphing of the American Mind." *New York Times* (Dec. 24, 1994): 25 Op. Ed.

33. Tousignant, *op. cit.*

34. Anon. "Multilingual Doll Has Retailer to Call Home." *Lansing State Journal* (Dec. 12, 2000): 8 C; Jegla, Melissa. "Tutor Toys: Gifts That Educate and Entertain." *Lansing State Journal* (Dec. 17, 2000): 1S.

35. Porterfield, *op. cit.*

36. Ridgeway, Nichole. "Robo-Therapy." *Forbes* (May 14, 2001): 216.

37. Kuznets, Lois R. *When Toys Come Alive.* New Haven, CT: Yale University Press, 1994.

38. Meeker, Mary. "Toys Before and After Christmas." *Gifted Children Today* 12 (6) (Nov.–December, 1989): 54.

39. Leshan, Eda. "Where Has the Magic Gone?" *PTA Magazine* (June, 1968): 2.

Chapter 6. Hazardous Toys

1. Howard, Dorothy. *Dorothy's World.* Englewood Cliffs, NJ: Prentice-Hall, 1977, 139–40.

2. Stratton, Joanna. *Pioneer Women: Voices from the Kansas Frontier.* New York: Simon and Schuster, 1981. P. 153.

3. Jackson, Charles. *The Buffalo Wallow: A Prairie Boyhood.* Univ. of Nebraska Press, Lincoln NE, 1982, 183.

4. Applegate, Jessie A. *A Day with the Cow Column in 1843.* Chicago: The Caxton Club, 1934. P. 60.

5. Applegate, ibid, P. 161–4.

6. Beard, Dan. *Hardly a Man Is Now Alive.* New York: Doubleday, 1939. P. 75.

7. Howells, William Dean. *A Boy's Town.* New York: Harper, 1918. P. 128–9.

8. Hale, Edward. *A New England Boyhood.* Boston: Little, Brown and Company, 1964. P. 45.

9. Anon. "Helium Balloons Popular at Central Park; Toothpowder Can Gave Idea for 'Kelly Comet.'" *New York Times* (Nov. 21, 1938): 21.

10. Anon. "Holiday — For Danger?" *Ladies Home Journal* (Dec. 1945) 6.

11. Anon. "Industry to Fight Toy Bill in Albany." *New York Times* (Mar. 11, 1948): 47.

12. Dales, Douglas. "Senate at Albany Passes Bias Bill." *New York Times* (Mar. 15, 1949): 5.

13. Anon. "Warning Is Issued on Stuffed Duck Toys." *New York Times* (April 20, 1965): 25.

14. Anon. "Maker Says Tests Indicate Toy Does Not Cause Rashes." *New York Times* (May 19, 1963): L55.

15. Anon. "Text of the President's Message Requesting Wide Range of Consumer Safeguards." *New York Times* (Mar. 22, 1966): 22.

16. Anon. "Toy Safety Bill Signed by Nixon." *New York Times* (Nov. 11, 1969): 33.

17. Anon. "How to Be Sure a Toy Is Safe." *Good Housekeeping* (Nov., 1965): 177; Rakistis, Ted. R. "How Safe Are Your Child's Toys?" *Today's Health,* 45 (Dec., 1967): 21.

18. Swartz, Edward. *Toys That Don't Care.* Boston: Gambit, 1971; Swartz, Edward. *Toys That Kill.* New York: Vintage, 1986.

19. Anon. "A trial lawyer and his wife work to take the dangers out of children's playthings." *American Home* 75 (Jan., 1972): 12; Katz, Barbara. "Verbal Darts Tossed at Toys." *Washington Post* (Dec. 13, 1977): C 1,6.

20. Anon. "Toys Santa Shouldn't Bring." *Newsweek* (Dec. 13, 1982): 106.

21. Anon. "Food and Drug Policy." *Congressional Digest* 76 (Feb., 1997): 34–5; Knut-

son, Lawrence L. "Power Wheel Toy Is Recalled." *Lansing State Journal* (Oct. 23, 1998): 3A.
22. Loh, Sharon, and Elizabeth Levy. "Playing It Safe." *E Magazine* (Nov./Dec., 1998): 48; Anon. "PVC Toys Are Judged Safe, But So What?" *Modern Plastics* (Jan., 1999): P. 14.
23. Anon. "Toys Hold Lessons for Plastics Engineers." *Design News* (April 8, 1996): 37.
24. Heiman, Carolyn. "The Perils of Tiny Toys." *Macleans* (Dec., 1984): 48.
25. Koncius, Jura. "New Toys Designed to Battle Bacterial Bad Guys." *Lansing State Journal* (Feb. 17, 1997): 1D.
26. Necrgaard, Lauran. "Are Toys Encased in Chocolate Really OK?" *Lansing State Journal* (July 17, 1997): 1D. Anon. "Chocolate-Covered Toys May Pose Threat." *Lansing State Journal* (Aug. 28, 1997): 1D.
27. Lord, Mary. "Carnivore in the Cabbage Patch?" *US News and World Report.* 122 (2) (Jan. 20, 1997): 69.
28. Mayes, Caroline E. "Panel Deems Vinyl Toys Safe." *Washington Post* (June 16, 2001): E2.
29. Delgado, Ray. "Parents Warned About Unsafe Toys/Avoid Scooters, Group Urges Shoppers." *San Francisco Chronicle.* (Nov. 21, 2001): A23; Ho, David. "Nearly 10,000 Hurt on Scooters This Year." *Lansing State Journal* (Sept. 6, 2000): 5A.
30. Bernstein, Elizabeth. "Here's Yet Another Toy That Lets You Spend More Time in the Air." *Wall Street Journal* (Aug. 10, 2001): B1.
31. Schneider, John. "Spark Flies." *Lansing State Journal* (April 29, 1999): 1B.
32. Leung, Shirley. "Burger King Recalls 2.6 Million Kids Meal Toys." *Wall Street Journal* (Aug. 1, 2001): B2.
33. Spencer, Peter. "Label Mania." *Consumer Research* (Mar., 1992): 38.
34. Brooks, Andree'. "Warnings on Toys Are Often Ignored, Causing Injuries." *New York Times* (Mar. 13, 1997): C 2.
35. Babij, Bruce. "Lawn Darts: A Dangerous Game." *Trial* 21 (Feb., 1985): 14.
36. Streitfeld, David. "Deadly Serious Over Toys." *Washington Post* (Dec. 9, 1986): C 5.
37. Ibid.
38. Anon. "For Kid's Sake. Think Toy Safety." Washington, D.C. U.S. Consumer Product Safety Commission. Undated.
39. Monks, Viki. "If You Spray Pesticides in Your Home, They Might Coat Your Children's Toys." *National Wildlife* (April– May, 1999): 16–17.
40. Swartz, Edward. "Toys-R-Dangerous." *Trial* 18 (Feb., 1982): 28– 31, 75.

41. Anon. "Toy-Related Injuries Among Children and Teenagers— United States, 1996." *Journal of the American Medical Association* (Jan., 1998): 265.
42. Laudan, Larry. "It's Not the Toys, Stupid." *Consumer's Research* 80 (Feb., 1997): 36.
43. Aucain, Don. "Danger Is His Business." *Boston Globe* (Oct. 29, 2002): B7.
44. Hartland, Peter. "Documentary Sheds Light on Asthma." *San Francisco Chronicle* (Nov. 1, 2002): D3.
45. Ryan, Joan. "The Dirt on Dirt." *San Francisco Chronicle* (Sept. 21, 2002): A 27.
46. Mergenbagen, Paula. "Product Liability: Who Sues?" *American Demographics* 19 (June, 1995): 48–54.

Chapter 7. Racist Toys

1. King, Wilma. *Stolen Childhood: Slave Youth in Nineteenth Century America.* Bloomington: Indiana University Press. 1995. P. 45.
2. King, *ibid.*, p. 49.
3. King, *ibid.*, p. 46.
4. King, *ibid.*, p. 45.
5. Mergen, Bernard, *Play and Playthings. A Reference Guide.* Westport, CT: Greenwood Press, 1982. P. 46.
6. Jailer, Mildred. "Non-Traditional Dolls." *Antiques & Collecting* (Oct., 1991): 29.
7. King, *op. cit.*, p. 34.
8. King, *op. cit.*, p. 54.
9. King, *op. cit.*, p. 51.
10. Ibid.
11. Wiggins, David. "The Play of Slave Children in the Plantation Communities of the Old South, 1820–60." *Journal of Sport History* 7 (2) (1980): 21–39.
12. Mergen, *op. cit.*, p. 45.
13. Sears, Roebuck and Company Catalog. 1927. P. 594.
14. Fredrickson, George M. *The Black Image in the White Mind; the Debate on the Afro-American Character and Destiny, 1817–1914.* New York: Harper & Row, 1971. P. 46.
15. Fredrickson, *op. cit.*, p. 47.
16. Ibid.
17. Fredrickson, *op. cit.*, p. 52.
18. Dubin, Steven C. "Symbolic Slavery: Black Representations in Popular Culture." *Social Problems* 34 (2) (April, 1987): 123–40.
19. Honecker, Kristin. "Memorabilia May Reflect Racism." *Michigan State News* (Oct. 24, 1995): 3
20. Wilkinson, Doris. "Play Objects as Tools of Propaganda: Characterizations of the African American Male. *Journal of Black Psychology.* 7 (1) (Aug., 1980): 7.

21. Saunders-Watson, Catherine. "The British Empire Strikes Back." *Antiques & Collecting* 103 (2) (April, 1998): 32–6.
22. Jones, Lisa C. "Toys That Teach." *Ebony* XLIX (1) (Nov., 1993): 57.
23. Tobin, James. "Historical Doll Begins Life as a Southern Slave." *Lansing State Journal* (Sept. 5, 1993): 3B.
24. Ducille, Ann. "Dyes and Dolls: Multicultural Barbie and the Merchandising of Difference." *Differences, a Journal of Feminist Cultural Studies* 6 (1) (1994): 46–68.
25. Banks, W. Curtis. "White Preference in Blacks: A Paradigm in Search of a Phenomenon." *Psychological Bulletin* 83 (6) (1976): 1179–86.
26. Reid-Dove, Allyson. "With Mixed Blessings." *Black Enterprise* 19 (5) (Dec., 1988): 24.
27. Ibid.
28. Anon. "A Celebration of Black Identity Toys." *Ebony* 42 (2) (Dec., 1991): 23; Anon. "Ethnic Dolls Make Their Mark on Industry Growth." *Playthings* 91 (April, 1993): 31.
29. Anon. "Toys for Pride and Fun." *Ebony* 52 (1) (Nov., 1997): 44.
30. Anon. "New Boom in Ethnic Toys." *Ebony* 49 (1) (Nov., 1993): 66.
31. Anon. "Toys That Celebrate You." *Ebony* 52 (1) (Nov., 1996): 76.
32. Anon. "The Joys of Black Toys." *Ebony* 50 (1) (Nov., 1994): 52.
33. Ibid., P. 52.
34. Ibid. P. 54; Anon, 1997, op. cit., 47.
35. Yee, Albert. "Myopic Perceptions and Textbooks: Chinese Americans' Search for Identity." *Journal of Social Issues* 29 (2) (1973): 102.
36. Derig, Betty. "Celestials in the Diggings." *Idaho Yesterdays* 16 (3) (Fall, 1972): 2.
37. Wen, Patricia. "Barbie's Missing Face." *Boston Globe* (May 24, 2000): A 15.
38. Larruba, Evelyn. "Homies Toys Are Center of Debate Over Stereotypes." *Lansing State Journal* (June 13, 1999): 1D; Perez, George A., and C.T. Davis. "Controversy Over Homies." *Los Angeles Times* (May 31, 1999): B4.
39. Sharkey, Betsy. "Beyond Tepees and Totem Poles." *New York Times* (June 11, 1995): 2: 1.
40. Irvine, Martha. "Racially Diverse Dolls Gain Popularity with Kids." *Lansing State Journal* (Feb. 19, 2002): 7C.
41. Ibid.
42. Ibid.

Chapter 8. Gender Toys

1. Landells, E. *The Boy's Own Toy-Maker*. New York: Appleton, 1860. Intro. V11.
2. Oldenziel, Ruth. "Boys and Their Toys: The Fisher Body Craftsman's Guild, 1930–1968, and the Making of a Male Technical Domain." *Technology and Culture* 38 (Jan., 1997): 60–96.
3. Sissman, L.E. "Innocent Bystander." *Atlantic Magazine* 236 (5) (Nov., 1975): 26–7.
4. Teale, Edwin. "America's Five Favorite Hobbies." *Popular Science* 138 (May, 1941): 98–103; Beaubier, Edward. "Model Kits: A Boon to Education." *Today's Health* 39 (Nov., 1961): 72.
5. Ibid., 72.
6. Humphrey, Barbara. "Looking for a Hobby? Try Model Building." *Today's Health* 36 (Feb., 1958): 37.
7. Hinton, Walter. "What Lindbergh Is Doing for Education." *The Outlook* 146 (June 22, 1927): 246.
8. Anon. "How Little Lindbergs Test Their Wings." *Literary Digest* (Oct. 13, 1928): 74.
9. English, Charles H. "A Model Airplane Association and How It Grew." *Recreation* 28 (April, 1934): 6–11, 41–2.
10. Ibid., 9.
11. Anon. 1928, op. cit., 72, 74.
12. Costello, John. "Fliers Who Never Leave the Ground." *Nation's Business* 69 (Nov., 1981): 93–5.
13. McClary, Andrew, *Toys with Nine Lives*. North Haven, CT: Linnet, 1997. P. 130–1.
14. Sissman, *op. cit.*, 26.
15. Anon. "Teaching the Young Idea to Fly." *Literary Digest* (June 9, 1928); 41.
16. Anon. Advertisement. *Sports Illustrated* (Dec. 18, 1961); 35.
17. Dickson, Paul. "The Object at Hand." *Smithsonian* (2) (May, 1995): 26,28.
18. Karwatka, Dennis. "Technology's Past: The First Construction Toy. *School Shop* 43 (Feb., 1984): 42.
19. Pursell, Carrol. "Toys, Technology and Sex Roles in America, 1920–1940." P. 263 in Trescott, Martha M., *Dynamos and Virgins Revisited: Women and Technological Change in History*, 1979.
20. Anon. Advertisement. *The Ladies' Home Journal* XXXIII December, 1916): 85.
21. Anon. "Erector Sets." *Fortune* XIV (6) (Dec., 1936): 60; Nuhn, Roy. "Hello Boys! Make Lots of Toys." *American History Illustrated* 15 (Dec., 1980): 36–42.
22. Purcell, *op. cit.*, 260.
23. Purcell, ibid, 256.
24. Purcell, ibid, 257.

25. Purcell, ibid, 253.
26. Sears, Roebuck Catalog, 1926.
27. Dickson, *op. cit.*, 28
28. Allard, Denise M. *Hobbyist Source Book*. Detroit: Gale, 1990. P. 233.
29. Annicelli, Cliff. "Building Sets Break Apart." *Playthings* 93 (July 1995): 27.
30. Anon. "Lego Seeks New Image Through 'Girl Power' Toys." London, *Marketing* (Sept. 17, 1998): 8.
31. Greenwald, John. "Barbie Boots Up." *Time* (Nov. 11, 1996): 48–50.
32. Ibid., 49.
33. Hordern, Barbara. "Cyberbuzz: Computer Games Girls Can Relate To." *Working Woman* (Jan., 1996): 14.
34. Blasko, Larry. "Let Little Girls Take a Shot with Barbie's Camera." *Lansing State Journal* (Nov. 25, 1998): 1D.
35. Purdom, Candice. "Toying with Stereotypes." *Chicago Tribune* (Dec. 5, 2000): sect. 7, 03.
36. Anon. "High-Tech Savvy Girls Are Attracting Toymakers Looking for New Markets." *Wall Street Journal* (Sept. 18, 2000): B1, 8D.
37. Slatella, Michelle. "Inventor Fills Girls' Desire for Their Own Gadgets" *New York Times* (Sept. 30, 1999): G7.
38. Ibid.
39. Chase, Susan. "A Girl's Toy Trunk." *New York Times* (Jan. 25, 2000): A22.
40. Bradbard, Marilyn R., and Susan A. Parkman. "Gender Differences in Preschool Children's Toy Requests." *Journal of Genetic Psychology* 145 (2) (1984): 283–5.
41. Othes, Cele, Kyungseung Kim, and Young Chan Kim. "Yes, Virginia, There Is a Gender Difference: Analyzing Children's Requests to Santa Claus." *Journal of Popular Culture* 28 (1) Summer, 1994): 17–29
42. Eisenberg, Nancy, Edward Murray and Tina Hite. "Children's Reasoning Regarding Sex-Typed Toy Choices." *Child Development* 53 (1982): 81–6.
43. Blair, Gwenda. "Blame It on Barbie." *Self* 15 (Dec., 1993): 124–7, 167; Hall, Nancy. "Boys vs. Girls." *Parents* 71 (July, 1996): 64.
44. Pomerleau, Andree', et al. "Pink or Blue: Environmental Gender Stereotypes in the First Two Years of Life." *Sex Roles* 22 (5–6) (Mar., 1990): 359–67.
45. Etaugh, Claire, and Marsha B. Liss. "Home, School and Playroom: Training Grounds for Adult Gender Roles." *Sex Roles* 26 (3/4) (1992): 129–147; Fisher-Thompson, Donna. "Adult Sex Typing of Children's Toys." *Sex Roles* 23 (5–6) (1990): 291–303.
46. Jones, Marion. "Toy Story." *Psychology Today* 29 (6) (Nov./Dec., 1996): 12.
47. Blair, *op. cit.*,127.
48. Haffner, Debra W. "Toy Story: A Look Into the Gender-Stereotyped World of Children's Catalogs." *Siecus Report* 24 (4) (April/May, 1996): 20–1.
49. Horn, Jack. "The Sexist World of the Toy Store." *Psychology Today* 11 (11) (April, 1978): 125, 127.
50. Oppenheim, Joane. *The Best Toys, Books and Videos for Kids*. New York: Harper-Collins,1997. Unpaged.
51. Anon. *Scholastic News* (April 17, 2000): 7.
52. Davidson, Nicholas, P. 103–28 "The Rise and Fall of Cultural Determinism." In Davidson, Nicholas. Ed. *Gender Sanity*. Lanham, MD: University Press of America, 1989. P. 113.
53. Berenbaum, Sheri, and Melissa Hines. "Early Androgens Are Related to Childhood Sex-Typed Toy Differences." *Psychological Science* 3 (3) (May,1992): 203–6.
54. Blum, Deborah. *Sex on the Brain. The Biological Differences Between Men and Women*. New York: Viking, 1997; Petrikin, Jonathan S., Ed. *Male/Female Roles: Opposing Viewpoints* San Diego: Greenhaven, 1995; Pursell, *op. cit.*, 252–267.
55. The Editors. "Are Woman Better Leaders?" *U.S. News & World Report*. (Jan. 29, 2001): 10.

Chapter 9. Toys of the World We Have Lost

1. Anon. *Statistical Atlas*. Washington, D.C. Census Office, Department of the Interior, 1903.
2. Howard, *op cit.*, 111.
3. Wallace, Allie. *Frontier Life in Oklahoma*. Washington, DC: Public Affairs Press, 1964. P. 73
4. Dale, Edward. *The Cross Timbers*. Austin, TX: University of Texas Press, 1966. P. 40.
5. Parks, Annette. "Children's Work and Play on the Northwest Frontier." *Greenfield Village Herald* (Nov. 1, 1986) 3.
6. Rheingold, *op. cit.*, 462.
7. Dale, *op. cit.*, 8.
8. Coffin, Robert. *Lost Paradise*. New York: Macmillan, 1934, P. 222.
9. Howard, *op. cit.*, 82.
10. Parks, *op. cit.*, 34–5.
11. Ysenbaard, John H., and J. Hoffmann. "Between Hope and Fear. The Life of Lettie Teeple." *Michigan History* 58 (3) (1974): 230.

12. Alford, Thomas. *Civilization*. Norman OK: University of Oklahoma Press, 1936. P. 22.
13. Eastman, *op. cit.*, 69–70.
14. Swadish, Frances Leon. "Toys and Games." *Palacio* 81 (1) (Spring 1975): 31–5.
15. Dale, *op. cit.*, 82.
16. Catton, *op. cit.*, 46.
17. Larcom, Lucy. *A New England Girlhood*. Glouster, MA: Peter Smith, 1973. P. 90.
18. Miller, Max. *The Beginning of a Mortal*. New York: Dutton, 1933. P. 25.
19. Frank, Melvin. "In North Minneapolis: Sawmill City Boyhood." *Minnesota History* 47 (4) (Winter, 1980): 141–53.
20. Gardner, Don. "Yesterday's Kids Invented Fun." *Lansing State Journal* (Dec. 20, 1977): 2C.
21. Creevey, Caroline. *A Daughter of the Puritans*. New York: Putnams, 1916. P. 19.
22. O'Connor, Flannery. *Mystery and Manners*. New York: Farrar & Straus, 1969. P. 4.
23. Johnson, Anna. "Rough was the Road They Journeyed." *Palimpsest* 58 (3) (1977): 66–83.
24. Brody, Catharine. "A New York Girlhood." *American Mercury* (Nov., 1928): 57.
25. Burns, George. *Third Time Around*. New York: Putnams, 1980. P. 17.
26. Savo. *op. cit.*, 57.
27. Levinson, Sam. *Everything But Money*. New York: Simon and Schuster, 1966. P. 100.
28. Burns, *op. cit.*, 28.
29. Clark, John. G. "The Stoop Is the World." P. 260–80 in Hiner, N. Ray, and Joseph M. Hawes, *Growing Up in America: Children in Historical Perspective*. Urbana, IL: University of Illinois Press, 1985. P. 268–80.
30. Howard, *op. cit.*, 235.
31. Dale, *op. cit.*, 91.
32. Wallace, *op. cit.*, 51.
33. Osborn, Vera. *There Were Two of Us.*. New York: McGraw-Hill, 1944. P. 83.
34. Howard, *op. cit.*, 194; Teale, Edwin Way. *Dune Boy*. New York. Bloomington: Indiana University Press, 1957. P. 32.
35. Howard, *op. cit.*, 194.
36. Dale, *op. cit.*, 82.
37. Savo, *op. cit.*, 65.
38. Allen, Jennifer. "The Danger Years." *Life* 18 (9) (July, 1995): 40–45.
39. Koste, Virginia. *Dramatic Play In Childhood*. New Orleans: Anchorage, 1978. P. 65–6.
40. Pickler, Nedra. "Study says kids don't play enough." *Lansing State Journal* (Nov. 16, 1998.): 1B.
41. Mulrine. Anna. "What's your favorite class?" *U.S. News & World Report* (May 1, 2000): 50, 52.

42. Cowan, Ruth S. "The Industrial Revolution." in "The Home: Household Technology and Social Change in the 20th Century." *Technology and Culture* (Jan., 1976): 1–23; Vanek, Joann. "Household Technology and Social Status: Rising Standards and Status and Residence Differences in Housework." *Technology and Culture* (July, 1978): 361–75.
43. Sutton-Smith, Brian. "Ambivalence in Toyland." *Natural History* (Dec., 1985): 10.
44. Sutton-Smith, Brian, *Toys as Culture*. New York: Gardner Press, 1986. P. 37–8.
45. Kolata, Gina. "While Children Grow Fatter, Experts Search for Solutions." *New York Times* (Oct. 19, 2000): A1,6.
46. Stillman, Laurie. "We're teaching our children bad habits." *Boston Globe* (Jan. 14, 2001): D7.
47. Saul, Helen. "Fine Young Slobs?" *New Scientist* 142 (April 23, 1994): 24–5.
48. Anon. "Fitter Kids." *Futurist*. 23 (3) (May-June, 1993): 5; Neergaard, Lauran. "Test Has Kids Pedaling to Watch TV." *Lansing State Journal* (April 19, 1999): 2A.
49. Anderson, Leslie. "Making childhood fitness fun." *Boston Globe* (Aug. 12, 2001): GW 9; Axtman, Kris. "Find those gym shorts! Phys ed makes comeback. *Christian Science Monitor* (Jan. 22, 2002): 1,2.
50. Nabhan, Gary, and Stephen Trimble. *The Geography of Childhood*. Boston: Beacon Press, 1994. P. XV.
51. Rivkin, Mary. "The Great Outdoors: Restoring Children's Right to Play Outside." Booklet, ED 388414, 1995. P. 11.
52. West, Elliott. *Growing Up with the Country: Childhood on the Far Western Frontier*. Albuquerque, NM: University of New Mexico Press, 1989. P. 130–1; Snyder, Grace. *No Time on My Hands*. Lincoln, NE: University of Nebraska Press, 1963. P. 25.
53. Teale, *op. cit.*, 5.
54. West, *op. cit.*, 44–5.
55. Garland, *op. cit.*, 133.
56. Catton, *op. cit.*, 41.
57. Conklin, Henry. *Through "Poverty's Vale." A Hardscrabble Boyhood in Upstate New York, 1832–1862*. Syracuse, NY: Syracuse University Press, 1974. P. 59.
58. Sneller, *op. cit.*, 214.
59. Cobb, Edith. *The Ecology of Imagination in Childhood*. New York: Columbia University Press, 1977.
60. Mann, Leslie. "Natural activities for families." *Chicago Tribune* (July 22, 2001): 13:8; Grant, Tracy. "Back to Nature at Brookside." *Washington Post* (Sept. 21, 2001): WK 54; Rees, Brenda. "For Cool Fun, Night Is Right." *Los Angeles Times* (June 21, 2001): WK 38.
61. Lukashok, Alvin, and Kevin Lynch.

"Some Childhood Memories of the City." *Journal of the American Institute of Planners.* (Summer, 1956): 142–52.
  62. Hart, Roger. *Children's Experience of Place.* New York: Irvington, 1979.
  63. Dovey, Kimberly. "Refuge and Imagination: Places of Peace in Childhood." *Children's Environment's Quarterly* 7 (4) (1990): 16.
  64. Kirkby, Mary Ann. "Nature as Refuge in Children's Environments." *Children's Environment's Quarterly* 6 (1) (Spring, 1989): 7–12.
  65. Moore, Robin. "Plants as Play Props." *Children's Environment's Quarterly* 6 (1) (Spring, 1989): 3.
  66. Stein, Sarah. *Noah's Children: Restoring the Ecology of Childhood.* New York: Farrar Straus and Giroux 2001.
  67. Stocker, Carol. "Nurture children's outdoor instincts, specialist urges." *Boston Globe* (Jan. 10, 2001): H 1, 7.
  68. Rivkin, *op. cit.*, 79.
  69. Bixler, Robert P., and Myron F. Floyd. "Nature Is Scary, Disgusting, and Uncomfortable." *Environment and Behavior* (July, 1997): 443–65.
  70. Coffin, *op. cit.*, 223; Deland, Margaret. *If This Be I.* New York: Appleton, 1935. P. 73.

Chapter 10. The Commercialization of Toys

  1. Applegate, Jane. "Small Toymakers Find Their Niche." *Lansing State Journal* (Dec. 22, 1997): 2B.
  2. Stewart, *op. cit.*, 72–83.
  3. Collins, Glen. "A Toy Fair, a Feud, and the Industry's General Angst." *New York Times* (Feb. 10, 1996): 39.
  4. Ibid.
  5. Anon. "Shareholders Sue Hasbro Over Mattel Bid." *New York Times* (Feb. 5, 1996): L 7.
  6. Adams, Walter. "Mega-Mergers Present Illusion of Growth." *State News* (June 26, 1997): 4.
  7. Miller, G. Wayne. *Toy Wars: The Epic Struggle Between G.I. Joe, Barbie, and the Companies That Make Them.* New York: Times Books, 1998. P. XIV.
  8. Reyson, Frank. "Absence of Super-hits Puts Retailers to Test." *Playthings* 84 (11) (Oct., 1986): 37.
  9. Harkin, Tom. "No Cheer from Toys Made By Child Labor." *Los Angeles Times* (Dec. 22, 1994): 11.
  10. Holstein, William. "Santa's Sweatshop." *U.S. News and World Report* 121 (Dec. 16, 1996): 50–4, 56–7, 60.
  11. Burrell, Cassandra. "Toys Made With Child Labor Are Targeted in New Campaign." *Lansing State Journal* (Dec. 12, 1996): 6A; Razzi, Elizabeth. "Did Child Labor Make That Toy?" *Kiplinger's Personal Finance Magazine* 50 (Dec., 1996): 46–8, 50.
  12. Seiter, Ellen. *Sold Separately.* Brunswick, NJ: Rutgers University Press, 1993. P. 213.
  13. Holstein, *op. cit.*, 56.
  14. Foek, Anton. "Sweatshop Barbie: Exploitation of Third World Labor." *The Humanist* 57 (Jan./Feb. 1997): 9.
  15. Kelly, Florence. "A Five Cent Toy and the Two Morals It Teaches." *The Survey* 31 (Dec. 13, 1913): 290.
  16. Baumann, Paul. *Collecting Antique Marbles.* Radnor, PA: Wallace-Homestead, 1991. P. 51.
  17. McClintock, Inez, and Marshall McClintock. *Toys in America.* Washington, D.C.: Public Affairs Press, 1961: 193–7.
  18. Lyman, Rick. "Pokemon Is Catching and Keeping Them." *New York Times* (Nov. 13, 1999): 20; Segall, Rebecca. "Pokemon Challenges Docs." *Psychology Today* 33 (2) (Mar./April, 2000): 12.
  19. Wilson, Craig. "Running Circles Around an Old Toy, This New Hoop Is Making Waves." *USA Today* (April 28, 2000): D1.
  20. McGinn, Daniel. "The Making of a Fad." *Newsweek* (July 24, 2000): 38–9.
  21. Stipp, David. "Why People Often Act Like Sheep: The Theory of Fads." *Fortune* 134 (7) (Oct. 14, 1996): 49.
  22. McGinn, *op. cit.*, 38.
  23. McTernan, William. "Beanie Babies Bottoming Out." *Lansing State Journal* (Oct. 5, 1998): 1D.
  24. Eberhart, Tracy. "Fads: From Hot to Not." *Parenting* (Feb., 2000): 31; Scott, A.O. "The End of Innocence." *New York Times Magazine* (July 2, 2000): Sect. 6 P. 12.
  25. Stewart, *op. cit.*, 78.
  26. McNeal, James U. *Kids as Customers.* New York: Macmillan, 1992. P. 20.
  27. Tedesco, Richard. "CME Says Web Promos for Kids Don't Play Fair." *Telamedia Week* (April 8, 1996): 58.
  28. Wolfenstein, Martha. "The Emergence of Fun Morality." *Journal of Social Issues* 7 (1951): 15–25.
  29. Kaplan, David, and Adam Rogers. "It's a Pokemon Planet." *Newsweek* (Mar. 1, 1999): 48.
  30. Wollenberg, Skip, and Bob Kahn. "Toys were the main meal at many fast-food places." *Lansing State Journal* (Dec. 25, 1999): 7B.

31. Cross, Gary. "Too Many Toys." *New York Times* (Nov. 24, 1995): 35.
32. Henry, James S. "Why I Hate Christmas." *The New Republic* (Dec. 31, 1990): 21–4.
33. Botwinick, Stacy. "Top Ten." *Playthings* (Dec., 2000): 24–38.
34. Lemport, Phil. "Aging Boomers Set Pace for Holiday Gift Giving." *Advertising Age* (Dec. 9, 1996): 25.
35. Jensen, Bill. "Toys Get Religion." *Playthings* (Dec., 2000): 44–6.
36. Benjamin, Ludy T., Jacqueline F. Halls and Rosalie J. Hall. "Santa Now and Then." *Psychology Today* 13 (7) (Dec. 1979): 39.
37. Anon. "Parents admit: We're spoiling our kids" *Lansing State Journal* (Dec. 8, 1993): 5B.
38. Waits, William. *The Modern Christmas in America. A Cultural History of Gift-Giving.* New York: New York University press, 1993. P. 132.
39. *Ibid.* 25.
40. Anon. "Out of the Claus-et." *Time* (Dec. 22, 1997): 14.
41. Pennell, Greta. "What I Learned From Spying on Santa." *Good Housekeeping* 223 (6) (Dec. 22, 1996): 118–9.
42. Beck, Rachel. "No Single Leader on the Toy Shelf." *Lansing State Journal* (Nov. 27, 1995): 8B.
43. Othes, Cele, Chan Kim Young and Kim Kyungseung. "All I Want for Christmas: An Analysis of Children's Brand Requests to Santa Claus." *Journal of Popular Culture* 27 (4) (1994): 183–194.
44. Belk, Russell W. "A Child's Christmas in America: Santa Claus as Deity, Consumption as Religion." *Journal of American Culture* 10 (1) (Spring, 1987): 96.
45. Belk, *op. cit.*, 93.
46. Oppenheim, Joanne. *Buy Me! Buy Me!* New York: Pantheon, 1987: 41–2.
47. Kutner, Lawrence. "Parent & Child." *New York Times* (Dec. 16, 1993): C 10.
48. Baker, Mark. "How Kids Really Feel About Christmas." *Parents* 69 (Dec.1994): 96.
49. Miller, G. Wayne. *Toy Wars: The Epic Struggle Between G.I. Joe, Barbie, and the Companies That Make Them.* New York Times Books, 1998.
50. Mayhover, Stephen. Review of Miller *op. cit.. Library Journal* 123 (Feb. 15, 1998): 152.
51. Anon. Review of Miller *op. cit. Kirkus Reviews.* (Dec. 1, 1997): 1755.
52. Kline, Stephen. *Out of the Garden. Toys, TV and Children's Culture in the Age of Marketing.* New York: Verso, 1993.
53. Cross, *op. cit.* 1997.
54. Englehardt, 1997, *op. cit.*, 37.
55. Phillips Phil. *Turmoil in the Toybox.* Lancaster, PA: Stardust, 1986.
56. D'Innocenzio, Anne. "Toys aim to turn toddlers into tiny geniuses." *Lansing State Journal* (Mar. 17, 2001): 1D.
57. Gumbrecht, Jamie. "Treasured Toys." *Lansing State Journal* (July 30, 2002): 1,6E.
58. Gumbrecht, *op. cit.*, E.

Chapter 11. The John Burroughs Toy

1. Burroughs, John. "Corrupting the Innocents." *The Independent* 61 (Dec. 13, 1906): 1424–5.
2. Wiencek, Henry. "The World of Lego Toys." New York: Harry N. Abrams, 1987. P. 46.
3. Resnick, Mitchel. "Behavior Construction Kits." *Communications of the ACM* 36 (July, 1993): 64–71.
4. Young, Jeffery. "M.I.T. Scholar Brings Legos Into the Digital Age." *Chronicle of Higher Education* XLIV (12) (Nov. 14, 1997): A25–6.
5. Flatley, Kate. "She Builds Her Own R2D2 — Phew!" *Wall Street Journal* (Dec. 11, 1998): W 14.
6. Kotkin, Joel. "Of Dolls and Online Dollars." *New York Times* (Nov. 28, 1999): B 5.

Chapter 12. The Special Problem of Media Bias

1. Kreyche, Gerald. "Americans Are Running Scared." *USA Today* 123 (May, 1995): 98.
2. *New York Times Index.* 229 West 43d St. New York. 10036. Vol. 60 1972.
3. *Ibid.* 87 (1999): 1611–2.
4. Klaidman, Stephen. "How Well the Media Report Health Risks." *Daedalus* 119 (1990): 123.
5. Goldberg, Bernard. *Bias.* Washington, D.C.: Regency, 2000: 195ff.
6. McLaughlin, *op. cit.*, 3C.
7. Miller, *op. cit.* 1998; Kline, *op. cit.* 1993; Cross, *op. cit.* 1997.

Chapter 13. The Plight of the Parent

1. Hymowitz, Kay S. *Ready or Not: Why Treating Children as Small Adults Endangers*

Their Future — And Ours. New York: Free Press, 1999: 12.
   2. D'Innocenzio, Anne. "Toy Market Cools Down for Now." *Lansing State Journal* (Dec. 16, 2000): 9C.
   3. *Ibid.*
   4. Lane, Charles. "Tubby Ache." *New Republic* 22 (10) (Mar. 8, 1999): 4.
   5. Spiro, Melford. *Children of the Kibbutz.* Cambridge, Mass: Harvard, 1958.
   6. Oppenheim, Joanne. *op. cit.*, 1987.

Selected Bibliography

Andreas, Carol. "War Toys and the Peace Movement." *Journal of Social Issues.* 25 (1) (1967): 83–99.
Atfield, Judy. "Barbie and Action Man: Adult Toys for Girls and Boys, 1959–93." P. 80–7 in Kirkham, Pat, *The Gendered Object.* New York: Manchester University Press, 1996.
Barnes, John. "Heroic Figures May Top Holiday Wish Lists." *New York Times* (Sept. 26, 2001): C6–7.
Beard, D.C. *The American Boy's Handy Book.* Boston: Godine, 1983.
____. *The Outdoor Handy Book.* New York: Scribner's, 1925.
Beard, Lina, and Adelia Beard. *Handicraft and Recreation for Girls.* New York: Scribners, 1924.
____, and ____. *The American Girls Handy Book.* Boston: Godine, 1987.
Bloch, Marianne, and Anthony Pellegrini. *The Ecological Context of Children's Play.* Norwood, NJ: Ablex, 1982.
Bok, Sissela. *Mayhem: Violence as Public Entertainment.* Reading, MA: Allison-Wesley, 1998.
Brumberg, Jean Jacobs. *The Body Project.* New York: Random House. 1997.
Calvert, Karen. *Children in the House.* Boston: Northeastern University Press, 1992.
Clark, William. *Boy's Own Book.* New York: Miller, 1882.
Clepper, Irene. "What Toys Teach." *Parents* 44 (Nov. 1971): 50–1.
Cobb, Viki. "How To Make a Science Lesson Out Of Anything." *Instructor,* 90 (April, 1981): 44.
Coffin, Robert. *Lost Paradise.* New York: Macmillan, 1934.
Creevey, Caroline. *A Daughter of the Puritans.* New York: Putnam: 1969.
Cross, Gary. *Kid's Stuff.* Cambridge, MA: Harvard, 1997.
Culin, Stewart. *Games of the North American Indians.* New York: Dover, 1975.
Dale, Edward. *The Cross Timbers.* Austin: University of Texas Press, 1966.
Davies, Maire. *Fake, Fact and Fantasy: Children's Interpretation of Television Reality.* Mahwah, NJ: Erlbaum, 1997.
Eastman, Charles. *Indian Boyhood.* Rapid City, SD: Fenwyn Press, 1970.
Fallows, James. *Breaking the News: How the Media Undermine American Democracy.* New York: Pantheum, 1996.
Foley, Dan. *Toys Through the Ages.* New York: Chilton, 1962.
"For Kid's Sake, Think Toy Safety." Washington, DC: U.S. Consumer Product Safety Commission. Undated.
Fraser, Antonia. *A History of Toys.* New York: Delacorte Press, 1966.
Fredrickson, George. *The Black Image in the White Mind. The Debate*

Freeman, Larry. *Yesterday's Games*. Watkins Glen, NY: Century House, 1970.
Fritzsch, Karl, and Manfred Bachmann. *An Illustrated History of Toys*. London: Abbey, 1961.
Goldberg, Bernard. *Bias* . Washington, D.C: Regency, 2002.
Gordon, Leslie. *Peepshow into Paradise*. London: Harrap, 1953.
Grober, Karl. *Children's Toys of Bygone Days*. New York: Stokes, 1928.
Grossman, Dave. "We Are Training Our Kids to Kill." *Saturday Evening Post* (July/August, 1997): 64–72. (Sept./Oct. 1997): 54–5, 78–81.
Gura, Pat, Ed. *Exploring Learning: Young Children and Blockplay*. London: Paul Chapman, 1992.
Hale, Edward. *A New England Boyhood*. Boston: Little, Brown, 1969.
Harkin, Tom. "No Cheer from Toys Made By Child Labor." *Los Angeles Times* (Dec. 22, 1944).
Hewitt, Karen, and Louise Roomet. *Educational Toys in America: 1800 to the Present*. Burlington, VT: Queen City Printers Inc., 1979.
Hickey, Mary. "How the Power Rangers Stole Christmas." *Ladies Home Journal* (Dec. 1995): 126–7, 167–9.
Hiner, N. Ray, and Joseph M. Hawes. *Growing Up in America: Children in Historical Perspective*. Urbana: University of Illinois Press, 1985.
Hofstadter, Richard. "America as a Gun Culture." *American Heritage* (October, 1970): 4–11, 82–5.
Holstein, William. "Santa's Sweatshop." *U.S. News & World Report* (Dec. 16, 1996): 50–4, 56–7, 60.
Howard, Dorothy. *Dorothy's World*. Englewood Cliffs, NJ: Prentice Hall, 1977.
Howells, William Dean. *A Boy's Town*. New York: Harper, 1918.
Hymowitz, Katy S. *Ready or Not: Why Treating Children as Small Adults Endangers Their Future—And Ours*. New York: Free Press, 1999.
Jackson, Kathy Merlock. "Targeting Baby-Boom Children as Consumers. Mattel Uses Television To Sell Talking Dolls." In Eiss, Harry, ed. *Images of the Child*. Bowling Green, OH: Bowling Green State University Popular Press, 1994; pp. 187–91.
Johnson, Jeffery, et al. "Television Viewing and Aggressive Behavior During Adolescence and Adulthood." *Science* 295 (March 29, 2002): 2468–71.
Kantrowitz, Barbara. "The New Age of Anxiety." *Newsweek* (August 3, 1999): 39–40.
"Kids Ad Special Raises Eyebrows of Critics." *Advertising Age* 63(6) (Feb. 10, 1992): 5–14.
King, Wilma. *Stolen Childhood: Slave Youth in Nineteenth Century America*. Bloomington: Indiana University Press, 1995.
Kline, Stephen. *Out of the Garden: Toys, TV and Children's Culture in the Age of Marketing*. New York: Verso, 1993.
Koste, Virginia. *Dramatic Play in Childhood: Rehearsal for Life*. Los Angeles: Anchorage Press, 1978.
Kuznets, Kois Rostow. *When Toys Come Alive*. New Haven, CT: Yale University Press, 1994
Larcom, Lucy. *A New England Girlhood*. Gloucester, MA: Petersmith, 1973.
Lee, Martin A., and Norman Solomon. *Unreliable Sources*. New York: Lyle Stuart, 1990.
Lord, M.G. *Forever Barbie*. New York: William Morrow, 1994.
Marzollo, Joan, and Janice Lloyd. *Learning Through Play*. New York: Harper & Row, 1972.
McClintock, Marshall, and Inez McClintock. *Toys in America*. Washington, DC: Public Affairs Press, 1961.
McGinn, Daniel. "The Making of a Fad." *Newsweek* (July 24, 2000): 38–9.

Selected Bibliography 195

McNeal, James U. *Kids as Customers.* New York: Macmillan, 1992.
Mergen, David. *Play and Playthings: A Reference Guide.* Westport, CT: Greenwood Press, 1982.
Miller, G. Wayne. *Toy Wars: The Epic Struggle Between G.I. Joe, Barbie, and the Companies that Make Them.* New York: Times Books, 1998.
O'Brien, Richard. *The Story of American Toys.* New York: Artebras, 1990.
O'Dell, John. *The Great American Depression Book of Fun.* New York: Harper & Row, 1981.
O'Kieffe, Charley. *Western Story: The Recollections of Charley O'Kieffe, 1884–1898.* Lincoln: University of Nebraska Press, 1960.
On the African-American Character and Destiny, 1817–1914. New York: Harper and Row, 1971.
Othes, Cele, Chan Kim Young and Kim Kyung Seung. "All I Want for Christmas. An Analysis of Children's Brand Requests to Santa Claus. *Journal of Popular Culture* 27 (4) (1994): 183–94.
Parks, Annette. "Children's Work and Play on the Northwest Frontier." *Greenfield Village Herald* (Nov. 1, 1986): 37.
Provenzo, Eugene, and Asterie Provenzo. *Easy-to-Make Old-Fashioned Toys.* New York: Dover, 1979.
Quilitch, H. Robert. "Can Toys Really Teach?" *Saturday Review World*, 2 (Nov. 16, 1974): 60–2.
Qwen, David. "Where Toys Come From." *Atlantic* (Oct. 1986): 65–78.
Razzi, Elizabeth. "Did Child Labor Make That Toy?" *Kiplinger's Personal Finance Magazine* 50 (12)(Dec. 1996): 46–8, 50.
Sawyers, Janet, and Crosby S. Rodger. *Helping Young Children Develop Through Play.* Washington, DC: National Association for the Education of Young Children, 1988.
Schnacke, Dick. *American Folk Toys: How to Make Them.* New York: Penguin, 1982.
Schwartzman, Helen B., Ed. *Play and Culture.* West Point, NY: Leisure Press, 1980.
Singer, Dorothy, and Jerome Singer. *The House of Make-Believe: Children's Play and the Developing Imagination.* Cambridge, Mass: Harvard, 1990.
Stein, Sarah. *Noah's Children: Restoring the Ecology of Childhood.* New York: Farrar Straus and Giroux, 2001.
Stewart, Douglas. "In the Cutthroat World of Toy Sales, Child's Play Is Serious Business." *Smithsonian* 20 (9) (Dec., 1989): 75–83.
Stipp, David. "Why People Often Act Like Sheep: The Theory of Fads." *Fortune*, 134 (7)(Oct. 14, 1996): 44.
Sutton-Smith, Brian. "Ambivalence in Toyland." *Natural History* (Dec., 1986): 6–16.
____. "The Role of Toys in the Instigation of Playful Creativity." *Creativity Research Journal.* 5 (1992): 3–11.
____. *Toys As Culture.* New York: Gardner, 1986.
Swartz, Edward. *Toys That Don't Care.* Boston: Gambit, 1991.
____. *Toys That Kill.* New York: Vintage, 1986.
Teale, Edwin Way. *Dune Boy.* Bloomington: Indiana University Press, 1957.
Turner, Ray. "100 Years of Physics and Toys: Balancing Toys." *The Physics Teacher* 30 (Dec. 1992): 642–3.
Waits, William. *The Modern Christmas in America. A Cultural History of Gift-Giving.* New York: New York University Press, 1993.
Wallace, Allie. *Frontier Life in Oklahoma.* Washington, DC: Public Affairs Press, 1964.
Weininger, Otto, and Susan Daniel. *Playing To Learn.* Springfield, IL: Charles C. Thomas, 1992.

West, Elliott. *Growing Up with the Country: Childhood on the Far Western Frontier.* Albuquerque, NM: University of New Mexico Press, 1989.

Wigginton, Eliot. *Foxfire 6.* New York: Anchor, 1980.

Wilkinson, Doris. "Play Objects as Tools of Propaganda: Characteristics of the African-American Male." *Journal of Black Psychology* 7 (1) (August, 1980): 4–16.

Wolfenstein, Martha. "The Emergence of Fun Morality." *Journal of Social Issues* 7 (1951): 15–25.

Index

Action figures: and aggression 40–41; change to meet changing views of war 42; early examples 39; story line dependent on movies, television 40; as turn-ons for drug use 42
Advertising toys: deceptive toy ads 46; early toy ads 157; fun morality and toy ads 157–58
African-American children: had fewer toys 94; had to make their own toys 94; whites used black children as playthings 94–95
African-American racism: protests against 99; views of northern whites 98–99; views of southern whites 94–99
African-American toys in change: as vehicles for power and pride 103; Barbie as an African-American 101; toys designed for African-American interests 102
Airgo 87
"Alive," definition of 43
Andy Gump 39
Animals: as hazards 77
Animals as toys: chickens a favorite 130; elaborate festivals for animals 131; Lettie Teeple's frog doll 131; taming prairie dogs, possums and badgers 131
Applegate, Charlie, and battles with Indians 8–9
Asian-Americans and toy racism 104
Astro-blaster 67
Attfield, Judy 32

Barbie: and anorexia 34; as career girl 36; as a dumb blonde 35; her affordability 31; her early success 33, 40; her figure 34; Mattel's view of their Barbie doll 28; for President 37; primary users today 38; and segmentation 33; and swappers 35
Barney Google 39
Barney the dinosaur 52–53
BB guns: as a harmless family toy 12, 14; Joe Brown: "It's no longer a toy" 14; Morris Wright 12
Beard, Dan 10
Berg, Liz, and her Barbie 31
B.I.O. Bugs 50–51
Bleeds leads syndrome 173–74
Bow and arrow 11, 17–18
The Boy's Own Toymaker 107
Bratz 38
Brownies 39
Brumberg, Joan, and her Barbie 31
Burroughs, John 166
Byrne, Chris: toy consultant 57

Cabbage Patch Kids 85
Cap guns 14
Captain Kangaroo 49
Carlsson-Paige Nancy 40–41
Catton, Bruce 17
Cereal boxes as toys 133
Charness, Wayne 48
Charon, Peggy 175
Chemistry sets 115
Child labor: making toys abroad 150–52
Child-made toys as hazards 76–79
Children and racism 105

Children's allowances 44
Chores 128–28
Christiansen, Ole, and Lego 166–69
Christmas: and commercialism 162–64; and stress 159; as year-round holiday 164–65
Civil War: replaying it 17
Coffin, Miriam 129
Columbine shooting 23
Combat play 16–18
Commission on Product Safety 82
Computer and video games 26–27
Computer created toys 169
Conklin, Ed 143
Conroy, Jack 9
Consumerism 81
Cox, Michael: playing "Roman soldier" 10–11
Crandall, Charles, and "Pigs in Clover" 152
Cultural determinists and sociobiologists 122–23

Dale, Ed 128, 134–35
Da Vinci, a robotic dog 56
Davis, Arthur 9
Davis, Marie, and children's understanding of TV 47
Derr, Margaret 67
Dewey, John 61
Dolls: Amaryllis 30–31, 33; Autoperpatetikos 51; Baby Go Boom 55; Baby Luv N' Care 2; Baby Walk N' Play 52; Barbie 30–38 *see also* under Barbie; Bratz 38; Edison's doll 52; French fashion doll 29; Ken 31, 35; Laila 38; Lettie Teeple's frog doll 31; Lilli Doll 28; Mommy-To-Be 70–71; New Friends 69–70; Niya 73; Noma 52; paper 28–29; Peggy Pen-Pal 52; Queen Victoria Doll 29–30; rag 128; Shirley Temple 30; Wheelchair Becky 37, 40; Zaadi 68
Dolls and dentistry 69
Dolls and handicapped children: Education for All Handicapped Children Act 69; Mattel's Wheelchair Becky 70; New Friends doll 69–70
Dolls and increasing ethnic diversity 105
Dorothy's World (Dorothy Howard) 127

Dramatic Play in Childhood (Virginia Koste) 137

Early baseball 132
Early country houses 128
Eastman, Charles 7, 132
Edgeworth, Maria 59
Educational toys: Counting Pal 73; problems of defining 58; teaching language 73; teaching reading 73; teaching numbers 73; today's views 60–61
Ellard, Mr. 13–14
Englehardt, Tom 47, 72
Erector Set 113–15, 166
Exercise: as a problem with children 141–42

Fad toys: Crazy Daisy 153; Hula Hoops 153; Pigs in Clover 152; Razor Scooter 154; Tickle-me Elmo 154; Virtual pets 155
Federal Communications Commission 49
Fiery hoop of death 64
Fireball toys: as hazards of early America 78
Fishing through gutter grates 132–32
Flipperdinger 67
Focus groups: and children 155–56
Froebel, Friederich: his building blocks 61; influence on Frank Lloyd Wright 60; as philosopher and mystic 59
Fun morality: and parental decisions about toys 49; replacing older Puritan ethic 157

Gangster films 18
Garland, Hamlin 17
Garland, Harriett 17
Gender toys: boys' toys 106–115; computer games and girls 118; girls' toys 115–116; parental influences 120; peer influences 121; television and its influence 122; toy companies and their influence 121–2; two views of toy choice 122–4
German toy makers 5
G.I. Joe 42, 46
Gilbert, A.C. 113–115
G-Men 18

Index

Goldberg, Bernard, and his view of bias 175
Goodwin, Candice 92
Graces 63–64
Grahame, Kenneth, and *Wind in the Willows* 49
Greenpeace 83
gun culture, America as 22

Hale, Edward 9
Halick, Dr. Lynn 69
Halley's Comet 79
Hamilton, Clarence 12
Handcapper dolls 70–71
Handler, Ruth 28
Handmade toys: and hazards 76
Handmade toys of early America: animals as playthings 130–33; chairs as wagons 134; lima beans and corn kernels for checkers 134; melon rinds into false teeth 135; oatmeal boxes into telephones 133; onions as noisemakers 130; paper into butterflies 135; plants as toys 128–29; rags into dolls 128
Harkin, Senator Tom: and views of toys made abroad 150–52
Harmless pistol 12
Hasbro: and deceptive advertising 46; disclaims view that TV brainwashes children 48
Haugland, Kristina 30
Hazards of early American play: Dorothy Howard hurt while sewing 76; fireballs 78–9; homemade cannon 78; jack knives 77–78; Jesse Applegate and the ox stomach 77; pyrotechnic toys 78–79; snakes 77; spear fights 10–11
He-Man and the Masters of the Universe 45
Hearst, James 11
History of Children's Play (Brian Sutton-Smith) 11
Holland, Barbara 18
Homemaking toys for today's girls 115–16
Homies: Chicano toys 104
Hoops as all-purpose toys: Dio Lewis and "Hoop Drill" 64; Ernst Balch and "The Fiery Hoop of Death" 64; graces, an early hoop 63–64; hoop drill 64; the hula hoop as a fad 65, 153; Melvin Frank and hoop races 133; Thomas Alford and the "hat game" 131; Whamo invents the hula hoop 65
Horsewhips as weapons 16–7
Howard, Dorothy: growing up in Sabine Bottom, Texas 76; had a dozen toys in her "pretty box" 5; indoor play 134; paper dolls 28
Howells, William: and fireballs 78; and the German boys across the street 9; stoning German children in town 17
Hymowitz, Kay, and peer group power 177–78

I Cybie 50–51
Incredible Hulk 40
Indian Wars 17–18
Indians: replaying their ways 17
Indoor play of early America 134–35
Indoor play of today: can lead to isolation 139; most of today's toys are for indoor use 138; requires less exercise, thus children are overweight 141
Industrial Revolution: and new kinds of toys 136; becomes a reality for most Americans 30; changes appearance of toy weapons 16; changes work-play habits 106; creates a world of change 86

Javelins 11
Jones, Wendy 31

Kernan, Michael 18
Kibbutz 179
Kid's Stuff (Gary Cross) 159
Kindergarten boys: suspended from school for cops and robbers play 24
Kline, Stephen 47,179
Kuznets, Lois 74

Lady's squirt gun 12
Landells, E. 107
Larcom, Lucy 132
Legos 118, 167–68
Leotard toy 49
Leshan, Edna 75

Levin, Dianne 40
Licensing 33, 158
Lincoln Logs 166
Lindbergh's flight 110
Lion-Lamb project 24, 55
Little Gym cassettes 141
Little House on the Prairie 43
Locke's blocks 58–59
Lord, M.G., and *Forever Barbie* 34

MacCracken, Henry 9, 17
Machine-Gun Kelly 18
Machine-made toys hazards: children's views 136; flammable materials 81; plastics can cause rashes 81; toy ducks carried germs 81
Madigan, Dick and Pauline, and their walking doll 51
Maggie and Jiggs 39
Martin, Sella, as a marble player 95
Massachusetts General Hospital 68
Mattel: and merger mania 148–9; and Mickey Mouse Club TV show 45; and toy safety 84; segmentation and licensing 33
Mattel-A-Time Clock 62
Mean World Syndrome 22
Mechanical banks 95; as racist toys 95–97
Media bias 174–75
Mickey Mouse Club 45
Model airplane contests 111–12
Model yacht contests 112–13
Morris, Wright 12
Mud-willow fights 7

Nader, Ralph 174
Napoleonic Coach 107–8
National Environmental Trust 84
Native Americans: and toy images 104–5; and toy racism 104–5
Northern whites: views of African-Americans 98

O'Dell, John 18
O'Kieffe, Charley 7, 8
Olney, Don 148
Oppenheim, Joanne, on parental role in toy choice 180
Out of the Garden (Stephen Kline) 47

Outdoor play in early America: hazardous toys 76–79; outdoor toys were handmade 128–32; outdoor recess at school 138
Outdoor play today: children still create toys from scratch 137; most of today's outdoor toys are machine-made 137; outdoor play is less common than in early America 137–38; wild places are diminished today 137

Paige, Nancy 40–41
Parents: and toy choice 120, 178
Peace activists 22
Peashooters in school 9
Peers-influence on toy choice 121
Phillips, Phil 48
Physical fitness toys 63–65
Physics toys 65–68
Pigs in Clover 152–53
Plantation play and racism 97–98
Plants as toys 132
Pokemon 153
Poo Chi 50
Popeye 39
Powell, Josephine 20
Power Rangers 40
Power Wheel toy 83
Powered models 110–13
Pregnant dolls 70–71
Protests: against racist toys 99
PVC controversy and toys 83

Quiltech, Robert 62

Rabbit transit toy 157
Racing toys 113
Rautman, Arthur 20
Readers' Guide to Periodicals 6
Revolutionary War 17
Robotic toys: Aibo 56; Da Vinci 56; Furby 50, 54, 56–57; as irritating 53–4; Leotard sand toys 49; as poor taste; and problems of bonding 56–57; seen as "alive" by adults 56; seen as "alive" by children 50–51; as teachers 73–74
"Roman Soldier" 11
Rosie O'Donnell Show 55
Rowan 87

Rubber band guns: as fancy toy weapons 18; in safe battles 12, 14

Safety problems: Boomerang Links 84; chocolate-covered toys 85; Consumer Product Safety Commission 83; Flubber and skin rashes 81; hazardous toys and government control 80–82; how safe are today's toys? 91–92; Microban and safety problems 85; parents' role in toy safety 88; Pogo sticks as hazards 87; presidents Johnson and Nixon on toy safety 81–82; product liability suits and toys 92; scooter injuries 87; Snacktime Kid and hair pulling 85–86; toy ducks and salmonella 81
Santa Claus: children's belief in 161–62; letters to 119; as salesman 161
Savo, Jimmy 9, 133
Scale models: Fisher Body 107–8; Lindberg on model-making 110; model airplane contests 111–12; Sissman and model making problems 108, 112; *The Boy's Own Toymaker* (1866) 107
Schools and toy guns 24
Science kits 115
Shawnee Indians: and hoop game 131
Singer, Dorothy and Jerome 54
Sioux Indians: and top games 132
Sissman, L. E., and problems in model making 108, 112
Sling shots: Charley O'Kieffe's sling shot 7, 8; Dan Beard's sling shot 17; at school 9–10
Sneller, Ann, and country play 17, 143
Snow, Al 55
Snowballing 9
Soap Box Derby 113, 117
Soldiers: Dan Beard's clothespin soldiers 17; Eleanor Abbot's soldiers 14; Robert Rutland's soldiers 14–15
Spock, Dr. Benjamin 54
Squirt gun fights 12, 14
Star Wars 16
Stirn, Carl P., Company 28
Stivender, Ed, and war play 19

Stoop as play place 134
Suction cup guns 14
Super Soakers 16
Sutton-Smith, Brian: all frontier societies have similar play 11; children don't mindlessly mimic TV 41; solitary play may not be entirely bad 140; toys are passive, it is children who are creative 62; we project our anxieties onto children 35
Swartz, Edward: as a media celebrity 83; ideas about toy misuse and dangerous toys 90; "There is a death trap in the toy house" 82; the Tyke Bike is dangerous 89

Teddy 68
Teenage Mutant Turtles 16
Teeple, Lettie 131
Television: and family solidarity 43; instills bad values in children? 48–49
Tinker Toys 59, 166
Top play by Indian children 132
Town gangs and trouble 8
Toy choice 119–121
Toy guns 22–25
Tuff Talking wrestlers 55
Turmoil in the Toy Box (Phil Phillips) 48
Turtle Park 23

UNICEF 72

Video games: and violence 26
Viet Nam War: and toy weapons 21–22

Wallace, Allie 127, 135
War play 12, 17–20
Wellness toys 68–71
Whamo Toy Company 65
When Toys Come Alive (Lois Kuznets) 74
World Wrestling Foundation: and wrestler toys 55
Wright, Frank Lloyd 60

Zeiger, Lisa, and Barbie 31–32

www.ingramcontent.com/pod-product-compliance
Ingram Content Group UK Ltd.
Pitfield, Milton Keynes, MK11 3LW, UK
UKHW042005140426
5217IPUK00015B/996